# ALBUM OF
# AMERICAN HISTORY

# ALBUM OF AMERICAN HISTORY

## VOLUME II
### 1783-1853

**James Truslow Adams**
*Editor in Chief*

**R. V. Coleman**
*Managing Editor*

Thomas Robson Hay
*Associate Editor*

Atkinson Dymock
*Art Director*

NEW YORK
CHARLES SCRIBNER'S SONS
1945

N preparing and presenting the second volume of the *Album of American History*, the editors have been much encouraged by the reception accorded by the public to the first.

The editorial policy will, in general, follow that already established. The treatment, however, comes to be somewhat different. Beginning, as we do in this volume, with the formation of the United States as a nation, the presentation can be a more unified one than was possible when we were dealing with individual colonies with widely varied backgrounds and interests.

On the other hand, the period from 1783 to 1853, covered in this volume, was one of national growth and ever-widening boundaries. The frontier in a large measure influenced the life of the time, and thus demands a proportionally prominent place in our work.

Again, the preparation of this volume has posed one editorial problem quite different from that encountered in the first one. In the earlier period the difficulty was to find an adequate supply of contemporary and authentic pictorial material. Increasingly, with the opening of the 19th Century, such material has multiplied to so great an extent that the difficulty now becomes one of decision as to what may be left out.

The criticism may be made that important pictures have been omitted or that significant events have been slighted. We can only hope that within the limits of the space to which we have necessarily had to limit ourselves, we have provided a true and representative picture of how our history *looked* between 1783 and 1853.

Although the *Album* is intended to present its story without reference to other more detailed works, yet, particularly where exploration is concerned, we believe the *Atlas of American History* will be found useful as a supplement to the *Album*. Equally for a wider knowledge of some of the facts necessarily treated briefly in the *Album*, the *Dictionary of American History* will provide a fuller understanding.

In securing the pictorial material used in this volume, we have, as in the previous one, been helped at every turn by the libraries, museums and scholars of the country. To them we are indebted not only for the privilege of using their treasures but for their advice as to what should be used. Credit for our source has been given with practically every picture, and elsewhere in these pages we have made especial acknowledgment to those who have helped us greatly. To all the others, and they are many, we herewith express our gratitude.

As Editor in Chief, I wish to take this opportunity of again expressing my deep appreciation of the invaluable aid given by the Managing Editor, Mr. R. V. Coleman, to whose other responsibilities has been added that of writing the running text. I can only repeat and emphasize what I said of his help in the first volume. His knowledge, like that of Ulysses, "of many men and many cities," and I may add, of the vast variety of historical characters, episodes, periods and conditions with which we have had to deal, has very largely helped to achieve such success as we may have attained in dealing with the mass of material now becoming available.

An Editor knows how much he owes to those who have worked with him, and I wish to express my heartfelt thanks also for the assistance rendered in their fields by our Associate Editor, Mr. Thomas R. Hay, and the Art Editor, Mr. Atkinson Dymock, both of whom have ably met the many intricate and technical difficulties which have daily confronted them in one way and another.

Warm appreciation is also due to E. Graham Platt, Marion G. Barnes, Ethel M. Watson and Mary Wells McNeill who have searched the museums and libraries of the country for pictorial material and have checked both the facts and the form of presenting them.

JAMES TRUSLOW ADAMS

January 2, 1945

# ACKNOWLEDGMENT

IN THIS as in the previous volume the editors have been assisted by the advice and cooperation of museums, libraries and individuals throughout the country. In general, proper credit has been given in the case of each picture reproduced but particular acknowledgment for especial help is due the following:

Prof. Randolph G. Adams, William L. Clements Library, Ann Arbor, Mich.
American Antiquarian Society, Worcester, Mass.
Boatmen's National Bank of St. Louis, Mo.
Brooklyn Museum, Brooklyn, N. Y.
The Bucks County Historical Society, Doylestown, Pa.
Buffalo Historical Society, Buffalo, N. Y.
Lawrence J. Burpee, International Joint Commission, Ottawa, Canada
The Society of California Pioneers, San Francisco
Public Archives of Canada, Research and Publicity Division, Ottawa
Carolina Art Association, Charleston, S. C.
The Charleston Museum, Charleston, S. C.
Chase Bank Collection of Moneys of the World, New York City
Chicago Historical Society, Chicago, Ill.
William L. Clements Library, University of Michigan, Ann Arbor, Mich.
Colt's Patent Fire Arms Manufacturing Co., Hartford, Conn.
The Library of Congress, Washington, D. C.
The Corcoran Gallery of Art, Washington, D. C.
Eames Collection, The New York Public Library
Eno Collection, The New York Public Library
Enoch Pratt Free Library, Baltimore, Md.
The Essex Institute, Salem, Mass.
University of Georgia, Athens, Ga.
Henry E. Huntington Library and Art Gallery, San Marino, Calif.
Illinois State Historical Society, Springfield

Institut Francais de Washington, Washington, D. C.
Thomas Jefferson Memorial Foundation, Monticello, Charlottesville, Va.
Church of Jesus Christ of Latter Day Saints, Salt Lake City, Utah
The Jockey Club, New York City
Landis Valley Museum, Lancaster, Pa.
Louisiana State Museum, New Orleans, La.
Mr. A. S. McQueen, Folkston, Ga.
Mr. George F. Macdonald, Windsor, Canada
Marine Research Society, Salem, Mass.
The Mariners' Museum, Newport News, Va.
Maryland Historical Society, Baltimore, Md.
The Metropolitan Museum of Art, New York City
The Mirabeau B. Lamar Library, University of Texas, Austin
Missouri Historical Society, St. Louis, Mo.
Municipal Museum of the City of Baltimore, Md.
Nacogdoches Historical Society, Nacogdoches, Texas
The National Archives, Washington, D. C.
National Park Service, U. S. Department of the Interior, Washington, D. C.
The New-York Historical Society, New York City
The Society of The New York Hospital, New York City
The New York Public Library, New York City
New York State Library, Albany, N. Y.
The Ohio State Archaeological and Historical Society, Columbus, Ohio
Peabody Institute, Baltimore, Md.
Peabody Museum, Salem, Mass.
The Historical Society of Pennsylvania, Philadelphia
The Pennsylvania Hospital, Philadelphia
Carnegie Library of Pittsburgh, Pa.
Dr. Milo M. Quaife, Detroit Public Library, Detroit, Mich.
Rhode Island State Archives, Department of State, Providence, R. I.
Rochester Historical Society, Rochester, N. Y.
City Art Museum, St. Louis, Mo.
St. Louis Mercantile Library Association, St. Louis, Mo.
The H. V. Smith Collection, New York City
Smithsonian Institution, Washington, D. C.
South Carolina Historical Society, Charleston
Stokes Collection, The New York Public Library
Transportation Library, University of Michigan, Ann Arbor, Mich.
Uniontown Free Public Library, Uniontown, Pa.

U. S. Coast and Geodetic Survey, Washington, D. C.

U. S. National Museum, Washington, D. C.

Mr. R. W. G. Vail, New York City

Vincennes Public Library, Vincennes, Ind.

Walters Art Gallery, Baltimore, Md.

The Western Reserve Historical Society, Cleveland, Ohio

The William Henry Smith Memorial Library of the Indiana State Historical
    Society, Indianapolis

William Rockhill Nelson Gallery of Art, Kansas City, Mo.

State Historical Society, Madison, Wis.

The Historical Society of York County, York, Pa.

# CONTENTS

# 1
# THE NEW NATION
## 1783-1789

**"The United States of America"**

Such was the self-chosen title of the New Nation, and the title by which it was recognized by the former mother country in the treaty of peace signed at Paris, Sept. 3, 1783.

The greatest of republics had been born and christened.

Its boundaries swept from the St. Croix River on the north

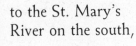
*Courtesy, New Brunswick Government Information Bureau*
St. Croix River

to the St. Mary's River on the south,

*Courtesy, Mr. A. S. McQueen, Folkston, Ga. and his History of Charlton County*
St. Mary's River

and westward to the rolling Mississippi.

*Courtesy, Free Public Library and Chamber of Commerce, Hannibal, Mo.*
Mississippi River

**The Border Forts**

On the north, the boundary followed a line through the Great Lakes, placing within the United States such important frontier forts and posts as

**Oswego**

at the end of the long portage route through central New York to Lake Ontario,

VIEW OF OSWEGO AND THE FORT IN 1798.

From a drawing by Dewitt, surveyor general.

B. J. Lossing, *Pictorial Field-Book of the Revolution.* 1851

**Fort Niagara**

where the Niagara River, after plunging over the Falls, flows placidly into Lake Ontario,

*The Port Folio, October, 1812*

View of Fort Niagara from the Canadian Side

### Detroit

that strategically situated, far-famed and much fought over sometimes trading post, sometimes fort, still mostly French, between Lake Erie and Lake Huron,

Courtesy, Detroit Public Library, Detroit, Michigan
Drawing of Detroit, by David Meredith (1790?)

### and Michilimackinac

meeting place of the Indians from the West and of the traders from the East, beautiful, but with a bloody past, where the waters of Lake Huron, Lake Michigan and Lake Superior meet.

Swett.                                    Lith. of Pendleton
VIEW of MICHILIMACKINAC

Thomas L. McKenney, *Sketches of a Tour to the Lakes.* 1827

But—it was thirteen years, after much diplomatic wrangling, and after many packs of furs had gone to Montreal rather than New York, before these frontier posts were surrendered to the United States.

## Demobilization

As the field service in the Revolution came to an end, the Continental Army was concentrated in the Highlands of the Hudson—mostly around the village of New Windsor.

A view of the camp grounds, looking up the Hudson River

Benson J. Lossing, *The Pictorial Field-Book of the Revolution.* 1852

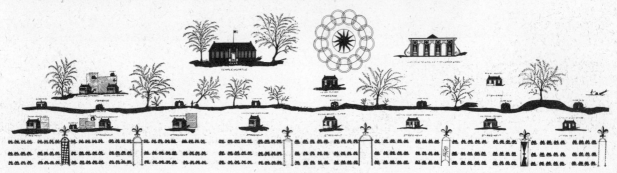

Courtesy, Historical Society of Newburgh Bay and The Highlands, Newburgh, N. Y.

*Above* is a view of the encampment at New Windsor, drawn in 1783 by William Tarbell, who was one of the men encamped there.

In the upper part of the picture *above*, is shown a building (the one with the flag) named the Temple of Virtue. This building was erected by the soldiers, with the approval of General Washington, as a gathering place for the men, where religious services could be held and social activities take place. The impending demobilization was not without its heartburnings. Would Congress, could Congress, see that the claims of the soldiers were met? The Newburgh Addresses, setting forth the discontent of the Army, circulated in March, 1783. It was at the Temple that Washington made his reply, urging his officers to hold fast to the principles for which war had been fought. It was here, and in this address, that Washington, taking his spectacles from his pocket, said, "You see, gentlemen, that I have not only grown gray, but blind in your service."

Benson J. Lossing, *The Pictorial Field-Book of the Revolution.* 1852
The Temple

## Boston

was the great New England seaport. At the entrance of its harbor stood this lighthouse.

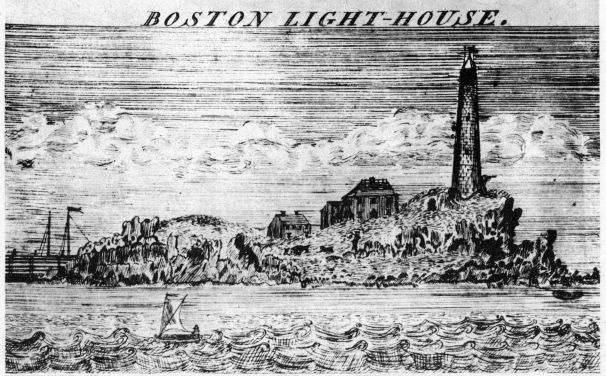

From sketch in *Journal of "Hercules".* 1792  *Courtesy,* The Essex Institute, Salem, Mass.

And here is a view of the town itself as it looked during this period.

*A View of the Town of Boston the Capital of New England.*

*Columbian Magazine,* December, 1787
*Courtesy,* The New-York Historical Society, New York City

## Faneuil Hall

was surrounded by hitching posts, and we see not only one of the many crooked streets of Boston, but the usual means of transportation and the way the people dressed at the time.

*Massachusetts Magazine, 1789   Courtesy, The New-York Historical Society, New York City*

In Boston, as in Salem and other New England towns, the character of the business carried on in a shop was often indicated by some such sign as the one to the *right*, which designated a tannery.

*Courtesy, Essex Institute, Salem, Mass.*

Lighting was still largely by candles of one sort or another, but the use of whale oil was not uncommon.

Benjamin Butterworth, *The Growth of Industrial Art.*
1892

*Left,* Adjustable candle-stick table

Courtesy, The Metropolitan Museum of Art, New York

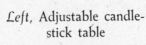
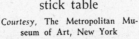

**At Home**

There might have hung on the wall a looking glass such as this, with mahogany and gilt frame.

My lady might have viewed herself in a dress such as we see *opposite*.

*Right*, Flowered Silk Brocade Dress

*Courtesy*, Essex Institute, Salem, Mass.

Luke Vincent Lockwood, *Colonial Furniture in America.* 1926

And in the better homes would have been found a bed such as this, in Sheraton style.

Luke Vincent Lockwood, *Colonial Furniture in America.* 1926

Beside the bed at night might have been found shoes such as these.

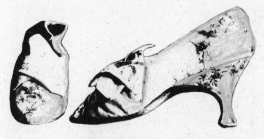

*Courtesy*, Essex Institute, Salem, Mass.

## The Charles River Bridge

was one of the great engineering feats of that period. It was completed in 1786 and opened with due ceremonies.

*View of the BRIDGE over CHARLES RIVER.*

Massachusetts Magazine, or, Monthly Museum, September, 1789    Courtesy, The New-York Historical Society, New York City

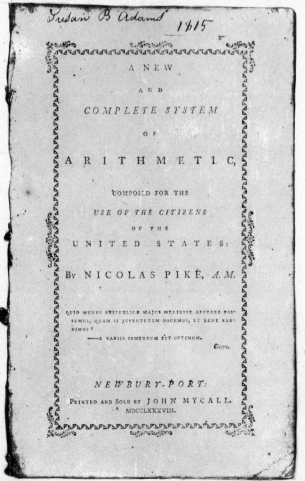

### Recommended by George Washington

At Newburyport in 1788, John Mycall printed the first edition of *Nicholas Pike's Arithmetic*.

The book was recommended by the presidents of Yale, Harvard and Dartmouth, and even by George Washington, to whom the editor sent a copy.

It went through eight editions; was widely used as a text in schools throughout the country; and was an outstanding contribution to American education.

## An Agricultural Depression

as usual, followed the ending of the war. Despite this prosperous looking farm at Worcester, times were not good in western Massachusetts.

*Massachusetts Magazine*, November, 1792   *Courtesy*, The New-York Historical Society, New York City

Home of Moses Gill at Worcester

Commonwealth of Massachusetts.

By His EXCELLENCY

James Bowdoin, Esq.

GOVERNOUR OF THE COMMONWEALTH OF

MASSACHUSETTS.

A Proclamation.

WHEREAS by an Act passed the sixteenth of February instant, entitled, "An Act describing the disqualifications, to which persons shall be subjected, which have been, or may be guilty of Treason, or giving aid or support to the present Rebellion, and to whom a pardon may be extended," the General Court have established and made known the conditions and disqualifications, upon which pardon and indemnity to certain offenders, described in the said Act, shall be offered and given ; and have authorized and empowered the Governor, in the name of the General Court, to promise to such offenders such conditional pardon and indemnity :

I HAVE thought fit, by virtue of the authority vested in me by the said Act, to issue this Proclamation, hereby promising pardon and indemnity to all offenders within the description aforesaid, who are citizens of this State ; under such restrictions, conditions and disqualifications, as are mentioned in the said Act : provided they comply with the terms and conditions thereof, on or before the twenty-first day of March next.

GIVEN at the Council Chamber in Boston, this Seventeenth Day of February, in the Year of our LORD One Thousand Seven Hundred and Eighty Seven, and in the Eleventh Year of the Independence of the United States of AMERICA.

JAMES BOWDOIN.

By His Excellency's Command,
JOHN AVERY, jun. Secretary.

BOSTON : Printed by ADAMS & NOURSE, Printers to the GENERAL COURT.

From copy in Massachusetts Historical Society, Boston.
Winsor, *Narrative and Critical History*, 1888

In the summer of 1786 discontent broke into open rebellion and gave the authorities of Massachusetts considerable trouble. From the name of one of its leaders, it came to be known as Shays' Rebellion.

So grateful were the people of eastern Massachusetts to General Shepard, who crushed the Rebellion, that they commissioned Paul Revere to make him a silver bowl.

*Courtesy*, Mabel Brady Garvan Collection, Yale University Art Gallery, New Haven

## Health Insurance

At Exeter, N. H., Ananias Tubbs was sick from July 31, 1786, to July 31, 1787, and got five pounds eight shillings as compensation from the State.

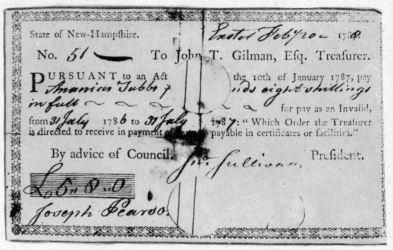

Courtesy, Chase National Bank Collection of Moneys of the World, New York

## Prisons

In 1799, so the story goes, a man named Brunton was sent to Newgate Prison, in Connecticut, for counterfeiting. While there, he made this picture of that prison. Elsewhere, over the country, thousands of people were in almost equally bad prisons for less serious offences. Inability to pay a trifling debt often resulted in indeterminate confinement in a filthy prison.

*Left*, Newgate Prison

A. C. Bates, *An Early Connecticut Engraver and his Work*, 1906

## Farms

At Canaan, Conn., not far from Newgate, life went peacefully on in the valleys between the hills. Here we get a glimpse of a country road in 1789. Even in gravelly Connecticut it must have been practically impassable for wheeled vehicles after the spring thaw.

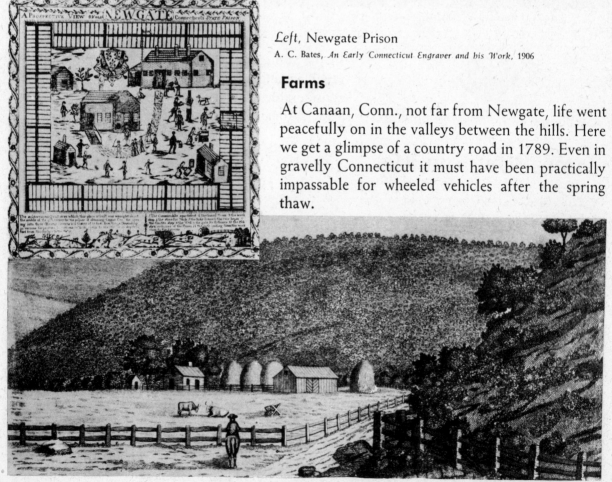

*Columbian Magazine*, March, 1789   Courtesy, The New-York Historical Society, New York City

## The Blacksmith Shop

At the old Cooke Tavern, in Plainville, Conn., stood this forge. Similar ones all over New England provided latches, hinges and the thousand and one things needed around a house.

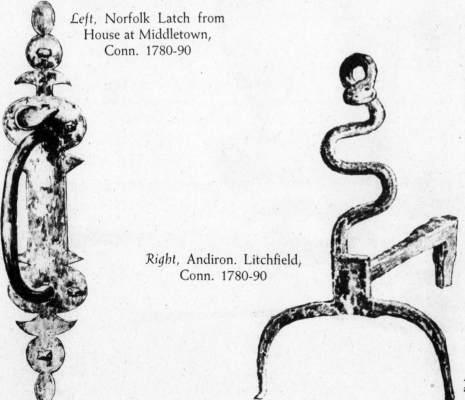

*Left*, Norfolk Latch from House at Middletown, Conn. 1780-90

*Right*, Andiron. Litchfield, Conn. 1780-90

All illustrations on this page are from Albert H. Sonn, *Early American Wrought Iron.* 1928

## And the Silversmith

Teapot by Abraham Dubois, 1780-1790

*Below*, Bowl by Ephraim Brasher, 1775-1800

Beakers by Cary Dunn. Late 18th Century

Mug by Stephen Emery, 1775-1800

*Left*, Creamer by Daniel Van Voorhis. Late 18th Century

*Below*, Spoon by John Burger. Late 18th Century

Coffeepot by John Vernon ca. 1790

Ladle by Joseph Anthony, 1785-1800

All illustrations on this page are by *courtesy* of the Metropolitan Museum of Art, New York

## Down the Hudson

At Albany the Dutch influence was still evident in the stepped roofs of the brick houses.

At Poughkeepsie, Henry Livingston, recently released from British captivity, had a country home.

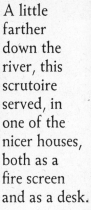

*Columbian Magazine*, December, 1789
Courtesy, The New-York Historical Society, New York City.

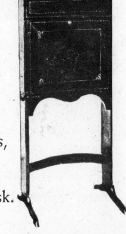

A little farther down the river, this scrutoire served, in one of the nicer houses, both as a fire screen and as a desk.

Luke Vincent Lockwood,
*Colonial Furniture in America.* 1926

*New-York Magazine; or, Literary Repository*, May, 1791
Courtesy, The New-York Historical Society, New York City

At West Point, where one of the big chains (b) had been stretched across the river during the war, there was still a fort, but no military academy as yet.

*West Point viewed from the North as it appeared at the Close of the War*

*New-York Magazine; or, Literary Repository*, March, 1791 Courtesy, The New-York Historical Society, New York City

## New York City

was creeping up Manhattan Island, while Brooklyn, across the East River, was taking on the appearance of a village.

*Courtesy, The New-York Historical Society, New York City*

St. Mémin's view of the city and harbor of New York from Mount Pitt, the seat of John R. Livingston, esq., 1794.

Trinity Church was already beginning to be down town.

Stokes *Iconography of Manhattan Island, 1915-28*

Another church, humbler but of great potentiality, also had a place in New York—on John Street.

*Courtesy, Stokes Collection, The New York Public Library*

Old Methodist Church in John Street

## Hospital

At 319 Broadway, between Duane and Worth Streets, stood the New York Hospital, opened in 1776, one of the early though not the first in the United States.

*Courtesy,* The Society of The New York Hospital

## Shipping

New York was primarily a seaport and shipping was its life. Near the waterfront, sailmakers were busily at work.

*Courtesy,* The New-York Historical Society, New York City

## The China Trade

This Philadelphia item, in a Baltimore newspaper, announcing the sailing of the *Empress of China* from New York in February, 1784, was of greater importance than the editor realized. Across the Atlantic, around Cape Horn and through the Indian Ocean went the *Empress of China* to the fabulous East.

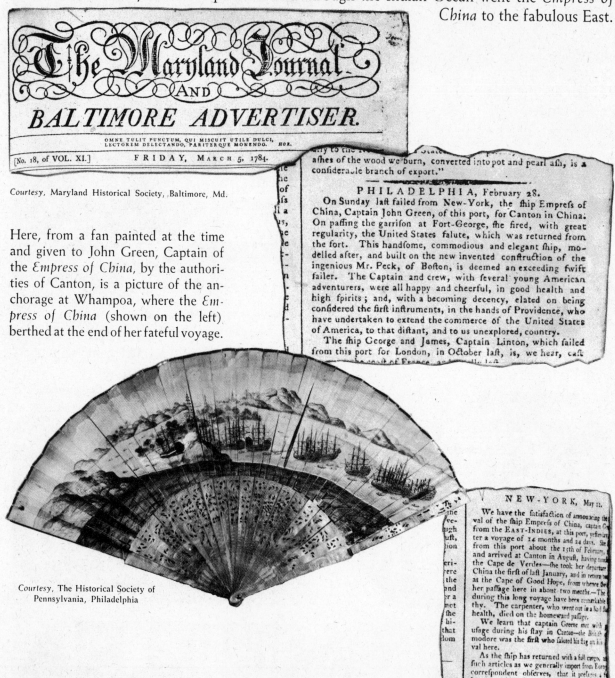

*Courtesy*, Maryland Historical Society, Baltimore, Md.

Here, from a fan painted at the time and given to John Green, Captain of the *Empress of China*, by the authorities of Canton, is a picture of the anchorage at Whampoa, where the *Empress of China* (shown on the left) berthed at the end of her fateful voyage.

*Courtesy*, The Historical Society of Pennsylvania, Philadelphia

PHILADELPHIA, February 28.

On Sunday laſt ſailed from New-York, the ſhip Empreſs of China, Captain John Green, of this port, for Canton in China. On paſſing the garriſon at Fort-George, ſhe fired, with great regularity, the United States ſalute, which was returned from the fort. This handſome, commodious and elegant ſhip, modelled after, and built on the new invented conſtruction of the ingenious Mr. Peck, of Boſton, is deemed an exceeding ſwift ſailer. The Captain and crew, with ſeveral young American adventurers, were all happy and cheerful, in good health and high ſpirits; and, with a becoming decency, elated on being conſidered the firſt inſtruments, in the hands of Providence, who have undertaken to extend the commerce of the United States of America, to that diſtant, and to us unexplored, country.

The ſhip George and James, Captain Linton, which ſailed from this port for London, in October laſt, is, we hear, caſt

NEW-YORK, May 11.

We have the ſatisfaction of announcing the arrival of the ſhip Empreſs of China, captain Green, from the EAST-INDIES, at this port, yeſterday, after a voyage of 14 months and 24 days. She ſailed from this port about the 15th of February, and arrived at Canton in Auguſt, having touched the Cape de Verdes—ſhe took her departure from China the firſt of laſt January, and in return touched at the Cape of Good Hope, from whence ſhe made her paſſage here in about two months.—The crew during this long voyage have been remarkably healthy. The carpenter, who went out in a bad ſtate of health, died on the homeward paſſage.

We learn that captain Greene met with good uſage during his ſtay in Canton—the Britiſh commodore was the firſt who ſaluted his flag on his arrival here.

As the ſhip has returned with a full cargo, of ſuch articles as we generally import from Europe, a correſpondent obſerves, that it preſages a happy period of our being able to diſpenſe with burdenſome and unneceſſary traffick, which before we have carried on with Europe—to the great prejudice of our riſing empire, and future happineſs and proſpects of ſolid greatneſs: And that whether not, the ſhip's cargo be productive of thoſe advantages to the owners, which their merits for the undertaking deſerve, he conceives it will promote the welfare of the United States in general, by inducing their citizens with emulation to equal, if not to exceed their mercantile rivals.

Some years ago, when the advantages of trade and navigation were better ſtudded and more valued than they are now, the arrival of a veſſel after ſo perilous a voyage, from ſo diſtant a part of our globe, would be announced by public thankſgiving and ringing of bells!—Should not this be our practice ſince Providence is countenancing our navigation to this new world? We hope in our next, to be able to give our readers a more perfect detail of this important voyage.

OMNE TULIT PUNCTUM, QUI MISCUIT UTILE DULCI, LECTOREM DELECTANDO, PARITERQUE MONENDO.    HOR.

[No. 18, of VOL. XI.]    FRIDAY, MARCH 5, 1784.

*Courtesy*, Historical Society of Pennsylvania, Philadelphia

Another small item—this time in the *Pennsylvania Packet* of May 16, 1785—announced the return to New York on May 11, of the *Empress of China* "with a full cargo". This was the beginning of the famous China Trade.

## New Jersey

West of the Hudson, toward Morristown in New Jersey, we find a well-kept countryside and comfortable farms.

*View upon the Road from New-Windsor, towards Morris Town JERSEY.*

*Columbian Magazine*, October, 1789 *Courtesy*, The New-York Historical Society, New York City

## And in Pennsylvania

near Philadelphia, we find an equally charming country scene.

*A View on Schuylkill, near Philadelphia.*

*Columbian Magazine*, October, 1789
*Courtesy*, The New-York Historical Society, New York City

## Philadelphia

then the largest city in the United States, was still in many ways only a village. Here is a view of the New Market taken from the corner of Shippen and Second streets. Note the town pump.

*A View of the New Market from the Corner of Shippen & Second streets Philada.*

Columbian Magazine, February, 1788
Courtesy, The New-York Historical Society, New York City

With unpaved, muddy streets, foot scrapers were useful as well as ornamental.

Albert H. Sonn, *Early American Wrought Iron.* 1928

At No. 13 South 6th Street, stood the building known as the Department of the United States for Foreign Affairs, in which was drafted the proclamation of peace in 1783.

Courtesy, Historical Society of Pennsylvania, Philadelphia

## Newspapers and Magazines

Here, in Philadelphia, was published *The Independent Gazetteer*

FRIDAY, JAN. 18, 1788.

# THE INDEPENDENT GAZETTEER;

## OR, THE

# CHRONICLE OF FREEDOM.

VOLUME VII. NUMBER 655.

*That the People have a Right to Freedom of Speech, and of writing, and publishing their Sentiments; therefore the Freedom of the Press ought not to be restrained.—*Pennsylvania Bill of Rights.
*Let it be impressed upon your Minds, let it be instilled into your Children, that the Liberty of the Press is the* PALLADIUM *of all the civil, political, and religious Rights of Freemen.*—Junius.

### TO THE PUBLIC.

THE subscriber being possessed of considerable real estate, consisting of houses and lots of ground in the city of Philadelphia, plantations and improvements in Bedford county and state of Pennsylvania, two rice plantations in the county of Essingham, and state of Georgia; together with various plantations in the county of Harrison, and state of Virginia; also lots of ground in the town of MONTGOMERY and county of Harrison aforesaid, proposes to transfer and dispose of the same in the following manner, that is to say:

1st. The property hereafter specified shall be drawn for by numbers to such persons as choose to become adventurers.

2d. The property and respective lots are warranted free of every incumbrance to the time of drawing.

3dly. The price to each number or TICKET, is eight dollars, specie, or the present medium of the state of Pennsylvania, or New-Jersey, as suits the purchaser.

4thly. There are NO BLANKS ... PRIZES.

Franks township, and county aforesaid, lying on and near the new road leading from Franks-Town to Chest valley, on the waters of Will's creek and Clearfield.

Ten plantations, each containing 175 acres, in the county aforesaid, situate on the waters of Middle Creek and Wolf's and Camp-Run. Most of the above plantations are in the neighbourhood of the Gledes, amid a wealthy settlement of Germans.

Fifty plantations, containing 200 acres each, in Harrison county, and state of Virginia, situate on the branches of Hughes's river, &c. within a few miles of Clarksburgh, Morgan-Town, and the town of Montgomery. • Vide the Reverend William Werth's certificate, with regard to the situation of Montgomery Town, and the soil of the last mentioned 50 plantations.

The remaining prizes consist of lots of ground in the said town of Montgomery, each of which are at least from 60 to 70 feet front on the main street, and in length or depth to 20 feet alleys, from 240 to 280 feet.

In order to remove, as much as possible, any suspicions ...

tween Third and Fourth-streets: Francis Swaine, Esquire, Sheriff, of Montgomery county: Colonel Henry Miller, York-Town: Major Jeremiah Talbot, Dr. Robert Johnston, of Franklin county: Thomas Grant, Esq. Sheriff of Northumber and county: William Antis and Daniel Montgomery, Esqrs. of Northumberland Town: Major Thomas Robinson, Pine creek: Mr. James Silverwood, Sunbury: James Martin, Esq. Bedford county, and of the subscriber, living in Walnut-street, Philadelphia.

Philadelphia, November 21, 1787.

THE Acting Committee of the Society for alleviating the miseries of Public Prisons, visiting, agreeably to their appointment, the Jail and Work-house of this city, have frequently wished that the funds of their institution would allow them to supply the *unhappy beings* there confined, with suitable cloathing, during this *inclement season*—But as this is ...

in the January, 1788, issue of which we find the advertisement of post coach carriages shown *opposite*.

The Philadelphia, Baltimore, and Eastern Shore

### Line of Post Coach Carriages.

THE subscribers beg leave to inform the public, that they have established a complete line of Post Coach Carriages, to convey the public mail and baggage for hire between Philadelphia and Baltimore. And in order to make it convenient for passengers travelling to and from Philadelphia and Baltimore, they will convey passengers for hire between Philadelphia and Susquehanna; and between Susquehanna and Baltimore, they will convey all such passengers (gratis) that favor them with their company between Philadelphia and Susquehanna.

The Post Coach Carriages will

Set off from the Baltimore and Eastern Shore Stage-Office, in Fourth street, nearly opposite the Old Indian Queen Tavern, in Philadelphia, and from Mr. Evans's Tavern, the corner of Calvert and Bank streets in Baltimore, during the winter season, on Monday and Thursday in each week, at 10 o'clock in the forenoon, and will arrive in Philadelphia and Baltimore, on Wednesdays and Saturdays in good season for dining. The said post coaches will stop with passengers on their way from Philadelphia the first night at Christiana Bridge, where the coach for the Eastern Shore will, on Friday morning in each week, take up the mail, passengers, and baggage, and arrive the same afternoon at Chester-Town, and set off from Chester-Town, on Tuesday morning, and arrive at Christiana ...

Courtesy, Historical Society of Pennsylvania, Philadelphia

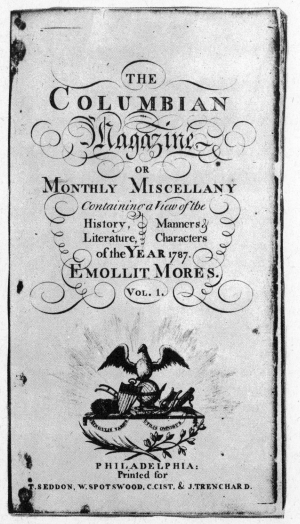

# THE COLUMBIAN Magazine

## OR

## MONTHLY MISCELLANY

*Containing a View of the*

History, Manners & Literature, Characters

of the YEAR 1787.

EMOLLIT MORES.

VOL. 1.

PHILADELPHIA: Printed for
T. SEDDON, W. SPOTSWOOD, C. CIST, & J. TRENCHARD.

Also at Philadelphia there was published at this time *The Columbian Magazine*, from which several of the illustrations in this volume are drawn (magazines were becoming important as a branch of journalism)

## Fire Insurance

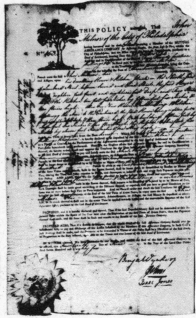

John Milnor, of the City of Philadelphia, had his dwelling, his "new house" and his "back building" and "kitchen" insured against fire loss for £300 by the Mutual Assurance Company. His policy was No. 153, and nailed to his house was this fire marker, carrying

the number of his policy. If he had a fire, the Mutual Assurance brigade, seeing the marker, would do its best to extinguish the fire, but the brigades of other fire insurance companies, having no concern in the matter, might sit down and watch the fun.

## Ladies' Hats

In 1784, the ladies wore hats as shown on the *left*. In 1785, they wore hats as shown on the *right*.

## And Bad Men

# A PROCLAMATION.

WHEREAS by the examination of a Negro boy named Jem, taken before the Hon. Francis Hopkinson, esq. Judge of the Admiralty, it appears, that on or about the 15th ult, a certain JAMES BURN did feloniously run away with, and carry off the Negro boy aforesaid, and a Sloop, called the *Bumper*, ——— Simpson master, the property of David King and William M'Dowal of the island of Antigua: And whereas it appears by the deposition of James Kennard, Pilot, taken as aforesaid, that on the 29th of August last, being near Lewis-Town, in the bay of Delaware, he found the Sloop aforesaid, at anchor, with the Negro boy Jem on board, (the said Burn having previously quitted the Sloop and gone ashore): And whereas it is of the utmost importance that the perpetrator of such atrocious crimes be brought to condign punishment, WE have thought fit to offer and do hereby offer a public reward of *One Hundred Dollars*, for the said James Burn, to any person, who shall apprehend and secure him, to be paid on his conviction for the same: And all judges, justices, sheriffs, and constables, are hereby strictly enjoined and required to make diligent search and enquiry after,

## Roads

Back of Philadelphia, to the West, lay the prosperous village of York, near which ran this road. Note the ruts, and the man on horseback.

*View from Bushongo Tavern 3 miles from York Town on the Baltimore road*

*Columbian Magazine*, July, 1788
Courtesy, The New-York Historical Society, New York City

On a house near Doylestown was this latch — made in the neighborhood.

Albert H. Sonn, *Early American Wrought Iron.*
1928

## The Hinterland

On west from York, toward Carlisle, the road over South Mountain looked like this in May, 1788.

*Columbian Magazine*, May, 1788
Courtesy, The New-York Historical Society, New York City

**The Frontier**

H. R. Schoolcraft, *Information respecting Indian Tribes of the United States*, 1851-57

Pittsburgh in 1790

Over the mountains, at the forks of the Ohio where old Fort Duquesne stood, was the frontier village of Pittsburgh, to become increasingly important as an outfitting place for the West.

**On the Lehigh River**

in northeastern Pennsylvania, was the Moravian village of Bethlehem.

Isaac Weld, *Travels through North America*, 1795-97

## Farming

was the occupation of about ninety percent of all Americans. Plows such as this, with cast-iron mould boards, were in use, though not too common.

*Courtesy*, Bucks County Historical Society, Doylestown, Pa.

Seed drills, homemade, simple but efficient, were to be found on many farms.

*Courtesy*, Bucks County Historical Society, Doylestown, Pa.

In the *Columbian Magazine* for December, 1787, was shown this plan for a newer and more scientific implement for drilling seed.

*Courtesy*, The New-York Historical Society, New York City

## The Old and the New

The scythe and cradle were still ordinarily used for harvesting grain,

Courtesy, Bucks County Historical Society, Doylestown, Pa.

but here, too, new methods were being thought of. *Below* seems to be the genesis of the "header" used in the great middle-western wheat fields a hundred years later.

*A new method of Reaping*

Columbian Magazine, September, 1788
Courtesy, The New-York Historical Society, New York City

New methods of storing grain were also being considered, if not tried, as is indicated by this plan of a granary appearing in the *Columbian Magazine* of 1786.

Courtesy, The New-York Historical Society, New York City

## On Chesapeake Bay

Annapolis was the capital of Maryland, and it was there, at the State House (shown *opposite*) that, in 1786, was held a meeting to discuss reform of the vexatious restrictions placed on interstate commerce by the various states, from which discussion resulted the Constitutional Convention of 1787 (see page 36).

David Ridgely, *Annals of Annapolis* (1841)
State House at Annapolis

At the theater in Baltimore "The Force of Love" was being tempered with the Christian religion.

*Courtesy,* The New-York Historical Society, New York City

James Williams was dealing in continental certificates and land,

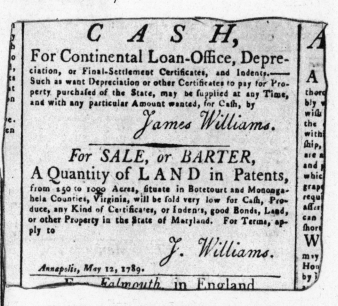

*Maryland Journal and Baltimore Advertiser,* June 9, 1789
*Courtesy,* Enoch Pratt Free Library, Baltimore, Md.

and Harry "a dark mulatto" was on the loose.

## South of the Potomac

On the indentations of Chesapeake Bay and on the James River, tobacco was the great industry.

The tobacco was hung in open sheds to dry,    and later packed in hogsheads for shipment

by barge

William Tatham, *Culture and Commerce of Tobacco.* 1800

by wagon

by rolling

to the wharfs where it was loaded in ocean-going vessels for shipment across the Atlantic.

*Right*, Virginia Tobacco Wharf

From a map of North America by Mathew Albert and George Lotter, 1784

## In the Carolinas

rice was still the staple crop.

Charles Fraser, *A Charleston Sketchbook,* 1796-1806    *Courtesy,* Carolina Art Association, Charleston, S. C.

The *above* sketch shows tidal rice fields developed on an old rice river by a system of ditches, banks and flood gates.

Charles Fraser, *A Charleston Sketchbook,* 1796-1806
*Courtesy,* Carolina Art Association, Charleston, S. C.

Some fifty miles west of Charleston, S. C., stood the Stony Creek Meeting House. Note the road with its deep ruts.

## A New Home

The home of Henry Laurens in South Carolina was burned during the Revolution. Laurens himself, while on the way to Europe to negotiate a loan for the colonies, was captured by the British and later exchanged for Cornwallis. On his return to South Carolina he built the house shown *below*.

Charles Fraser, *A Charleston Sketchbook*, 1796-1806    Courtesy, Carolina Art Association, Charleston, S. C.

The two mules on the *left* are of some interest in that, in 1785, the King of Spain presented to George Washington an Andalusian jack and jennies. Shortly after, Lafayette contributed a similar Maltese group. This stock accelerated the production of the mule in the United States.

Courtesy, The Charleston Museum, Charleston, S. C.

In Charleston, at the foot of Broad Street, stood the Exchange Building, on the steps of which George Washington made an appearance in 1791 and where the governors of South Carolina were proclaimed until the capital of the state was removed to Columbia.

## Money

What forms of money did the American of the 1780's use in his daily transactions?

Some of the old Continental currency still floated around, but was not worth much.

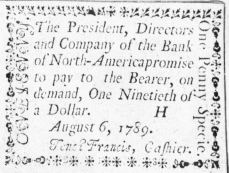

"Small change" notes such as this on the Bank of North America were common for small transactions.

Small coins, if they could be had, were mostly the old English ones.

George III Ha'penny

*Right*, George II Sixpence

George I Shilling

Queen Anne Crown

The commonest coin in circulation was the Spanish milled dollar.

The French Sou was also in circulation.

Louis XV Sou

## Gold Coins

were not common but there were a certain number in circulation—and their value, like the silver and copper coins, varied in the different states.

The Spanish Pistole went at
about $4.00

The Spanish Doubloon was worth
roughly $15.00

The Brazilian half-Joannes, commonly
known as half-joes, were worth
about $8.00

Some state coins had a limited circulation.

Connecticut Cent

## The First United States Coin

was the Fugio Cent, issued in 1787, but we still had no national coinage or national currency.

The Fugio Cent bore the injunction, "Mind your business."

## Banks

The first bank in the United States, founded by Robert Morris, was chartered December 31, 1781.

Here is the oldest known bank check in the United States, drawn simply on "The Bank."

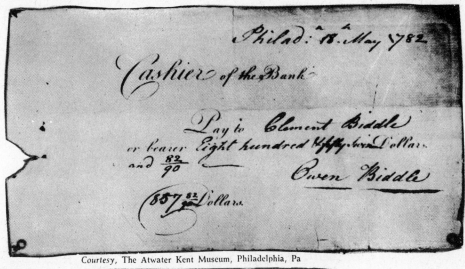

*Courtesy, The Atwater Kent Museum, Philadelphia, Pa*

Drafts on London were, of course, common. This one is signed by Robert Morris.

*Courtesy, Chase Bank Collection of Moneys of the World, New York*

## John Fitch and His Steamboat

In this same city of Philadelphia, where Owen Biddle was drawing a check and Robert Morris was endorsing a draft, there was a man named Fitch who had an idea, namely, that he could make the power of steam propel a boat. He got a watchmaker named Henry Voight to make an engine which he installed on a small boat with twelve paddles and tried it out on the Delaware River, but it did not work out too well and the age of steam had to wait.

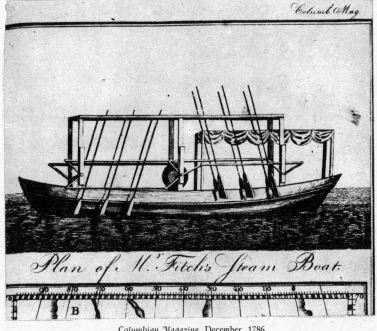

*Columbian Magazine, December, 1786*

## A Young Man Named Webster (First Name, Noah)

Right, First published in 1783 as *A Grammatical Institute of the English Language*

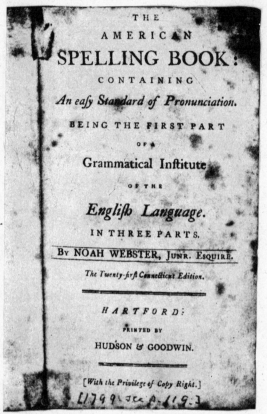

THE
AMERICAN
SPELLING BOOK:
CONTAINING
*An easy Standard of Pronunciation.*
BEING THE FIRST PART
OF A
Grammatical Inſtitute
OF THE
*Engliſh Language.*
IN THREE PARTS.
By NOAH WEBSTER, JUNr. ESQUIRE.
*The Twenty-firſt Connecticut Edition.*

HARTFORD:
PRINTED BY
HUDSON & GOODWIN.

[With the Privilege of Copy Right.]

A
Grammatical Inſtitute
OF THE
*Engliſh Language.*
COMPRISING
An eaſy, concise, and ſyſtematic Method of EDU-
CATION, designed for the Uſe of Engliſh Schools
in *America.*
IN THREE PARTS.
PART II.
CONTAINING
A plain and comprehenſive Grammar,
Grounded on the true Principles and Idioms of the Language.

By NOAH WEBSTER, jun. Eſq.

The Third Edition, reviſed and amended.

PHILADELPHIA:
Printed and ſold by YOUNG and M'CULLOCH, the
Corner of Cheſnut and Second-ſtreets.
M.DCC.LXXX.VII.

The author in 1788 changed the title to *The American Spelling Book,*

and, in 1788, we find this busy man employed as editor of *The American Magazine*, being published in New York,

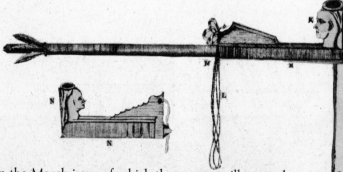

in the March issue of which there was an illustrated article on Indian pipes which had been presented to Congress.

( 195 )

THE
AMERICAN MAGAZINE,
For MARCH, 1788.

EXPLANATION OF THE PLATE.

A. THE Shank of the Calu-
met of Peace, a pipe,
5¾ inches in length. Preſented to Congreſs by the Pyanki-
ſhaws, an Illinois tribe.
B. The Bowl, of the ſize of that of
an ordinary pipe.
C. Two Circles cut round the
ſhank, near the end where the
ſtem enters it.
D. The Stem–The ſtems are from
2½ to 4 feet in length.
E. A String of leather, covered
with painted Porcupine quills.
F. Feathers curiouſly painted.
G. Strings of Wampum, wrought
out of ſhells, and deſigned to
faſten the ſhank and ſtem by
the ſtring E.
H. A Stone Pipe, 7¼ inches long
and an inch ſquare, diameter.
I. The Bowl 3 inches long.
K. The Figure of a man's face,
curiouſly wrought.
L. Strings of Wampum.
M. The Stem.
N. N. The Pipe without the
ſtem.

O. O. The Calumet without the
ſtem.
The *Calumet of Peace* is wrought
out of red ſtone, which is found in
one place only and is deemed ſa-
cred. None but chiefs are permitted to dig it and they at certain
times only. It is preſented to ce-
nemies on the ratification of a
peace.
The other pipe is for ordinary
uſe. It is wrought out of a ſoft
ſtone, of the color of clay, and fine
enough for a hone. The working,
poliſhing, drilling and carving of
figures, on theſe pipes, diſcover
great labor and ingenuity ; as do
the ſtrings of wampum, which are
compoſed of pieces of ſhell, wrought
into a cylindrical form, one third
of an inch in length, and pierced
with holes.
The *Indian red*, with which their
feathers, as well as many other articles, are painted, is a beautiful
color ; but the art of making it is
a ſecret with the natives.

BIOGRAPHICAL

## North of the River Ohio

From the Treaty of Fort Stanwix in 1768, this region had been recognized as Indian territory. But, during the Revolution, the Indians had sided with the British—and now came the penalty.

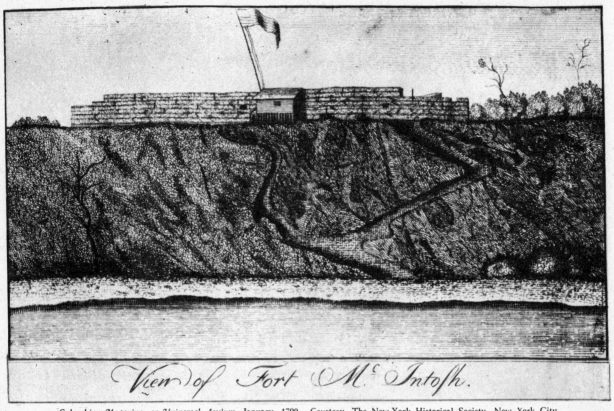

*View of Fort McIntosh.*

*Columbian Magazine, or Universal Asylum,* January, 1790   Courtesy, The New-York Historical Society, New York City

In 1778, Fort McIntosh had been established as the headquarters of the Western Department of the Revolutionary Army. There, in 1785, the government negotiated with the somewhat cowed Indians a treaty by which they relinquished some of their territory north of the Ohio—a treaty which was to make plenty of trouble later as we shall see in Chapter II.

However, as a result of this cession by the Indians, the Government, in the autumn of 1785, built Fort Harmar on the northerly side of the Ohio, just where the Muskingum comes in and on the westerly side of that river, and in 1787 created the Northwest Territory. Thus was established the entering wedge of settlement in the hitherto untouched Indian Country.

FORT HARMAR in 1790

*American Pioneer.* 1843

## The Ohio Company of Associates

With Ohio land available, the move for settlement was not long delayed. In 1786, a company, largely promoted by General Rufus Putnam, was organized in Boston to ask Congress for a grant of land "northwesterly of the river Ohio."

The Rev. Manasseh Cutler was selected to put the deal through Congress—and succeeded admirably. He not only got a million and a half acres for the Ohio Company, but he also got 5,000,000 acres for another group, known as the Scioto Company, headed by the Secretary of the Treasury Board.

William P. and Julia P. Cutler, *Life, Journals and Correspondence of Rev. Manasseh Cutler.* 1888

In 1788, the first settlement in the new Northwest Territory was made at Marietta, just across the Muskingum River from Fort Harmar, and within a palisaded area known as Campus Martius.

CAMPUS MARTIUS, IN 1791.

*American Pioneer.* 1844

And, in the same year, the Ohio Company of Associates established a land office which was the headquarters of General Putnam as Superintendent of the Company and as Surveyor-General of the United States.

*Courtesy, Ohio State Archaeological and Historical Society, Columbus*

Land Office, Marietta, Ohio

## General Putnam's Home

## The Miami Purchase

followed swiftly upon the Marietta settlement. Judge John Cleves Symmes of Morristown, N. J., was the promoter of this enterprise which often bears his name. Through a contract with the Treasury Board in 1788, Judge Symmes purchased, with Continental certificates and military warrants, a million acres on the northerly side of the Ohio, between the Miami and Little Miami rivers, where Cincinnati shortly came into being.

No. 16

### MIAMI LAND-WARRANT.

THIS entitles *Jonathan Dayton* his Heirs or Assigns, to locate one Section, in which the Fee of 640 Acres shall pass, subject to the Terms of settlement.

Dated the *first* Day of *May* A.D. 178

Signed by *John Cleves Symmes*

Counterfigned by

While on the banks of the Maumee River sat, brooding, a Miami chief by the name of Little Turtle (see page 47).

### Little Turtle

## The Constitutional Convention

Since 1781, the government of the United States had been functioning under what was known as the Articles of Confederation. Experience was now making evident that a more efficient form of government was necessary.

In 1786, as noted on page 25, a meeting of state commissioners at Annapolis resulted in the decision to call a larger convention to be held in Philadelphia the following year.

Thus, in the late Spring of 1787, delegates from each of the states, Rhode Island excepted, met in the State House at Philadelphia, and there, with George Washington as president of the meeting, brought forth the Constitution of the United States.

The proposed constitution was received with varying degrees of enthusiasm, but over the signature "Publius" began appearing in the press a series of essays in support of the Constitution, which contributed in great measure to its ratification by a sufficient number of states to enable the new government to be established on March 4, 1789. The essays, by James Madison, Alexander Hamilton and John Jay, were published in book form under title of *The Federalist*, which is recognized as one of the major contributions of American thinking to the literature of government.

*Courtesy, Historical Society of Pennsylvania, Philadelphia*

State House in Philadelphia. 1778

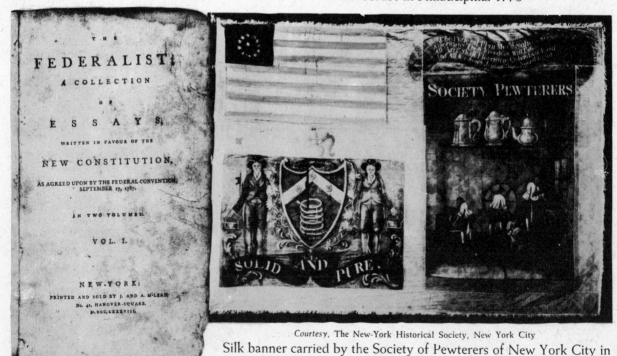

*Courtesy, The New-York Historical Society, New York City*

Silk banner carried by the Society of Pewterers of New York City in the Federal Procession, July 23, 1788, celebrating the impending ratification of the Constitution by New York State.

## The First President

There was no question as to who should be the first President of the new nation. George Washington was unanimously elected. On April 16th he started from Mt. Vernon for New York where the seat of government was then established. It was a triumphal journey with the people pouring out from every village and town to welcome him.

An East View of GRAY'S FERRY, near Philadelphia, with the TRIUMPHAL ARCHES, &c. erected for the Reception of General Washington. April 20th 1789.

*Columbian Magazine*, May, 1789    Courtesy, The New-York Historical Society, New York City

Philadelphia met the president-elect at Gray's Ferry on the Schuylkill River. The rude bridge was transformed into a triumphal arch as shown *above*.

View of the TRIUMPHAL ARCH, and the manner of receiving General Washington at Trenton on his Route to New York April 21st 1789.

*Columbian Magazine*, May, 1789    Courtesy, The New-York Historical Society, New York City

At Trenton, N. J., the scene was repeated. It was the 23rd of April when, rowed across the bay from Jersey to New York, amid thunderous salutes, Washington set foot in New York.

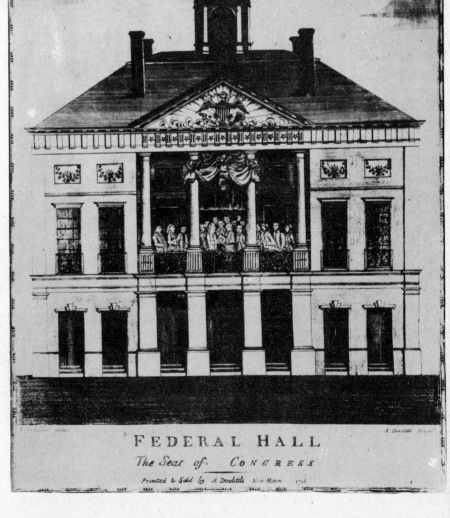

## The First Inauguration

On April 30, 1789, standing on the balcony of Federal Hall in New York, Washington took the oath of office from the Chancellor of the State of New York.

From a rare mezzotint made by Charles Willson Peale from his portrait from life in 1787.

J. C. Fitzpatrick, *Writings of George Washington*

After the oath was administered, the Chancellor turned to the packed throngs filling Wall and Broad streets and cried "Long Live George Washington, President of the United States", and from the people thundered back the cry "LONG LIVE GEORGE WASHINGTON, PRESIDENT OF THE UNITED STATES".

Courtesy, Stokes Collection, The New York Public Library

FEDERAL HALL
The Seat of CONGRESS

Printed & Sold by A. Doolittle New-Haven 1790

# 2
# THE FEDERAL PERIOD
## 1789-1800

### New York Was the Capital

Following Washington's inauguration, and the establishment of the government in New York, the President made his residence in a house at the corner of Pearl and Cherry streets.

*Courtesy, The New-York Historical Society, New York City*

Washington's Home
in New York, 1789

The Vice-President, John Adams of Massachusetts, lived in a house at Charlton and Varick streets.

*Left,* John Adams' Home in New York, 1789

*Courtesy, The New-York Historical Society, New York City*

At Broadway, near Bowling Green, lived the Minister from France, and from the upper windows of his apartment his sister, the Marquise de Brehan, made a watercolor view (*below*) of Paulus Hook, across the Bay.

*Vue de Paulushook prise de l'apartement de Mr. et Mme. de Brehan à Newyork.*

*Courtesy, Stokes Collection, The New York Public Library*

The ship in the foreground is probably the French frigate *l'Active.*

## The Bill of Rights

Courtesy, The New-York Historical Society, New York City

A View of City Hall, New York, 1792

At Federal Hall, the new Congress debated many things—and agreed upon some momentous measures. Foremost among them was that shown below and beginning—

CONGRESS OF THE UNITED STATES, begun and held at the City of New-York, on Wednesday the fourth of March, one thousand seven hundred and eighty-nine.

THE Conventions of a number of the States, having at the time of their adopting the Constitution, expressed a desire, in order to prevent misconstruction or abuse of its powers, that further declaratory and restrictive clauses should be added: And as extending the ground of public confidence in the Government, will best ensure the benificent ends of its institutions.

RESOLVED by the Senate and House of Representatives of the United States of America, in Congress assembled, two thirds of both Houses concurring, that the following Articles be proposed to the Legislatures of the several States, as Amendments to the Constitution of the United States, all, or any of which Articles, when ratified by three fourths of the said Legislatures, to be valid to all intents and purposes, as part of the said Constitution; viz:

Then followed twelve proposed Amendments. The first two, having to do with representation and the payment of salaries, were not ratified by the States, but the third, reading,

"Congress shall make no law respecting an establishment of religion, or prohibiting the free exercise thereof; or abridging the freedom of speech, or of the press, or the right of the people peaceably to assemble, and to petition the Government for a redress of grievances"

through the 12th, reading,

"The powers not delegated to the United States, by the Constitution, nor prohibited by it to the States, are reserved to the States respectively, or to the people"

were ratified and became the first ten amendments to the Constitution. They are commonly spoken of as the Bill of Rights. The facsimile *opposite* is from one of the original engrossed copies of the resolution of Congress. It bears the signatures of Frederick Augustus Muhlenberg, Speaker of the House of Representatives, and of John Adams, Vice-President of the United States, and President of the Senate.

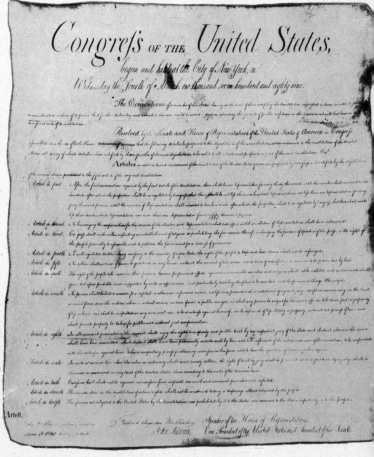

Courtesy, Rhode Island State Archives, Department of State, Providence

## Washington Takes A Trip

In the autumn of 1789, the President made a tour through New England. At Boston, while Governor Hancock stood on his dignity as to who should first call on whom, the people erected an arch and colonnade in honor of the President,

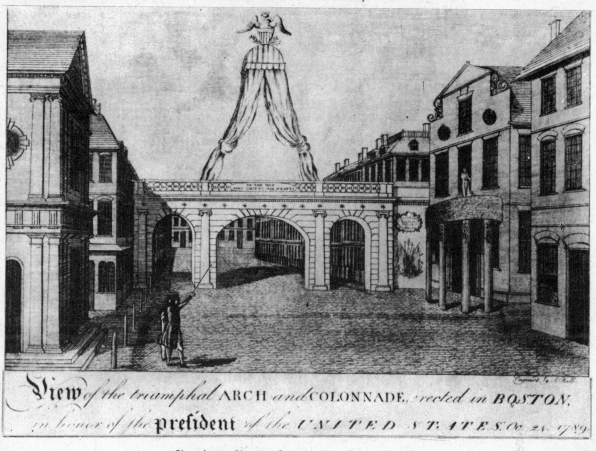

View of the triumphal ARCH and COLONNADE, erected in BOSTON, in honor of the president of the UNITED STATES Oct. 24, 1789

*Massachusetts Magazine*, January, 1790
Courtesy, The New-York Historical Society, New York City

and near the State House, when not himself being the center of attraction, he would have viewed a scene such as that shown *opposite*.

A S.W. View of the STATE HOUSE in BOSTON.

*Massachusetts Magazine*, July, 1793
Courtesy, The New-York Historical Society, New York City

## Assumption and Funding of the Debt (and the Location of the National Capital).

During the Revolutionary War, and subsequently, the Federal government had piled up a debt of over $42,000,000, owed to foreign creditors and to its own citizens in all sorts of ways.

Courtesy, Chase Bank Collection of Moneys of the World, New York

Bond of the Revolution, June 29, 1779

Courtesy, Chase Bank Collection of Moneys of the World, New York

Military Due Bill, May 15, 1784

The various states had accumulated debts of over $18,000,000, and expenses still went on.

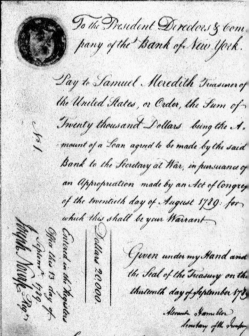

Alexander Hamilton, who was Secretary of the Treasury, recommended that the new Federal government take over the entire National and State debt and thus establish our credit upon a firm basis. And at the same time, the southern states wanted the permanent capital established on the Potomac. A bargain was struck by which Hamilton got his way with the debt, Philadelphia was to be the capital for ten years and, meantime, the permanent capital was to be built on the shores of the Potomac (see pages 49 and 84).

United States Treasury Warrant No. 1

Courtesy, Chase Bank Collection of Moneys of the World, New York

## Philadelphia—the Temporary Capital

In accordance with the bargain made in New York (see page 42) when Congress reassembled late in 1790, it met at Philadelphia, and there the government remained until 1800. Looking down Chestnut Street from the State House the legislators saw the masts of ships in the river.

Courtesy, The Historical Society of Pennsylvania, Philadelphia

State House, Philadelphia

ARCH STREET FERRY, PHILADELPHIA

Courtesy, The Historical Society of Pennsylvania, Philadelphia

At the Arch Street ferry they found activity such as that shown *opposite*.

And, at the High Street market, their wives shopped as we see in this picture made at the time.

*Right*, High Street Market House in 1800

Courtesy, The Historical Society of Pennsylvania, Philadelphia

## Around Town

From an engraving by W. Birch. 1799

Franklin Library in 1800

Swedes Church Southwark

PHILADELPHIA BANK in Fourth Street PHILADELPHIA.

All illustrations on this page by *courtesy* of
The Historical Society of Pennsylvania,
Philadelphia

## A National Bank

With the public debt in order, a system of banking and coinage was next.

In 1791, the Bank of the United States was created by Congress, with one-fifth of the capital sub-scribed by the government. The bank opened its doors for business on December 12, 1791. High finance or no high finance, wood had to be sawed—and the ar-tist seems to be a little off on the date of the founding of the bank.

BANK OF THE UNITED STATES, in Third Street PHILADELPHIA

Courtesy, The Historical Society of Pennsylvania, Philadelphia

Courtesy, Chase Bank Collection of Moneys of the World, New York

Here is a check drawn on the bank by Thomas Pinckney, our Min-ister to Great Britain.

A glance at pages 29 and 30 will show why a National system of coinage was desirable. In 1792, Congress took the business in hand, agreed upon a decimal sys-tem of coins and directed that a mint be established at Philadelphia to make these coins.

Philadelphia Mint
Courtesy, Chase Bank Collection of
Moneys of the World, New York

## Dollars and Cents

By 1793 the new mint was in operation, but the only coins turned out that year were a copper half-cent and a copper cent.

Copper Half-Cent, 1793

Copper Cent, 1793

During the next three years, and as dated below, the following coins appeared

Half-Dime. Silver. 1794

Dime. Silver. 1796

Half-Dollar. Silver. 1794

Dollar. Silver. 1794

Quarter-Eagle. $2.50. Gold.
1796

Half-Eagle. $5.00. Gold.
1795

Eagle. $10.00. Gold.
1795

## Indian Troubles in the Northwest Territory

To protect the settlers in the Miami Purchase (see page 35) Fort Washington was established in 1789, where Cincinnati was soon to grow up. From this fort (see location on map) Governor St. Clair started northward in 1791 to chastise the Indians. At the point where Fort Recovery is shown on the map, the Indians under Little Turtle (see page 35) completely defeated St. Clair's army and sent it reeling back to Fort Jefferson.

FORT WASHINGTON.

Henry A. Ford and Mrs. Kate B. Ford, *History of Cincinnati, Ohio.* 1881

*Right,* A Manuscript Map of Wayne's Campaign of 1794, by John Graves Simcoe, Lieutenant-Governor of Upper Canada

Courtesy, William L. Clements Library, Ann Arbor, Michigan

On the northern shore of the Ohio River, between Fort Washington and Marietta, was Gallipolis, a settlement made up of French families lured to the New World by the over-optimistic promises of the Scioto Company (see page 34).

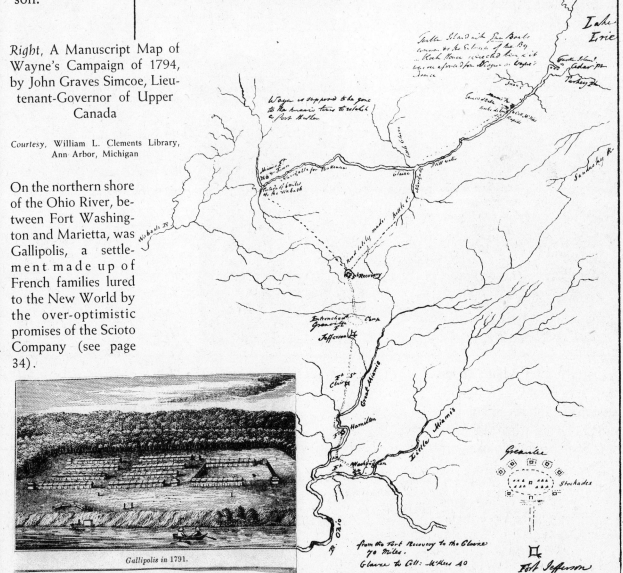

*Gallipolis in 1791.*

Henry Howe, *Historical Collections of Ohio.* 1847

## Wayne's Campaign

Partly for our self-respect and partly because the British were encouraging the
Indians, something had to be done. Accordingly, President Washington sent
General Anthony Wayne to Ohio to do
the job. In the autumn of 1793, Wayne
advanced from Fort Jefferson, built Fort
Recovery at the site of St. Clair's defeat,
and administered a preliminary beating to
the Indians. At Fallen Timbers, a few
miles below the entrance of the Maumee
River, Wayne finished the job — with
the British allies of the Indians looking on.
The map shown on page 47 was at this
time made by John Graves Simcoe, Lieutenant-Governor of Upper Canada, and
by him sent to Sir Henry Clinton from
among whose papers, now at the Clements
Library, University of Michigan, it is reproduced.

*Right,* Major-General Anthony Wayne
*Courtesy,* The Historical Society of Pennsylvania, Philadelphia

The Indians now were
ready for peace—which
they made with Wayne at
Fort Greenville.

*Left,* Greenville Treaty, 1795.
One of the soldiers in Wayne's
army was credited with this
work of art
*Courtesy,* Chicago Historical Society

Naturally, the Indians ceded
some more land, and by this
cession the mouth of the Cuyahoga River, where the City
of Cleveland shortly came into being, was opened to white
settlement.

*Right,* Sketch of the Mouth of the
Cuyahoga in 1800 by Captain
Allen Gaylord

*Courtesy,* The Western Reserve Historical
Society, Cleveland, Ohio

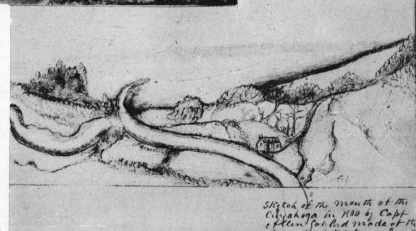

## The L'Enfant Plan

In 1791 Washington accepted the proffered services of Pierre Charles L'Enfant, a young French engineer and architect, in planning the new Capital on the Potomac. Although not wholly carried out, and often mutilated, the permanent plan of the City—with its circles and broad converging streets—deservedly retained the name of L'Enfant.

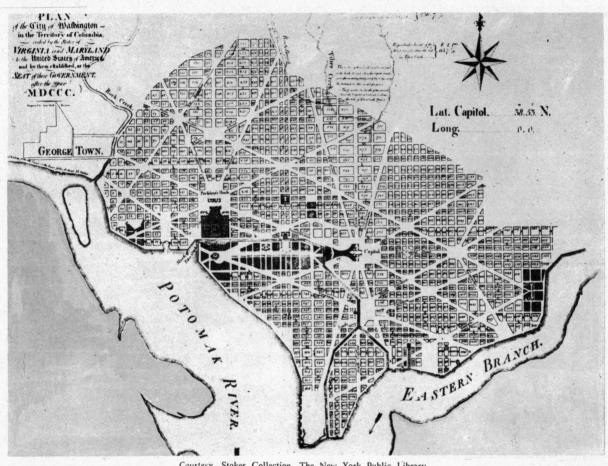

*Courtesy*, Stokes Collection, The New York Public Library

But, in 1795, the site of the future Capital appeared as shown below.

*Courtesy*, Stokes Collection, The New York Public Library

## Yellow Fever

Benjamin Rush, the leading doctor of Philadelphia, saw an unusual number of mosquitoes during the summer of 1793, but ascribed the fearful epidemic of yellow fever, which devastated the city, to spoiled coffee on the wharf.

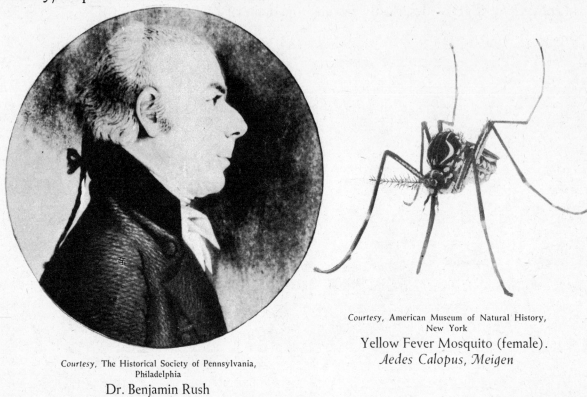

*Courtesy,* American Museum of Natural History, New York

Yellow Fever Mosquito (female).
*Aedes Calopus, Meigen*

*Courtesy,* The Historical Society of Pennsylvania, Philadelphia

Dr. Benjamin Rush

People died by the thousands. So terrified were those not infected that they refused care to the stricken. The hospital could not risk bringing the disease into its wards. A pest house away from the center of the city was demanded and Bush-Hill, the home of William Hamilton, was commandeered for the purpose.

BUSH-HILL,
*The Seat of William Hamilton Esq.ʳ near Philadelphia*

*Courtesy,* The Historical Society of Pennsylvania, Philadelphia

## The Pennsylvania Hospital

founded in 1751, had become an outstanding institution by the end of the century.

South Front of the Pennsylvania Hospital

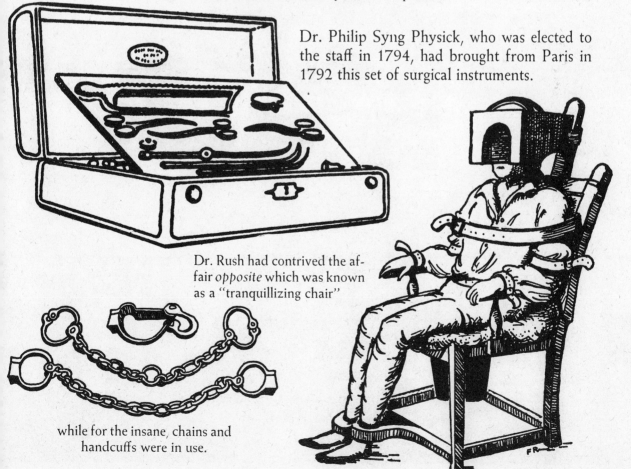

Dr. Philip Syng Physick, who was elected to the staff in 1794, had brought from Paris in 1792 this set of surgical instruments.

Dr. Rush had contrived the affair *opposite* which was known as a "tranquillizing chair"

while for the insane, chains and handcuffs were in use.

All pictures on this page are through the *courtesy* of The Pennsylvania Hospital, Philadelphia

## By Land and Sea

BOSTON and PROVIDENCE STAGE

THE Subscriber informs his friends and the Publick, that he for the more rapid conveyance of the MAIL STAGE-CARRIAGE, genteel, and easy, has good horses, and experienced, careful drivers.

They will start from *Boston* and *Providence*, and continue to run three times each week, until the first of *November*—Will leave *Boston* every Monday, Wednesday, and Friday, at 5 o'clock, A. M. and arrive at *Providence* the same days, at 2 o'clock, P. M.

They will leave *Providence* Tuesdays, Thursdays, and Saturdays, at 5 o'clock, A. M. and arrive at *Boston* the same days, at 2 o'clock, P. M.

The Price for each passenger, will be *Nine Shillings* only, and sets, if any other person will carry them for that sum. Twenty pounds of baggage gratis.

*Also*, a good new Philadelphia-built light WAGGON, to go the other days in the week, if wanted and as the Proprietor has been at such great expence to erect the Line, he hopes his exertions will give satisfaction, and receive the publick patronage.

Ladies and Gentlemen, who wish to take passage in his Stage, will please to apply for seats, at the house of the Subscriber, in Dock-Square, at Col Coleman's, or Mr. Gray's, State-street, as the Stage will set out from each of those places; books are there kept for entering passenger's names. The Stage will start from Coggeshall's Tavern, in *Providence*, formerly kept by Knight Dexter, Esq. THOMAS BEALS.

Boston, June 15, 1793.

*Courtesy*, Essex Institute, Salem, Mass.

Travellers could go from Boston to Providence in a "genteel" and "easy" manner, and in nine hours, by the mail stage-carriage. The fare was only nine shillings—less if anyone could beat it.

The sea was still the great highway, and from Salem, then a leading seaport, there went forth to the ports of the world such ships as the *America, below.*

*Courtesy* Peabody Museum, Salem, Mass.

while the country roads led through pleasant fields and villages— sometimes.

*New-York Magazine, or, Literary Repository,* June, 1796
*Courtesy*, The New-York Historical Society, New York City

## The Blacksmith's Art

This was a period when hardware for buildings meant something substantial—and generally artistic.

The barricaded door shown *opposite* guarded the Congregational Church at Little Haddam, Conn.; where also we find the handsome latch shown *below*—all made by the neighboring blacksmiths.

On the Sheaff House, near Philadelphia, was this farm bell with the bird above it,

and on a chest from the same house was the wrought iron hinge shown *opposite*, which carries the tulip motif so common throughout Pennsylvania.

All illustrations on this page are from Albert H. Sonn, *Early American Wrought Iron.* 1928

## Play and Work

The curative waters at Saratoga (N. Y.) were already well-known, and the vicinity was becoming a playground for the well-to-do. (Note the Negro boy bringing the drinks.)

*New-York Magazine, or, Literary Repository,* December, 1794
Courtesy, The New-York Historical Society, New York City

To western New York in 1792 came this plow, brought by the Rappalee family from New Jersey, to break the soil of a new frontier.

*Bulletin* 203—Department of Agriculture and Markets, State of New York, June, 1927

In the same general vicinity the village of Bath was growing up. (Note the house which has not yet been shingled. The construction of the bridge over the creek is also of interest). This settlement was in the Pulteney Purchase of 1791, one of the many land promotion schemes operating in the western country.

Colbert, Comte de Maulevrier, *Voyage dans l'Intérieur des Etats-Unis et au Canada* (1798)
Courtesy, Institut Français de Washington

**Down the Hudson**

we find the village of Catskill stretching out along the river bank

*New-York Magazine; or, Literary Repository*, September, 1797     *Courtesy,* The New-York Historical Society, New York City

and elsewhere farms and roads greet the eye.

*New-York Magazine; or, Literary Repository*, March, 1793     *Courtesy,* The New-York Historical Society, New York City

In New Jersey we find a road such as this, winding over the river and up a hill, with a mill utilizing the water power and substantial buildings adjoining. (Note the "buggy" at the crest of the hill.)

*New-York Magazine; or, Literary Repository*, November, 1794     *Courtesy,* The New-York Historical Society, New York City

## Near Philadelphia

we find well-kept fields and buildings with "paddock fences". Here, as in many of the pictures of this period, we see the prevalence of horseback travel.

*A View near Philadelphia*

*New-York Magazine; or, Literary Repository, August, 1795*
Courtesy, The New-York Historical Society, New York City

"Solitude", Mr. Penn's home, is a typical example of the better houses of the
period and locality.

*Solitude in Pennsylv.ᵃ belonging to Mr. Penn.*
*Drawn Engraved & Publish'd by W.Birch Springland near Bristol Pennsylv.ᵃ*

## And Far Up Where the Susquehanna Branches

we see the villages of Northumberland and Sunbury.

Colbert, Comte de Maulevrier, *Voyage dans l'Intérieur des Etats-Unis et au Canada* (1798)    Courtesy, Institut Francais de Washington

## Annapolis

presented this view to an unknown artist who made our picture near the end of the century.

*Courtesy*, Stokes Collection, The New York Public Library

## In South Carolina

Tidewater aristocracy was having to compromise with the democratic Piedmont, and in 1790 the capital was removed from Charleston to Columbia in the "up country".

Graved by James Akin Philad

The STATE HOUSE at COLUMBIA.

*Taken from Rivess Tavern. May 1794.*

John Drayton, *A View of South Carolina*. 1802

## Education

The buildings at Harvard were locally thought of as "ancient" even in 1788.

*View of the ancient Buildings belonging to Harvard-College, Cambridge, New England.*

Columbian Magazine, December, 1788
*Courtesy, The New-York Historical Society, New York City*

In 1791 young Noah Webster published a popular volume of informal essays "calculated to do the most good". We may note the stress laid on *Common Sense*, a characteristic of the late 18th century.

*Courtesy, The New-York Historical Society, New York City*

At Dartmouth the boys played a "bat-and-ball" game.

THE

PROMPTER;

OR A

COMMENTARY

ON

Common Sayings and Subjects, which are full of Common Sense, the best Sense in the World.

"To see all others faults and feel our own."

HARTFORD:
PRINTED BY HUDSON AND GOODWIN.
M,DCC,XCI.
[Published according to Act of Congress.]

THE

PREFACE.

A PROMPTER is the man who, in plays, sits behind the scenes, looks over the rehearser, and with a moderate voice, corrects him when wrong, or assists his recollection, when he forgets the next sentence. A Prompter says but little, but that little is very necessary and often does much good. He helps the actors on the stage at a dead lift, and enables them to go forward with spirit and propriety.

The writer of this little Book took it into his head to prompt the numerous actors upon the great theater of life; and he sincerely believes that his only motive was to do good. He cast about to find the method of writing calculated to do the most general good. He wanted to whip vice and folly out of the country—he thought of Hudibras and M'Fingal—and pondered well whether he should attempt the masterly field of those writings. He found this would not do—for

*A front View of DARTMOUTH COLLEGE, with the CHAPEL & HALL.*

Massachusetts Magazine, February, 1793   Courtesy, The New-York Historical Society, New York City

## Best Sellers of the 1790's

*The Farmer's Almanack*, begun in 1792, by Robert Bailey Thomas at Sterling, Mass., was destined to a longer continued life than any other American publication.

Courtesy, The New-York Historical
Society, New York City

A competing Almanac known as *The Astronomical Diary*, had a wide circulation but lacked the vitality of the *Farmer's*.

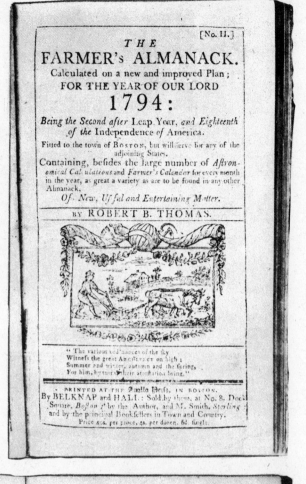

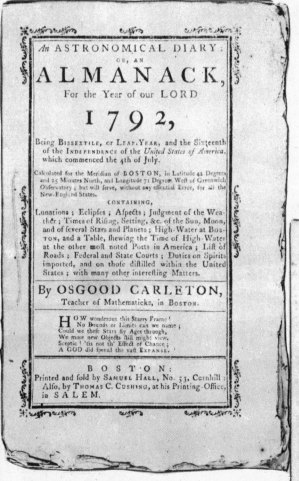

Courtesy, The New York Historical Society, New York City

But the literary sensation of 1794 was Thomas Paine's *The Age of Reason*, known as the "atheist's bible" and composed, in part, while its radical author was imprisoned in France as too conservative for the even more radical revolutionists.

## Three New States

In 1791 there was added to the original thirteen, the first new state, Vermont, which thus acquired the title of "The Fourteenth State".

*Right*, House in Rutland, Vt., where, from 1794 to 1804, the legislature of Vermont met from time to time

*Courtesy*, Vermont Historical Society, Montpelier

*New-York Magazine; or, Literary Repository*, July, 1796
*Courtesy*, The New-York Historical Society, New York City

State House, Frankfort, Ky.

Next came Kentucky in 1792. And in 1796, Tennessee, which, as the orphan child of North Carolina, had tried to go its way as the State of Franklin, came into the Union—imbued like Kentucky with a leaning toward Western separatism, while the federal government over the mountains appeared to be ignoring the interests of the "Men of the Western Waters".

Identified as an Indian attack upon a Tennessee station and applying to the period of its admission, the picture *opposite* appeared in the *Life of Andrew Jackson* by Amos Kendall, 1843. Its authenticity stands upon the fact that Jackson took a keen personal interest in the preparation of the book and presumably approved the picture as being a substantially correct portrayal of an event with which he was familiar.

## Cotton

In 1790, Samuel Slater, at Pawtucket in Rhode Island, contrived the first successful power-driven cotton spinning machines in America.

Cotton Carding Machine, made about 1790 by Samuel Slater

The demand thus created for raw cotton, led to the "invention" in 1793, of the cotton gin by Eli Whitney. *Left*.

*Below*, Benjamin Butterworth, *The Growth of Industrial Art.* 1892

The Whitney gin separated the seed from the fiber by running the cotton through a series of spikes. In 1796, Hodgen Holmes made a gin in which saw teeth removed the seed. *Right*.

Unquestionably Whitney's invention had a profound influence on the development of the cotton industry and the whole history of America. Whether it was a wholly new idea may be questioned in view of the picture *opposite*, ascribed to "one of the American islands" and shown in the *Universal Magazine* of July, 1764, where the machine is described as a mill to separate the seed from the cotton.

## Dreams

Oliver Evans, engaged in the milling business at Wilmington, Del., devised a flour mill, operated by water power and performing every necessary movement of the grain without manual labor. *Below* is Evans' view of the operation, beginning with (1) the wagoner emptying grain into scale pan—and whoso wishes to follow the operation in detail may find the story in *The Young Mill-wright and Miller's Guide*, published in 1795.

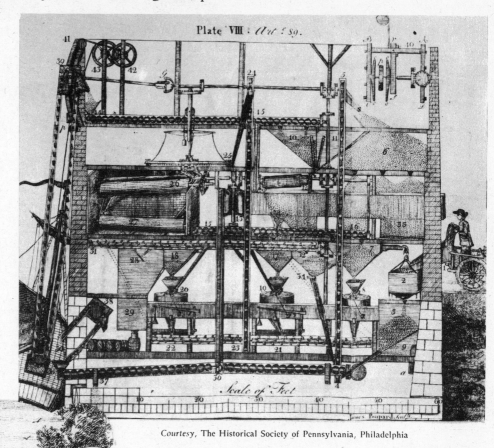

Courtesy, The Historical Society of Pennsylvania, Philadelphia

Benjamin Butterworth, *The Growth of Industrial Art.* 1892
Patents were pending for a cast-iron plow

And, in 1796, "Robert Fulton, Civil Engineer" in England, published his *Treatise on the Improvement of Canal Navigation* in which he showed "the numerous advantages to be derived from small canals".

## Bridges

began to render travel safer and easier.

A Bridge over the Merrimack River in the Commonwealth of Massachusetts

John Drayton, *Letters written during a Tour through the Northern and Eastern States of America.* 1794
*Courtesy*, The New-York Historical Society, New York City

*Left*, Bridge over the Mohawk River near Albany

Colbert, Comte de Maulevrier, *Voyage dans l'Intérieur des Etats-Unis et au Canada* (1798)

*Courtesy*, Institut Français de Washington

Colbert, Comte de Maulevrier, *Voyage dans l'Intérieur des Etats-Unis et au Canada* (1798)

*Courtesy*, Institut Français de Washington

VUE DU PONT ET DE LA VILLE D'YORK

## Ferries and Fords

were however still largely used.

Probably Wright's Ferry over the Susquehanna

A Ford on the Susquehanna.

Easton, Pa., on the Delaware River

All illustrations on this page are from Colbert, Comte de Maulevrier, *Voyage dans l'Intérieur des Etats-Unis et au Canada* (1798)  *Courtesy*, Institut Français de Washington

## The Whiskey Insurrection

In southwestern Pennsylvania the making of whiskey, in which form grain could profitably be transported over the mountains, was a leading industry. In 1791 Congress placed a tax on whiskey and trouble started immediately. Three years later a Federal marshal was attacked and the local militia assembled at Braddocks Field (see map).

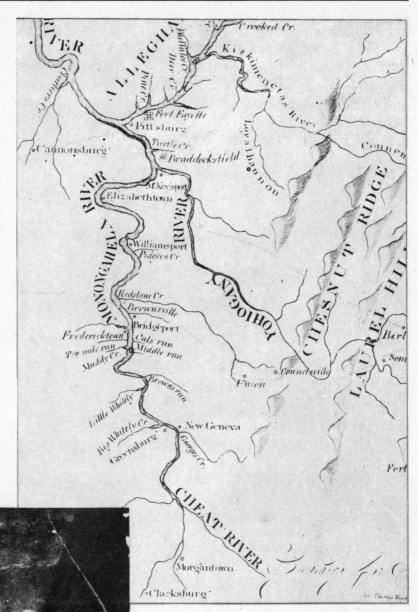

T. M. Harris, *Journal of a Tour.* 1805
Courtesy, Carnegie Library of Pittsburgh, Pittsburgh, Pa.

Washington called out the Eastern militia, the disaffected region was occupied, and the leaders of the Insurrection sent to Philadelphia where all were later acquitted, pardoned or dismissed for lack of evidence.

*The farewell previous to the WESTERN EXPEDITION*

Courtesy, Historical Society of Pennsylvania, Philadelphia

## Neutrality

In 1793, France, our old ally, which had become an aggressive revolutionary government, went to war with England. To America, in the frigate l'*Ambuscade* came Gênet as Minister from France, who proceeded to stir up trouble on land, while French men-of-war, by capturing British merchantmen within our territorial waters, made more trouble.

John Drayton, *Letters Written during a Tour through the Northern and Eastern States of America.* 1794
Courtesy, The New-York Historical Society, New York City

*Above* we see l'*Ambuscade* off the Battery in New York Harbor in 1793

NEW YORK.

and *opposite* is a view of lower New York made from the harbor at the same period.

Sketch by Archibald Robertson
Courtesy, The New-York Historical Society, New York City

The people were divided as to whether we should support France and be drawn into a war with England. President Washington met the situation temporarily by a proclamation of neutrality.

## The Jay Treaty

The difficulties created by the war in Europe, the unsettled details of the Treaty of Peace of 1783, and the lack of a commercial understanding between England and the United States made a further understanding with England necessary if we were to stay out of the general war. This was brought about by a treaty with Great Britain in 1794, negotiated on our part by Chief Justice John Jay and which has gone down in history as the Jay Treaty. Far from perfect, the treaty did at least help our commerce for the time being—and New York grew as a shipping point.

*Left,* John Jay

*Courtesy,* Mr. Peter A. Jay and the Metropolitan Museum of Art, New York

*View of the City of New York taken from Long Island*

Sketch by St. Mémin
*Courtesy,* Stokes Collection, The New York Public Library

## New York in the 1790's
### Government

*Courtesy, Stokes Collection, The New York Public Library*
City Hall, Broad and Wall Streets. 1797

### Church

St. Paul's Church and New
Presbyterian Meeting
House

From a watercolor by Archibald
Robertson

*Courtesy, The New-York Historical
Society, New York City*

### Business

The building to the *left* is the
famous Tontine Coffee House,
which in many ways came to
be the commercial center of
New York. Note the shipping
at the foot of the street.

*Courtesy, The New-York Historical Society,
New York City*

**From the Battery**

*Courtesy*, The Historical Society of Pennsylvania, Philadelphia

it was a long drive

From a painting by Robertson, 1798
*Courtesy*, The New-York Historical Society, New York City

*New-York Magazine, or Literary Repository*, October, 1795
*Courtesy*, The New-York Historical Society, New York City

but with many interesting sights

From a painting by
Robertson, 1798
*Courtesy*, The New-York
Historical Society,
New York City

to Harlem    *Courtesy*, The New-York Historical Society, New York City

## A New President

Having served two terms, Washington declined to be a candidate for re-election in 1796. The choice fell upon John Adams, the Vice-President, who, in 1797, was inaugurated as our second President.

*Left,* John Adams
Courtesy, Harvard University, Cambridge, Mass.

The Washingtons retired to Mount Vernon, and President and Mrs. Adams moved into the house which the Washingtons had occupied, as the President's home, in Philadelphia.

THE PRESIDENT'S HOME IN PHILADELPHIA.
[*The Robert Morris House*]

Mary J. Lamb, *The White House and its Memories* in *Magazine of American History,* May, 1887

The fans and the brocade shown at the *left* were carried and worn by Mrs. Adams.

Courtesy, Essex Institute, Salem, Mass.

## The Southern Boundary

The Treaty of Peace with England in 1783 had placed our southern boundary at 31°, from the Mississippi to the Chattahoochee, but Spain declined to recognize this boundary and continued to occupy northward to a line running from the mouth of the Yazoo (where Vicksburg later grew up) to the Chattahoochee.

*View of the Fort of the Natchez*

*Courtesy, The New-York Historical Society, New York City*

*Courtesy, Louisiana State Museum, New Orleans, La.*

While up and down the Mississippi, controlling that outlet for our Western states, sailed Gayoso, Spanish Governor of the recently established "Spanish District of Natchez."

*Below,* Plan of Gayoso's galley

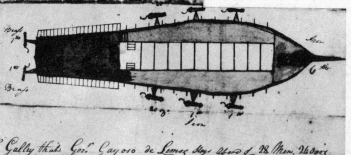

*Courtesy,* Eleanor Glasgow Voorhis Memorial Collection at the Missouri Historical Society, St. Louis

By the Treaty of San Lorenzo in 1795, Spain admitted our rights on the Mississippi and accepted 31° as the boundary between the United States and Florida. Three years later the boundary line was surveyed and finally established.

## Across the Mississippi

in Spanish Louisiana, was the town of St. Louis, established by the French when Kaskaskia and Cahokia, on the eastern side of the river, fell into the hands of England after the French and Indian War.

Courtesy, Missouri Historical Society, St. Louis

Plan de la ville de St. Louis des Illinois. 1796

Near the center of the map *above* will be seen the "fort." *Opposite* is a view of this fort as it appeared in 1794. It was built as much because the Spanish feared American expansion as because they feared Indian attacks.

F. L. Billon, *Annals of St. Louis in its Ear* *Days under the French and Spanish Domin* *tions.* 1886

In St. Louis lived Auguste Chouteau who ca ried on a vast fur-trading business in the Osag country and up the Missouri. *Opposite* we se the Chouteau Mansion in 1795.

F. L. Billon, *Annals of St. Louis in its Early Days under the Fren* *and Spanish Dominations.* 1886

## The Northeastern Boundary

Far "down east", where people were few and travel was by birch canoes, we were also having boundary controversies.

Patrick Campbell, *Travels in North America*
*Courtesy*, The Champlain Society, Toronto

The Treaty of Peace (see page 1) defined our Northeast boundary as the St. Croix River, but which of three rivers was the St. Croix? In 1798, a mixed commission settled the question of the river and, tracing it to its source, marked the spot with a cedar stake 5 feet 2 inches north of a yellow birch which was hooped by iron.

Joseph Bouchette, *The British Dominion in North America*. London, 1832

## The Theater

was still looked upon in New England as a child of the devil, and not until 1794 was a theater permitted in Boston. However, Washington attended the John Street Theater in New York, while living there as President, and theaters had been popular for nearly a century in the South, particularly in that center of the arts in colonial days, Charleston, S. C.

*A view of the NEW THEATRE in New York.*

*New York Directory for 1797*
*Courtesy, The New-York Historical Society, New York City*

### PETERSBURG THEATRE.

On WEDNESDAY Evening, November 13, 1799, will be presented,

A favorite COMEDY, in four Acts, called the

## CHILD OF NATURE;

OR, THE

## Happy Discovery.

Marquis Almanza,                                    Mr. J. West.
Duke Mercia,                                        Mr. Sully.
Count Valentia,                                     Mr. Hardinge.
Seville,                                            Mr. Bignall.
Granado,                                            Mr. Douglas.
Alberto,                                            Mr. Watts.

Amanthis                 (the Child of Nature)      Mrs. J. West.
Marchioness Merida,                                 Mrs. Douglas.

*Courtesy, The New-York Historical Society, New York City*

*Inside View of the New Theatre, Philadelphia.*

*New-York Magazine, or, Literary Repository, April, 1794*
*Courtesy, The New-York Historical Society, New York City*

## Museums, Circuses and Panoramas

provided both amusement and instruction for the public. Experiments in electricity were performed. There were moving wax figures. The guillotining of the King and Queen of France was a popular subject.

The advertisement *below* suggests a growing interest in natural history and art, and it is also worth noting, as a sign of increasing national feeling and unity, that a public in New York would pay 4s. each (children 2s.) to see a panorama of Charleston, S. C.

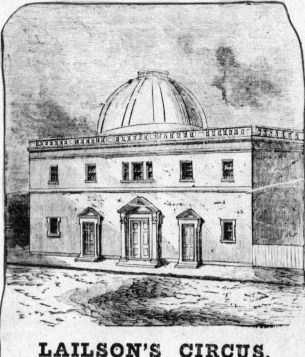

### LAILSON'S CIRCUS,

NORTHWEST CORNER OF FIFTH AND PRUNE STREETS.

First opened April 8, 1797. Destroyed, by falling in of the dome, July 6, 1798.

FROM A SKETCH BY THE LATE CHARLES DURANG.

*Courtesy,* The Historical Society of Pennsylvania, Philadelphia

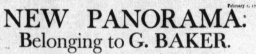

February 1, 1797

# NEW PANORAMA:
## Belonging to G. BAKER.

On Monday next, the 6th inst. will be opened in Greenwich-Street, near the bottom of Barclay-Street, the Panorama, or a natural and original view of the beautiful

## CITY of CHARLESTON

The capital of South Carolina, which is 110 feet in length by 20 feet in height, and contains upwards of 2000 square feet of canvass. *Accompanied with a grand*

## Automaton Bird Cage Clock,

which cost 300 dollars, where the Canary Bird and Bullfinch preserved from the life, are seen to sing and perform like living birds, by shewing all the motions of life; at the time the birds sing, a delightful cascade, or apparent falling of water is seen emerging from the perch on which the birds are standing. At the time the spectators are viewing the Panorama, they must consider themselves on a small low fund island, nearly opposite the centre of the city, surrounded by water. On the left is seen the boat where all vessels enter the port, 7 miles from the city; also, on the left is seen Ashly River, and on the right Cooper River; in the great space of water which appears, are a great number of vessels of all descriptions, and in all situations of sailing, and some saluting, and the fort returning the compliment, which makes the scene truly interesting. A complete and accurate description of the city will be handed the spectator at the time of visiting the Panorama.

Also, at the Panorama a room is set apart for the sale of

Prints, Paintings, and Natural History Subjects,

where are now to be seen nearly 200 different subjects in engravings, some of which are in elegant frames, and a number of most beautiful enameled paintings, executed in a most masterly style:
Also, a number of beutiful

## American Butterflies,

and other insects, in handsome frames, which are really very ornamental natural pictures.
PRINTS will be sold for half or less than half the usual price that has been asked in this city.

ONE VERY ELEGANT PAIR OF

## Glass Chandeliers,

With burnished gold supporters, and candle holders. Price *One Hundred Dollars* the pair, fitting for churches or large public rooms. CHARLESTON was executed by the masterly pencil of Mr. Winstanly, whose fame and abilities have shewn sufficiently conspicuous in his Panorama of the city of London, which was lately exhibited at the same place.

*The Panorama will be opened every day from Ten to Four o'Clock, and visitors can be admitted at all times as a family lives in the house.*

Admittance 4s. Children 2s.

N B. An AUTOMATON BIRD CAGE CLOCK, agreeable to the above description, for SALE, Price *Five Hundred Dollars.*

*Courtesy,* The New-York Historical Society, New York City

On January 9, 1793, Jean Pierre Blanchard, a Frenchman, made the first balloon ascension in America—at Philadelphia—with President Washington as one of the spectators.

*Courtesy,* American Antiquarian Society, Worcester, Mass.

## Chairs

Chairs and table (Francis Peabody, 1797) in J. H. Silsbee
House, Salem, Mass.

## And Clocks

"Martha Washington" chair

*Left*, Hepplewhite style chair,
1780-1800

Easy Chair, 1785-1790

Clock made by Nathan
Adams about 1790

*Left*, Clock, made by Burnap,
1790-1800

**Desk**  **Book Case**

Courtesy, The Metropolitan Museum of Art, New York City

Mahogany and Satinwood Desk
New York, ca. 1795

**Scrutoir**

Courtesy, The Metropolitan Museum of Art, New York City

Mahogany Bookcase, Salem, Mass. 1790-1800

**Chest**

Courtesy, Essex Institute, Salem, Mass.

Scrutoir, mahogany, New England,
ca. 1790

Courtesy, The Metropolitan Museum of Art, New York City

Mahogany and Satinwood Chest of Drawers
Portsmouth, N. H. Late 18th Century

**Sideboard**

*Courtesy,* Metropolitan Museum of Art, New York City
Mahogany Sideboard, 1790-1800

*Courtesy,* Essex Institute,
Salem, Mass.
Hepplewhite candle
stand ca. 1790

**Sofas**

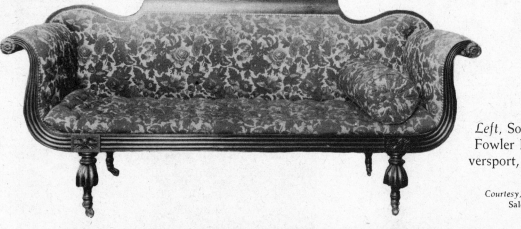

*Left,* Sofa in Samuel
Fowler House, Dan-
versport, Mass. before
1800
*Courtesy,* Essex Institute,
Salem, Mass.

*Courtesy,* Metropolitan Museum of Art, New York City
Mahogany and Satinwood Sofa, Massachusetts, 1790-1800

## Bulfinch, the Architect

Charles Bulfinch, born in Boston in 1763, early developed a taste for architecture, which was pointed by a tour of England and the Continent in 1785-87. From 1788 onward, his was a determining influence on New England architecture.

*Courtesy, Essex Institute, Salem, Mass.*

Rear Stairway of Ezekiel Hersey Derby House, 1799. By Bulfinch

Stairway of Harrison Gray Otis House, 1793. By Bulfinch

But his crowning contribution was the Massachusetts State House.

*Courtesy, Stokes Collection, The New York Public Library*

Bulfinch's plan (elevation) made in 1787 for the Massachusetts State House

The State House as finished, from Bulfinch's plan, in 1798

*Courtesy, Essex Institute, Salem, Mass.*

## Multiple Dwelling Architecture

The Tontine (or Franklin) Crescent was begun by Bulfinch in Boston in 1793. It consisted of sixteen connected houses. The Boston Library and the Massachusetts Historical Society were assigned rooms above the central arched entrance.

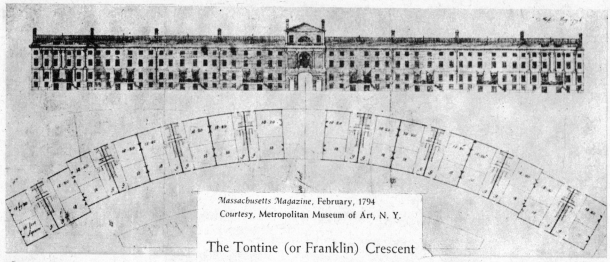

Massachusetts Magazine, February, 1794
Courtesy, Metropolitan Museum of Art, N. Y.

The Tontine (or Franklin) Crescent

## Thornton

Between 1798 and 1800, William Thornton, he who had provided the design for the wings of the Capitol at Washington, built in Washington, for John Tayloe, a home known as The Octagon, distinguished by circular rooms.

Courtesy, The Essex Institute, Salem, Mass.
Interior of the Octagon

Courtesy, The Essex Institute, Salem, Mass.
The Octagon

## L'Enfant

UNFINISHED HOUSE    PHILADELPHIA

At the same time that L'Enfant was busily engaged on his plan for the City of Washington (see page 49), he was commissioned by Robert Morris to build a house at Philadelphia. As the view *opposite* shows, the house followed the style of an earlier Paris, with nothing in it of the classical which was then becoming popular in America. The architect, with his usual prodigality, far outran the specifications of his wealthy client and with the crash of Morris' fortune, the house remained unfinished.

Courtesy, The Historical Society of Pennsylvania, Philadelphia

## Benjamin Latrobe

was a promising architect and engineer when he arrived in Virginia in 1796. He was soon busily engaged in his professions. In 1797 he completed the exterior of Jefferson's State Capitol at Richmond, Va.

*Courtesy*, Virginia State Library, Richmond

Perhaps Latrobe's most useful and most lasting work was in the field of engineering—the construction of the Philadelphia waterworks, fed from the Schuylkill River by a series of pumps.

*Left*, Center Engine House, Philadelphia Waterworks. 1799

*Courtesy*, The Historical Society of Pennsylvania, Philadelphia

*Right*, The Bank of Pennsylvania begun in 1799, from Latrobe's design, was completed in 1801.

*Courtesy*, The Historical Society of Pennsylvania, Philadelphia

"Sedgley," home of William Cramond, was designed and built at about the same time.

*Courtesy*, The Historical Society of Pennsylvania, Philadelphia

## "Hail Columbia"

Our relations with France had been steadily deteriorating, and, as a result of the XYZ episode in 1797, came an outburst of patriotic feeling. Joseph Hopkinson, a young lawyer, in 1798, made a prominent contribution to this feeling by composing a song entitled "Hail Columbia," set to the music of "The President's March." An immediate success, the song became a part of our national music.

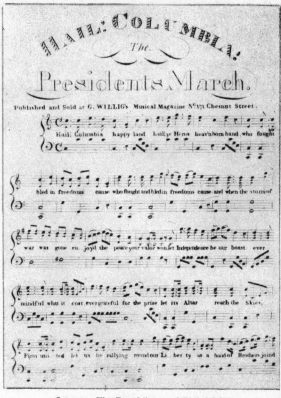

*Courtesy*, The Free Library of Philadelphia

War seemed imminent, and Washington accepted command of our land forces, though they never had to be mobilized. However, we did engage in

## An Undeclared Naval War With France

One of the more spectacular actions was that between the American frigate *Constellation*, commanded by Commodore Thomas Truxtun, and the French frigate *L'Insurgente*, in which action the latter was disabled and captured, February 9, 1799.

By E. Savage. From *Quasi War with France*, U. S. Naval Records and Library. *Courtesy*, Mrs. Charles H. Taylor, Boston, Mass.

## The Father of His Country Passes

In the midst of foreign misunderstandings and internal bickerings, the country was startled and shocked to learn of the sudden death—on December 14, 1799—of George Washington. Congress adjourned to do honor to him who was "first in war, first in peace, first in the hearts of his countrymen."

*HIGH STREET, From the Country Market-place PHILADELPHIA.*

*with the procession in commemoration of the Death of GENERAL GEORGE WASHINGTON, December 26th 1799.*

Courtesy, The Historical Society of Pennsylvania, Philadelphia

Not only in Philadelphia, but throughout the country, services and processions expressed the deep sorrow of the people.

He was buried at Mt. Vernon and his tomb has become a national shrine.

## Washington City on the Potomac

The great leader had fallen, but so well had he wrought and so strong were the foundations on which he had built, that the Nation continued on its march of destiny. The change from the old to the new was marked by the removal of the National Capital, in the year 1800, from Philadelphia to the new city of Washington on the Potomac (see pages 42 and 49).

Courtesy, The Library of Congress, Washington, D. C.

The city may, in 1800, have looked somewhat as this print *above*, published in 1804, indicated, but sure it is that the two wings of the capitol stood at that time as shown in the William Birch view *opposite*, without being connected and without a dome, either high or low. (Birch made the drawing for use as a title-page of a book, which explains the presence of the eagle in his view.)

On the way from Baltimore to Washington, President and Mrs. Adams got lost and "wandered two hours without find-

Glenn Brown, *History of the United States Capital, 1900*

ing a guide or a path". They found the President's House appearing externally much as we see it in the picture *opposite*, but, in the words of Mrs. Adams, "Not a single apartment finished . . . not the least fence, yard, or other convenience, without, and the great unfinished audience-room I made a drying-room of, to hang up the clothes in. . . . We have, indeed, come into a *new country*".

# 3
# JEFFERSONIAN DEMOCRACY
### 1801-1811

On March 4, 1801, Thomas Jefferson became the third President of the United States—the first to take the oath of office in the City of Washington.

*Right*, Thomas Jefferson
From a water color portrait made from life
while President, by Robert Field
Courtesy, The New-York Historical Society, New York City

That he rode up Capitol Hill unattended, tied his horse to the fence and, entering the Senate Chamber, took the oath of office, is a popular but untrue story. However, as the picture *below* indicates, travel to Washington was largely by horseback, and even within the City the condition of the streets often made carriage travel impossible.

Drawn by G. Beck.   Courtesy, Stokes Collection, The New York Public Library
Washington at the time of Jefferson's Inauguration

*Above*, Albert Gallatin
Portrait by James Sharples.
Courtesy, The Metropolitan Museum of Art,
New York City

Jefferson had been swept into office by democratic dissatisfaction with the administration of John Adams. And from the democratic west the President selected his Secretary of the Treasury, Albert Gallatin, whose home was in western Pennsylvania where the Whiskey Insurrection had occurred in 1794 (see page 65).

*Right*, Gallatin's Home in Western
Pennsylvania
Courtesy, Uniontown Public Library, Pa.

## The Back Country

In Pittsburgh, Hugh Henry Brackenridge was publishing *The Tree of Liberty* and supporting the Republican (Jeffersonian) Party in the West.

The Tree of Liberty

AND THE LEAVES OF THE TREE WERE FOR THE HEALING OF THE NATIONS *REV? 22. 2.*

Vol. 1.                    Saturday, *August 30th*, 1800.                    No. 3.

*Latest Foreign Intelligence.*

OPERATIONS IN ITALY.

OFFICIAL BULLETINS.

*Bulletin of the army of reserve dated Milan, June 3.*

" The division of Gen. Lannes, which had been the advance guard from St. Bernard to Ivrea, was advancing to Chivasso to make the enemy believe that it was our intention to make a junction with Gen. Thureau, who was between Rivoli and

son made a counter march, and moved towards Cremona, to make himself master of the numerous magazines the enemy have in that place, then to pass the Po, and to join the corps of gen. Murat at Placenza."

Letter from Gen. Buonaparte, First Consul of the republic, to the two Consuls.

" Milan, June 9.

" You will see, Citizens Consuls, by the letters of gen. Melas, which are annexed to my preceding letter, that gen. Ott re-

the head of the bridge of Plaisance, defended by 600 men and twenty pieces of cannon. But the enemy having cut from the coast of the town some bridges of boats, and defended the passage with 18 pieces of cannon, he sought another passage. The General procured some barks, that served him to carry over the 9th and 59th, and with these forces he attacked Plaisance, which he took on the 7th. He found considerable magazines, and made 600 prisoners. A party of the enemy's cavalry had just

dered Gen. Lannes to quit the position of Bronni, to attack the enemy at that point, where he should meet him, and general Victor to support him with his corps.

" General Watrin met the first posts of the enemy at San Diletto ; the principal force of the enemy occupied Casteggio, & the heights on the right, having much artillery in their positions, presenting a force of about 15,000 men. The 28th demi brigade, the 6th, 22d, and 40th, having repulsed the enemy's advanced guard, at-

*Courtesy,* Carnegie Library of Pittsburgh, Pa.

The picture shown *below*, and which found a prominent place in *The Port Folio* of January-June, 1810, indicates that the fur trade, the industry which always lay beyond the frontier, was not a distant interest.

Return of the Trapper

From Sketch by Alex. Wilson

Between the settled districts and the unbroken forests lay a section of far-separated houses, where the camp meeting was a great event, affording a vent for not only religious but long pent-up human social emotions starved by loneliness.

Joseph Smith, *Old Redstone.* 1854

SACRAMENTAL SCENE IN A WESTERN FOREST

## Merino Sheep

*Report of the Commissioner of Agriculture for the year 1864*

When, in 1801, David Humphreys, Minister to Spain under the late "aristocratic" administrations of Washington and Adams, was recalled by the "democratic" Jefferson, he brought back to Derby, Conn., a flock of Spanish Merino sheep, the multiplication of which had a tremendous influence on the industries of New England. The Massachusetts Society for Promoting Agriculture gave Humphreys a gold medal in recognition of his contribution.

*The Miscellaneous Works of David Humphreys. 1804*

But Humphreys' "democratic" successor, James Bowdoin, wore this handsomely embroidered coat of French manufacture while in Europe.

## Carriage Taxes

Legislation passed during Washington's second term, placed a Federal tax on carriages. This was contested in the courts but sustained and, in 1802, Eben Thompson, Jr., of Durham, N. H., paid $3.00 for the privilege of driving a "one-horse shay".

*Courtesy, Museum of Fine Arts, Boston, Mass.*

*Courtesy, Chase National Bank Collection of Moneys of the World, New York*

## Ohio

became a state in 1803 and the remainder of the vast Northwest Territory was organized as Indiana Territory. The first capital of Ohio was at Chillicothe.

*American Pioneer, 1844*

CHILLICOTHE COURTHOUSE, ETC. IN 1801.

Marietta (see page 34) was taking on the appearance of a village.

Victor Collot, *Voyage dans l'Amerique. Atlas.* 1826

Marietta. About 1800

**A RICH FARM FOR SALE.**

A GOOD BARGAIN will be given of 66 2-3 acres of land, 40 of which are cleared, situate about 7 miles from Cincinnati on Duck creek—a number of bearing apple trees, a good spring, and several cabins thereon. It is an excellent seat for a tanner or distiller. For particulars apply to the Editor of this paper.

*August 4*

This advertisement in the Cincinnati *Liberty Hall* of August 11, 1806, indicates that, where in 1789 there was only a frontier fort (see page 47), fruit trees were being set out, cabins built and industries considered.

Courtesy, The Ohio State Archaeological and Historical Society, Columbus

*Below,* View of Cincinnati. 1807

Courtesy, The Historical Society of Pennsylvania, Philadelphia

## The Mound Builders

The early settlers of Ohio could not help observing and wondering about great artificial mounds such as this. Marietta had been planted in the midst of a mound city. There were literally hundreds of these mounds, great and small, up and down the river valleys. Both Gen. Putnam and William Henry Harrison wrote accounts of them.

*Courtesy*, The Ohio State Archaeological and Historical Society, Columbus

The Miamisburg Mound, Montgomery Co., Ohio (north of Cincinnati). It is a burial mound, and almost 70 ft. high.

Effigy stone pipe found in the Adena Mound, Ross Co., Ohio.

*Courtesy*, The Ohio State Archaeological and Historical Society, Columbus

*Courtesy*, The Ohio State Archaeological and Historical Society, Columbus

Great Serpent Mound, Adams Co., Ohio. Over 1300 feet in length.

Later excavations brought to light many interesting objects which had been buried in the mounds.

Some of the mounds were in the form of living creatures such as the serpent shown *above*.

## Indiana Territory

created in 1800 and enlarged in 1802, comprised, as we have seen, all the old Northwest Territory except Ohio. William Henry Harrison was appointed as the first governor and established his official residence at the territorial capital of Vincennes. *Below*, is a view of his residence, built in 1804.

*Courtesy*, The Vincennes Public Library, Indiana

The Legislative Hall, or capitol building of Indiana Territory, at Vincennes, was the modest building shown at the *right*.

*Courtesy*, The Vincennes Public Library, Indiana

## Far to the Northwest

but within the Indiana Territory of 1800-1805, was the strategic water passage known as Sault Ste. Marie, or St. Mary's River, connecting Lake Huron and Lake Superior.

From a watercolor by Edward Walsh. *Courtesy,* William L. Clements Library, Ann Arbor, Mich.

### Falls of St. Mary's River

VIEW of the GRAND PORTAGE on LAKE SUPERIOR.

From Map of the Provinces of Upper and Lower Canada by Joseph Bouchette. 1815.
*Courtesy,* Public Archives of Canada. Research and Publicity Division, Ottawa.

While on the northern shore of Lake Superior was the trading post of Grand Portage, depot for furs received from and supplies destined to the great trapping country beyond.

Subsequent to the Treaty of Peace of 1783, the British had retained control of these western posts, but after the signing of Jay's Treaty (see page 67), sovereignty passed to the United States. Accordingly, the British fur traders established Fort William, or Fort Kaministiguia, a few miles within the Canadian boundary, and Grand Portage fell into disuse.

Reproduced from a copy of the Original Painting in the possession of Dr. VanCortland, Ottawa.

### FRONT VIEW OF THE FORT KAMINISTIGUIA, NORTH-WEST COMPANY, JUNE 15, 1805.

*Courtesy,* Lawrence J. Burpee, International Joint Commission, Ottawa, Canada

## Michigan Territory

consisting only of the Lower Peninsula, was carved out of Indiana Territory in 1805. *Below,* we have a picture of Detroit as it appeared in 1804.

Courtesy, William L. Clements Library, Ann Arbor, Mich.

From a watercolor painting made in 1804 by Dr. Edward Walsh, stationed in upper Canada with His Britannic Majesty's 49th Regiment. The view is from the Canadian side of the river.

## Westward the Course of Empire . . .

From the eastern states to these new territories in the West came a steady stream of settlers.

*Eighty Years' Progress of the United States.* 1868

The forest was giving way to clearings and log cabins.

*The Genesee Farmer,* January, 1851

## The Louisiana Purchase

Spanish control of the mouth of the Mississippi had long been a disturbing factor in our western settlement. The people of Ohio, Kentucky and Tennessee wanted free access to the sea for the products of their farms.

From a painting by J. L. Bouquet de Woiseri. *Courtesy*, Chicago Historical Society

New Orleans, 1803

When, during the Napoleonic wars in Europe, title to "Louisiana" passed to France, President Jefferson made an offer to buy New Orleans. To Jefferson's, and to the country's, amazement, Napoleon sold us (1803) not only New Orleans but the whole great, undefined territory west of the Mississippi to which the French and Spanish had applied the name "Louisiana".

*Left*, Cypress, Tupelo and Red Maple, Louisiana
Photo by U. S. Forest Service

After the Purchase, the area which later became the State of Louisiana was organized as the Territory of Orleans.

The Duplantier Mansion, shown *below*, was occupied by Gen. James Wilkinson as headquarters during the Burr episode (see page 100).

*Courtesy*, The Historical Society of Pennsylvania, Philadelphia

Duplantier Mansion, near New Orleans. 1808

## The Missouri Country

That part of the Purchase which lay north of the Territory of Orleans, and which soon came to be known as Missouri Territory, was at the time officially named the District or Territory of Louisiana.

*Courtesy,* Pierre Chouteau Collection in the Missouri Historical Society, St. Louis

Bull Boat

Here, from St. Louis as a center, the Chouteaus and others carried on a far-flung fur trade with the Indians, using bull boats and mackinaw (or cordelle) boats on the shallow rivers.

*Courtesy,* Pierre Chouteau Collection in the Missouri Historical Society, St. Louis

Mackinaw or Cordelle Boat

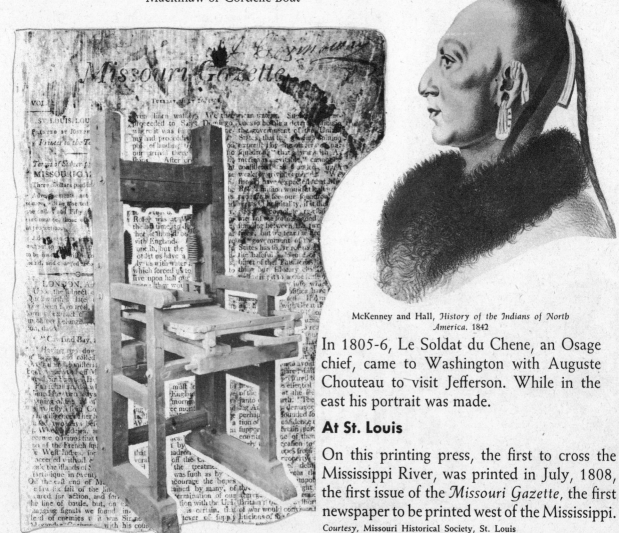

McKenney and Hall, *History of the Indians of North America.* 1842

In 1805-6, Le Soldat du Chene, an Osage chief, came to Washington with Auguste Chouteau to visit Jefferson. While in the east his portrait was made.

## At St. Louis

On this printing press, the first to cross the Mississippi River, was printed in July, 1808, the first issue of the *Missouri Gazette,* the first newspaper to be printed west of the Mississippi.

*Courtesy,* Missouri Historical Society, St. Louis

## A Famous Duel

In 1804, Aaron Burr, Vice-President of the United States, was a candidate for the governorship of New York. His defeat, which he largely charged to Alexander Hamilton, led Burr to challenge Hamilton to a duel. The challenge was accepted and on July 11 the opponents met on the duelling ground in Weehawken, N. J.

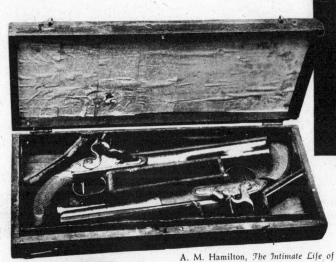

*Courtesy,* The New-York Historical Society, New York City

Alexander Hamilton

Each fired one shot and Hamilton fell mortally wounded.

A. M. Hamilton, *The Intimate Life of Alexander Hamilton.* 1910

Pistols used by Hamilton and Burr

Burr fled the jurisdiction of New York and was soon engaged in the scheme which history has labelled the "Burr Conspiracy" (see page 100).

W. H. Safford, *The Blennerhasset Papers.* 1864

Aaron Burr

Where Hamilton Fell

*Courtesy,* Stokes Collection, The New York Public Library

## Trouble with Tripoli

The Barbary States, along the southern shore of the Mediterranean, had long exacted tribute from vessels entering that sea. The United States followed the example of the older nations and made annual payments.

Cap! STERRETT in the Sch! ENTERPRISE paying tribute to TRIPOLI, August 1804

*Opposite*, we see an American ship paying its tribute to Tripoli, which, in 1801, declared war upon us.

From an engraving by M. F. Corné
Naval Documents. *Barbary Wars: Operations*. 1939-42

Two years later, we sent a small squadron against the Barbary States, but one of our ships, the *Philadelphia*, becoming stranded on a reef, was captured by the Tripolitans.

From a drawing by Capt. Wm. Bainbridge Hoff
Naval Documents. *Barbary Wars: Operations*. 1939-42

THE CAPTURE OF THE U. S. FRIGATE PHILADELPHIA.

THE BURNING OF THE U. S. FRIGATE PHILADELPHIA.

The following February, 1804, Stephen Decatur and eighty American officers and men, in a small boat, entered the harbor of Tripoli, and, under the guns of the castle, recaptured the *Philadelphia* and burned her.

From an engraving by F. Kearny
Naval Documents. *Barbary Wars: Operations*. 1939-42
*Courtesy*, Dr. Eugene H. Pool, New York

A close blockade of, and constant attack upon, the harbor during the summer and autumn of that year brought the Tripolitans to agree upon an end of tribute from the United States.

From a painting by M. F. Corné
Naval Documents. *Barbary Wars: Operations*. 1939-42

ATTACK ON TRIPOLI. 3 AUGUST 1804.

## The Lewis and Clark Expedition

The acquisition of Louisiana (see page 93) prompted President Jefferson to send an expedition to explore the western country. The party, under the leadership of Meriwether Lewis and William Clark, assembled near St. Louis in the autumn of 1803.

### The Missouri River

George Catlin, *Letters and Notes on the Manners, Customs, and Condition of the North American Indians.* 1841

Victor Collot, *Voyage dans l'Amerique. Atlas.* 1826
### Flatboat

The following Spring they ascended the Missouri in flatboats, picking their way among uprooted trees and hidden snags.

The Winter of 1804-5 was spent near the Mandan villages, on the Missouri River, in present North Dakota.

George Catlin, *Letters and Notes on the Manners, Customs, and Condition of the North American Indians.* 1841
### Mandan Village

In the *Journal of Voyages and Travels under Lewis and Clark,* by Patrick Gass, 1812, who accompanied the expedition, we find this picture of how their shelters were put up.

*Captain Clark & his men building a line of Huts*

## The Lewis and Clark Expedition (Continued)

Westward, to the source of the Missouri, went the expedition.

The leaders met and talked, as best they could, with the Indians.

*Captain Lewis & Clark holding a Council with the Indians.*

Patrick Gass, *Journal of Voyages and Travels under Lewis and Clark.* 1812

"AN AMERICAN, HAVING STRUCK A BEAR BUT NOT KILLED HIM, ESCAPES INTO A TREE."

From Gass' *Journal*
*Courtesy,* Wisconsin State Historical Society, Madison

Amusing incidents occurred.

Still westward, over the mountains, they went, to the Clearwater River, into the Snake River, and from that to the Columbia.

Maximilian, *Travels in the Interior of North America.* 1843

View of the Rocky Mountains

On Nov. 7, 1805, they gazed upon the broad Pacific, and established a claim which extended our boundaries from ocean to ocean.

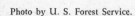

Photo by U. S. Forest Service.

## Pike's Expeditions

While the Lewis and Clark party was toiling over the mountains, between the rivers, another exploring expedition was starting from St. Louis, under the leadership of Lt. Zebulon M. Pike.

Lt. Zebulon M. Pike
Z. M. Pike, *Expeditions to the Sources of the Mississippi and through the Western Part of Louisiana.* 1810

Up the Mississippi, beyond the mouth of the St. Peters (or Minnesota) River he went.

VALLEY OF THE ST. PETERS, Minnesota.
PUBLISHED BY LIPPINCOTT, GRAMBO & CO. PHILAD.

H. R. Schoolcraft, *Information respecting Indian Tribes of the U. S.* 1851-57

He talked with the Indians, established the authority of the government, and selected the site for Fort Snelling.

H. R. Schoolcraft, *Information respecting Indian Tribes of the U. S.* 1851-57

INDIANS TRAVELLING

The following year, 1806, Pike led another expedition westward from St. Louis, through the Pawnee country, and along the eastern edge of the Rockies, where he saw at a distance the snowy peak which has since borne his name.

Seeking the headwaters of the Red River, Pike, by mistake, crossed the upper Rio Grande, and was captured by the Spaniards.

Pikes Peak
John C. Fremont, *Report of the Exploring Expeditions of 1842 and 1843-44*

## The Burr Conspiracy

Following the duel with Hamilton and the expiration of his term as Vice-President, Aaron Burr found himself bankrupt and almost a fugitive. His ambitious thoughts turned to the west, where he talked of establishing a colony in Spanish territory, while others said he planned to create an empire.

Harman Blennerhasset, a wealthy but eccentric Irishman, living on an island in the Ohio River near Marietta, not only helped to finance Burr's operations, but allowed his island to be used as a base for men and supplies going westward under Burr's direction.

Harman Blennerhasset
W. H. Safford, *The Blennerhasset Papers.* 1864

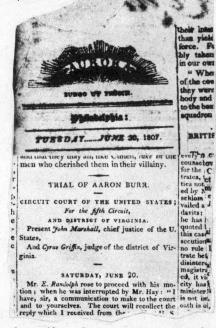

W. H. Safford, *The Life of Harman Blennerhasset.* 1850
Blennerhasset's Mansion

Burr, himself, on his way West, was the subject of almost panicky interest by the Federal Government; was arrested; brought back to Richmond, Va., for trial; and acquitted—to the unconcealed displeasure of President Jefferson.

St. Mémin's View of Richmond, Va.

## Impressment

The British Navy had traditionally manned its ships by means of the "press gang". To the practice of pressing idle seamen in British ports, there came to be added that of boarding ships and removing seamen believed to be British subjects.

PRESS GANG.

S. F. Holbrook, *Threescore Years: An Autobiography.* 1857

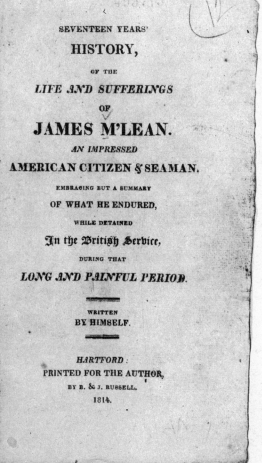

SEVENTEEN YEARS'

HISTORY,

OF THE

LIFE AND SUFFERINGS

OF

JAMES M'LEAN.

AN IMPRESSED

AMERICAN CITIZEN & SEAMAN.

EMBRACING BUT A SUMMARY

OF WHAT HE ENDURED,

WHILE DETAINED

In the British Service,

DURING THAT

LONG AND PAINFUL PERIOD.

WRITTEN
BY HIMSELF.

HARTFORD:
PRINTED FOR THE AUTHOR,
BY B. & J. RUSSELL.
1814.

The fact that thousands of British seamen, lured by higher pay, deserted from the Royal Navy and signed up on American ships, and were encouraged to do so by American captains, made misunderstandings and injustices inevitable.

Many *bona fide* Americans were "pressed", by sea or in ports, for service in the British Navy. To protect American nationals from seizure, certificates of citizenship were issued by American officials and carried by American seamen, and all too often bartered in foreign grogshops.

EXAMPLE OF AN AMERICAN SEAMAN'S PROTECTION PAPER
SIGNED BY WILLIAM R. LEE, COLLECTOR OF THE PORT OF SALEM
From the collections of the Essex Institute Library

Courtesy, The Essex Institute, Salem, Mass.

## The *Chesapeake-Leopard* Incident

An appalling case of impressment occurred on June 22, 1807, when the British man-of-war *Leopard* fired upon the American frigate *Chesapeake*, off Hampton Roads, and removed three American sailors along with one British deserter.

The American press mildly reflected the anger of the people, but a prompt repudiation by England enabled Jefferson to avert war.

Courtesy, The Bailey Collection, The Mariners' Museum, Newport News, Va.

*Leopard* and *Chesapeake*

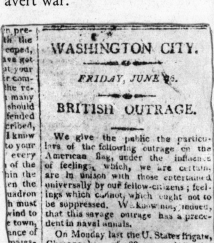

WASHINGTON CITY.

FRIDAY, JUNE 26.

BRITISH OUTRAGE.

National Intelligencer, June 26, 1807

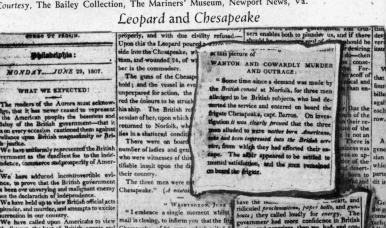

### Embargo

Courtesy, The Essex Institute, Salem, Mass.

Crowninshield's Wharf, at Salem, during Embargo

But a series of restrictions upon our shipping by the European belligerents, each trying to throttle the other, resulted in an Embargo Act, passed by Congress in December, 1807, by which all shipping from America to Europe was forbidden— and by which our merchant fleets were tied up in our harbors.

## Navigation and Coast Survey

Whatever the effects may have been on the warring nations of Europe, the Embargo was a stunning blow to American shipping, which had reached to all parts of the world. In 1802, Nathaniel Bowditch had issued his *American Practical Navigator*, which became the textbook of American seamen; going through edition after edition; and subsequently (1866) being taken over by the Hydrographic Office of the Navy.

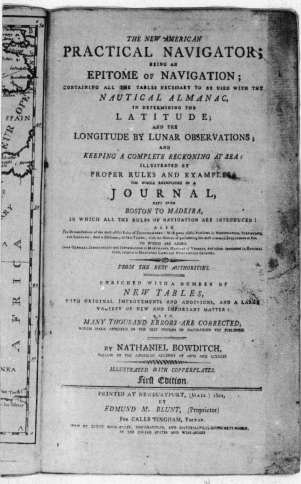

THE NEW AMERICAN
PRACTICAL NAVIGATOR;
BEING AN
EPITOME OF NAVIGATION;
CONTAINING ALL THE TABLES NECESSARY TO BE USED WITH THE
NAUTICAL ALMANAC,
IN DETERMINING THE
LATITUDE;
AND THE
LONGITUDE BY LUNAR OBSERVATIONS;
AND
KEEPING A COMPLETE RECKONING AT SEA:
ILLUSTRATED BY
PROPER RULES AND EXAMPLES:
THE WHOLE EXEMPLIFIED IN A
JOURNAL,
KEPT FROM
BOSTON TO MADEIRA,
IN WHICH ALL THE RULES OF NAVIGATION ARE INTRODUCED;
ALSO
FROM THE BEST AUTHORITIES.
ENRICHED WITH A NUMBER OF
NEW TABLES,
WITH ORIGINAL IMPROVEMENTS AND ADDITIONS, AND A LARGE
VARIETY OF NEW AND IMPORTANT MATTER:
ALSO
MANY THOUSAND ERRORS ARE CORRECTED,
BY NATHANIEL BOWDITCH,
FELLOW OF THE AMERICAN ACADEMY OF ARTS AND SCIENCES
ILLUSTRATED WITH COPPERPLATES.
First Edition.
PRINTED AT NEWBURYPORT, (MASS.) 1802,
BY
EDMUND M. BLUNT, (Proprietor)
For CALEB BINGHAM, BOSTON.

*Opposite*, from the Bowditch of 1802, we see the rigging of the various ships of the time.

A few months before the Embargo went into effect, Congress authorized the Survey of the Coast (subsequently the Coast and Geodetic Survey). F. R. Hassler, the first Superintendent, was directed to go to England for suitable surveying instruments, but his sailing was delayed until 1811 by the Embargo, and then his return was delayed by the War of 1812. Thus it was 1815 before the theodolite, shown *opposite*, and used in his first survey, reached America.

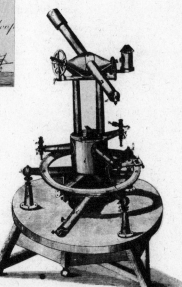

*Courtesy,* U. S. Coast and Geodetic Survey, Washington, D. C.

## Roads and Canals

During several months of the year, roads were impassable, and beyond the main routes between cities, there was no satisfactory means of communication at any time. The country was tending to break apart politically through the lack of physical ties.

Courtesy, Stokes Collection, The New York Public Library

# BOSTON,
## *Plymouth & Sandwich*
# MAIL STAGE,
### *CONTINUES TO RUN AS FOLLOWS:*

LEAVES Boston every Tuesday, Thursday, and Saturday mornings at 5 o'clock, breakfast at Leonard's, Scituate; dine at Bradford's, Plymouth; and arrive in Sandwich the same evening. Leaves Sandwich every Monday, Wednesday and Friday mornings; breakfast at Bradford's, Plymouth; dine at Leonard's, Scituate, and arrive in Boston the same evening.

Passing through Dorchester, Quincy, Wyemouth, Hingham, Scituate, Hanover, Pembroke, Duxbury, Kingston, Plymouth to Sandwich. *Fare,* from Boston to Scituate, 1 doll. 25 cts. From Boston to Plymouth, 2 dolls. 50 cts. From Boston to Sandwich, 3 dolls. 63 cts.

The Santee Canal, connecting the Cooper and Santee rivers in South Carolina (completed in 1800) was one of the few operating canals.

Charles Fraser, *A Charleston Sketchbook, 1796-1806*
Courtesy, Carolina Art Association, Charleston, S. C.

Santee Canal. 1803

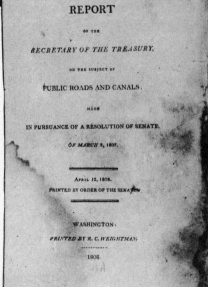

REPORT

OF THE

SECRETARY OF THE TREASURY,

ON THE SUBJECT OF

PUBLIC ROADS AND CANALS,

MADE

IN PURSUANCE OF A RESOLUTION OF SENATE,

OF MARCH 2, 1807.

APRIL 12, 1808.

PRINTED BY ORDER OF THE SENATE

WASHINGTON:
PRINTED BY R. C. WEIGHTMAN.

1808.

In 1808, Albert Gallatin made his famous *Report* recommending the building by the Government of a great connecting network of canals and roads, from the Atlantic to the midwestern rivers. Private enterprise within a few years carried out his program.

## Bridges

The Schuylkill River Bridge, begun in 1799, was completed in 1804.

From a drawing by W. Birch.   *Courtesy*, The Historical Society of Pennsylvania, Philadelphia

The first suspension bridge in America was erected by James Finley in 1801. In an article in *The Port Folio* for 1810, Finley says "There are eight of these bridges now", and adds, "The exclusive right was secured by patent in the year 1808".

View of the Chain Bridge invented by James Finley, Esq.

In 1811, Thomas Pope, in *A Treatise on Bridge Architecture*, visioned a bridge across the Hudson River, as shown *below*. One hundred and twenty-one years later such a bridge (the George Washington) did span the Hudson.

## The World of Tomorrow

William Tatham, who as a young man had lived in the region where The Tennessee Valley Authority contrived its great works one hundred and sixty years later, published a book in 1799 in which he foresaw canals such as this — running over and under one another, through tunnels and beside roads.

*The Lock System of Canals.*

William Tatham, *Political Economy of Inland Navigation, Irrigation and Drainage; etc.* 1799

He foresaw, also, the inclined plane which within a few decades was in practical operation.

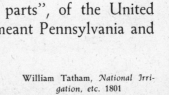

*Section & Front View of the German lifting Wheel used in America*

In another book, published in 1801, he described a water lifting wheel used for irrigation "in the interior parts", of the United States, by which he meant Pennsylvania and Virginia.

William Tatham, *National Irrigation, etc.* 1801

## "Fulton's Folly"

Several steamboats had been built before Fulton's but his *Clermont*, built and launched in 1807, was the first to prove physically and financially successful. It made the 150 mile run from New York to Albany in thirty-two hours—and a new era in water transportation began. *Below* we see the *Clermont* steaming past West Point, where, in 1802, had been established the U. S. Military Academy.

*Courtesy, Stokes Collection,*
*The New York Public Library*

The western rivers, soon to see the steamboat, were already being described in detail for the navigator. In 1801, Zadok Cramer, of Pittsburgh, began the publication of *The Navigator*, the title page of the Fifth Edition of which is shown *opposite.*

*Courtesy, The New-York Historical*
*Society, New York City*

THE
NAVIGATOR:
OR THE
Traders' useful Guide
IN NAVIGATING THE
MONONGAHELA, ALLEGHENY,
OHIO, AND MISSISSIPPI
RIVERS;
CONTAINING AN AMPLE ACCOUNT
OF THESE MUCH ADMIRED WATERS,
FROM THE HEAD OF THE FORMER TO THE MOUTH OF THE
LATTER;
A CONCISE DESCRIPTION OF THEIR
TOWNS, VILLAGES, HARBOURS, SETTLEMENTS, &c.
WITH PARTICULAR DIRECTIONS
HOW TO NAVIGATE THEM,
IN ALL STAGES OF THE WATER.
POINTING OUT THEIR
ROCKS, RIPPLES, CHANNEL, ISLANDS,
BLUFFS, CREEKS, RIVERS, &c.
AND THE DISTANCES FROM PLACE TO PLACE.
ILLUSTRATED WITH THIRTEEN ACCURATE MAPS OF THE
MISSISSIPPI, AND ONE OF PITTSBURGH.
THE FIFTH EDITION, MUCH IMPROVED AND ENLARGED.
TO WHICH IS ADDED,
AN ACCOUNT OF LOUISIANA;
AND A NOTICE OF THE
MINES, MINERALS, NATURAL CURIOSITIES, &c.
COPY RIGHT SECURED ACCORDING TO LAW.

PITTSBURGH;
FROM THE PRESS OF ZADOK CRAMER.
1806.

GENERAL DESCRIPTION
OF THE
RIVERS.

*MONONGAHELA.*

THIS river rises at the foot of the Laurel Mountain, in Virginia, thence meandering in a N. by E. direction, passes into Pennsylvania, and receives Cheat river from the S. S. E. thence winding to a N. by W. direction, separates Fayette and Westmoreland from Washington county, and passing into Allegheny county receives the Youghiogheny river from the S. S. E. and unites with the Allegheny river at Pittsburgh, fifteen miles below the mouth of the former, and by land, fifty-five below Cheat. The Monongahela is about 450 yards wide at its mouth, measuring from the top of bank to bank, and in the fall and spring freshes has water enough to carry ships of 400 tons burthen; these, however, subside quickly and render the navigation for such vessels very precarious. One great difficulty attending the navigation of vessels of burden down this river arises from the almost impossibility of keeping them in the proper channel, it being in many places very narrow, and full of short turns around points of islands which are numerous. This observation will also apply to the Ohio, especially as low down as Wheelen, ninety miles below Pittsburgh.

This river runs through a rich and well settled country; the lands on its banks sell for from twelve to thirty dollars per acre; its waters are in freshes very muddy; its banks are very generally firm, bearing numerous large trees of the button-wood, sugar-maple, walnut, hickory, black-oak, &c. these afford a good supply of logs to the saw-mills erected on the creeks emptying into it. Boards from these are frequently floated down to Pittsburgh, Wheelen, &c. where they sell for about

A

## Among the Books and Magazines

In 1800, Noah Webster announced a plan for three dictionaries, one for businessmen, one for elementary schools and one for scholars. In 1806, the first of these, *A Compendious Dictionary*, appeared.

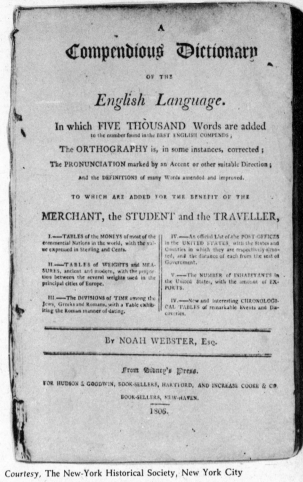

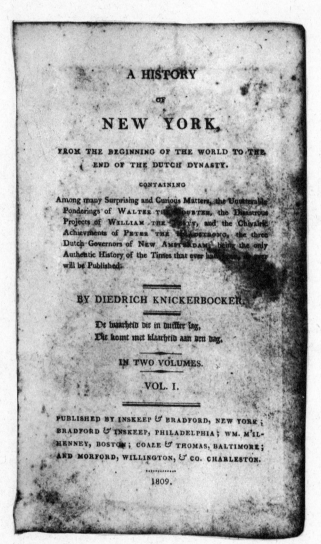

Courtesy, The New-York Historical Society, New York City

Washington Irving, who had tried, not too hard, to be a lawyer, finished in 1809, America's "first great book of comic literature"— Knickerbocker's *A History of New York*.

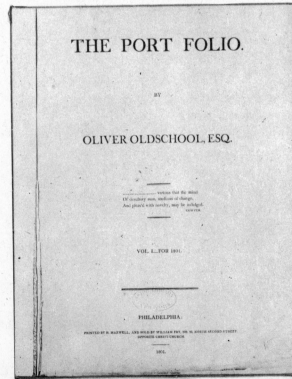

Outstanding among the magazines was *The Port Folio*, which has supplied its quota of illustrations for the present work.

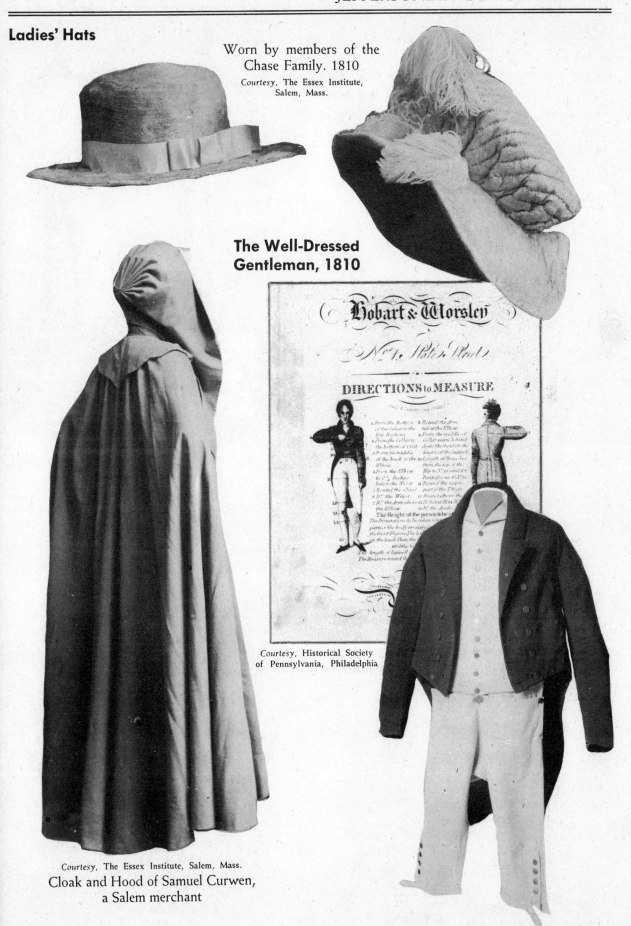

**Ladies' Hats**

Worn by members of the
Chase Family. 1810
*Courtesy,* The Essex Institute,
Salem, Mass.

**The Well-Dressed
Gentleman, 1810**

*Courtesy,* Historical Society
of Pennsylvania, Philadelphia

*Courtesy,* The Essex Institute, Salem, Mass.
Cloak and Hood of Samuel Curwen,
a Salem merchant

*Courtesy,* The Essex Institute, Salem, Mass.
Breeches and Coat, 1800-25

## Clocks

The "Banjo Clock" was invented by Simon Willard or his brother, Aaron, in 1802. The example shown *opposite* is 39 inches high. The case is of mahogany. The works are of brass, driven by a weight. The dial is of metal painted white with the numerals in black. The hands are made of iron.

**Silver**

*Left*, Sugar Urn by John Sayre. About 1800. New York City

*Courtesy*, The Metropolitan Museum of Art, New York City

Photo by Paul G. Darrot
Owned by Mr. Walter F. Keller, Scarsdale, N. Y.

**Pewter**

*Courtesy*, The Metropolitan Museum of Art, New York City
Pewter Plate by Samuel Kilbourn, Baltimore. Early 19th Century

*Left*, Candlesticks by Isaac Hutton. 1800-1825. Albany

*Courtesy*, The Metropolitan Museum of Art, New York City

**Chairs**

*Courtesy*, The Metropolitan Museum of Art, New York City

Mahogany Arm Chair, probably from the workshop of Duncan Phyfe, New York. Early 19th Century

*Courtesy*, The Metropolitan Museum of Art, New York City

Mahogany Side Chair ("Duncan Phyfe" Style), New York City. 1805-1815

**Table**

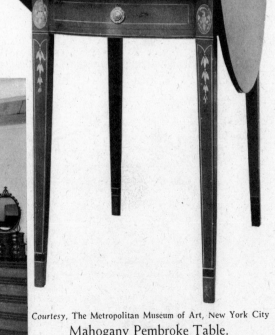

**Trundle Bed**

During the day it was pushed under the larger bed. At night it was pulled out, as shown *below*, and served for the younger children.

*Courtesy*, The Metropolitan Museum of Art, New York City

Mahogany Pembroke Table. About 1800

*Courtesy*, Brooklyn Museum, Brooklyn, N. Y.

Trundle Bed. Early 19th Century

**Ironwork**

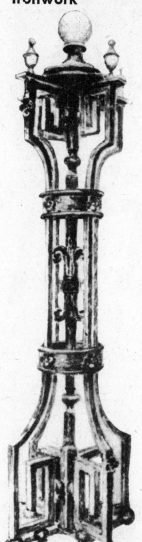

Main Gate of Colt Mansion, Bristol, R. I. 1810

*Left*, Newel Post. House on Bleecker Street, N. Y. 1800-1810

Gates of St. Michael's Cemetery, Charleston, S. C.
Work of A. W. Iusti. Early 19th Century

All illustrations on this page are from Albert H. Sonn, *Early American Wrought Iron.* 1928

Weathervane on Brick Meeting
House, Canandaigua, N. Y. 1803

## James Madison

was inaugurated as President on March 4, 1809.

James Madison. From a Portrait by
Gilbert Stuart
*Courtesy*, Bowdoin College Museum of Fine Arts, Brunswick, Maine

The National Capitol still stood as two unconnected wings.

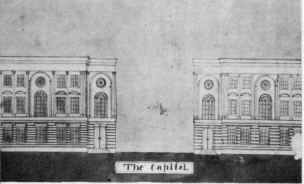

*Courtesy*, The Historical Society of Pennsylvania, Philadelphia

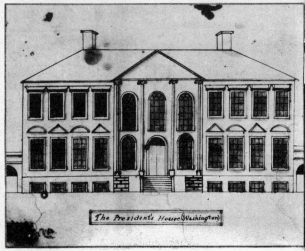

*Courtesy*, The Historical Society of Pennsylvania, Philadelphia

Mrs. Madison, however, found the President's House somewhat improved over the conditions which Mrs. Adams had encountered.

*Courtesy*, The New-York Historical Society, New York City
Dolly Madison

## Jefferson Retired

to his beloved Monticello, on a "little mountain" near Charlottesville, Va.

Monticello

Entrance Hall, Monticello

Dining Room, Monticello

Stable, with Law Office at *right*, Monticello

## New York In 1810

From an original drawing by the Baroness Hyde de Neuville.   *Courtesy*, Stokes Collection, The New York Public Library

### Corner of Greenwich Street

Note the small boy at the pump, the man sawing wood in the street, *and the trees.*

## Fire Fighting Equipment

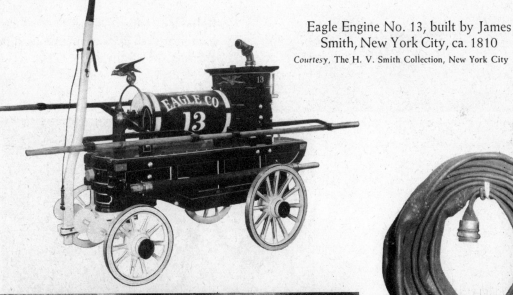

Eagle Engine No. 13, built by James
Smith, New York City, ca. 1810

*Courtesy*, The H. V. Smith Collection, New York City

*Courtesy*, The H. V. Smith Collection, New York City

Hose (1808). Single riveted seam;
double rivets at leather joinings.
Length of hose approximately forty
feet. Brass couplings.

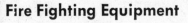

*View of the* BOTANIC GARDEN *at* ELGIN *in the vicinity of the* CITY *of* NEW YORK.

The Port Folio, January-June, 1810

## Philadelphia

as seen from the ferry (across the Delaware River) at Camden, N. J.

By J. L. Bouquet de Woiseri.    *Courtesy*, Stokes Collection, The New York Public Library

*Above*, and slightly to the right of the stage wagon, may be seen a steamboat, built shortly after the *Clermont* (see page 107).

The Market Street Bridge, Philadelphia, 1805

From a painting by John James Barralet
*Courtesy*, The Historical Society of Pennsylvania, Philadelphia

In the left center (*opposite*) is a Durham boat such as Washington used in crossing the Delaware in 1776.

Charles Willson Peale, the portrait painter, had become interested in natural history. His museum, which contained among other things, the bones of a mastodon dug up near Newburgh, N. Y., was one of Philadelphia's show places. The picture *opposite* is from a portrait of the artist and his Museum made by the artist himself.

*Courtesy*, The Pennsylvania Academy of the Fine Arts, Philadelphia

**Around About Philadelphia**

*View of Seconde Street, north from Market Street, with Christ Churche.*

*High Street, Philadelphiae, with an American Stage waggon*

*Philadelphia Theatre in Chesnut Streete.*

All illustrations on this page are from Charles Wilson Janson, *The Stranger in America.* 1807

## Umbrellas, Hats, Shoes

**Cheap                Umbrellas**

AND                *PARASOLS.*

WILLIAM            RICHARDSON,

OFFERS FOR SALE AT      HIS MANUFACTORY,

### No, 6, S.        Third street,

Seven doors below Market street, (west side,)
A LARGE and complete assortment, comprising some hundred dozens of UMBREL-
LAS and PARASOLS, of the latest and most approved fashions, and of *superior manufacture,*
which he will sell at as low prices, as any establishment in the United States, and will warrant his manufacture to be equal, if not superior to any offered for sale in this city.

All goods retailed are kept in repair one
year gratis.

ON HAND,

1000 Umbrellas suitable for shipping, and
any quantity supplied at short notice.
Also, Green, Blue and Crimson Senshaws
and Sarsnets, for sale by the case or piece.
Do. White and assorted Sewings.
march 3—dtf

### YOUNG's

PATENT ANATOMICAL DANCING

# SHOES.

DEDICATED TO THE LADIES AND GENTLEMEN

## OF PHILADELPHIA.

Such are the admirable qualities of this shoe, that it would
be a crime in the author not to delineate them. Ease united with
elegance, are qualities in science rarely to be found in any country; happy Americans this friendly genius originates with you. Hyperbole upon hyperbole; health and duration claims a part in this
admirable plan. Corns, twisted heels, and lacerated insteps shall
no more agonize human nature; no more shall the aged witness
the aid of the crutch, the middle aged shall walk with certain
sure and easy step, the young shall skip as an hart, and never
know their accumulated horrors; this shall deserve more of our
country than all the celebrated corn plaster physicians; for these
maladies shall cease to exist: wonderful! that the genius of
Crispen should have made so happy a discovery; the foot
looses in its appearance one third of its size, as to a side view
thereof, making it to appear exceedingly neat.

The celebrated Mr. Whale has authorized me to say that he has not in Europe seen any shoe so
complete to fit the foot and for dancing, as Young's Patent Anatomical shoe. The facility of dancing
in those shoes are so superior to any ever offered to the public, that none but the wearer of
them can possibly have an idea of the advantage derived from them. Ladies appartment in
private, who will be waited upon for the purpose of measuring them, by one of their own sex.
Gentlemen's appartment below in the back room; the author has been these ten years study
ing this principle, and has but just accomplished its end.

WILLIAM YOUNG. No. 31, Walnut Street.

*LADIES LOOK WELL TO YOUR LAST.*

Never did nature assume a more smiling aspect, than those who wear Young's Patents, they
more then smile, they laugh and trip it as they go on the light fantastic toe.
N. B. Price of fitting five dollars, in advance, as every Lady and Gentleman must have a
pair of lasts made particularly for their own feet, and reserved solely for their own use; which
will entitle them to be kept fitted let what fashion will occur. Young Ladies and Gentlemen
whose feet are not done growing to be kept fitted also. Elegant Cossack Boots upon a new
construction. No please no pay.

If there is any ques-
tion as to the demand
for parasols, see pages
116 and 119.

### NEW HAT STORE.

THE Subscriber having
taken a Store in the new
building, at the North-
East corner of Chesnut &
Third streets, No. 45, S.
Third street, where he in-
tends keeping a handsome
and general assortment of
fashionable hats, such as
Gentlemen's Beaver, Castor and Roram Hats.
Youths, and Children's Hats.
Reading Wool, Black & White, do.
Children's Morocco, do.
Ladies Misses, and Children's Beavers.
All of which will be sold on the most accom-
modating terms, wholesale and retail.
Orders from Country & Shipping Merchants,
promptly attended to.

### John Stuckert.

feb 10—dtf

### Wholesale and Retail

*FASHIONABLE*

# HAT MANUFACTORY,

## No. 134, MARKET STREET, between

Fourth and Fifth streets.

THE subscriber respect-
fully informs his friends and
the public, that he has con-
stantly on hand, a general assortment of HATS, as fol-
lows—Gentlemens' Beaver,
Castor and Roram Hats,
Boy's and Children's Hats,
Reading Wool & Children's
Morocco Hats, which he will
dispose of wholesale or retail, for cash or approved
paper.
Shipping and Country Merchants are invited to
call and examine for themselves, before purchasing
elsewhere.

### Lemuel B. Glover,

feb 19—dtf        Successor to S. Messinger.

### PATENT IRON-BOUND

# Boots, Bootees and Shoes.

### JOHN BEDFORD, *Philadelphia,*

RESPECTFULLY informs the public in general, and store-keepers
in particular, that he is now prepared to supply them with the a-
bove valuable goods, wholesale and retail, on moderate terms.

Shoemakers, also, may be supplied with patent-rights, on easy terms,
which they will find it highly their interest to obtain, as they can, by
this improvement, make four times the quantity of shoes, with their usual
number of hands; for example, the usual work of three men is only three
pair of common shoes per day; whereas, in the improved way, 3 men
with the assistance of a boy, can make from twelve to fifteen pair per day.
Thus the advantages resulting from this improvement, are evidently of
the most essential importance: in the first place, three-fourths of the la-
bour is saved: in the second place, half the leather is saved, for one pair
of shoes made in this way, will wear as long as two pair made in the
usual way, and in the third place, there is a saving of flax, at the rate of
one pound, to 24 pair of shoes, they are also much more water-proof
than the others, and easier mended.

These are well ascertained facts, proved by actual experience. The
patentee therefore hopes, that an improvement, fraught with such important public utility, will not only engage the attention, but the encouragement of every friend to the infant manufactures of this country. It
may not be amiss to remark, that the country shoemaker in particular,
may derive incalculable advantages from this improvement, as he can
supply his customers in one-fourth of the time he has usually devoted to
that purpose, and have the other three-fourths for the cultivation of his
farm or other avocations.

Price of patent-rights for the country, 100 dollars. For states, districts or towns, in proportion.

Nov. 15, 1809.

All illustrations on this page are through the *courtesy* of The Historical
Society of Pennsylvania, Philadelphia

## Among the Friends (Quakers) in Pennsylvania

*Friends' meeting House at Merion.*

*American friends going to meeting in summer.*

*American friends going to meeting in a settled frost*

*A Farm House in the Back Settlements*

All illustrations on this page are from Robert Sutcliff, *Travels in Some Parts of North America, 1804, 1805 and 1806.*
1815
*Courtesy,* The New-York Historical Society, New York City

## Carpenter and Artist

At York, Pa., lived Lewis Miller, who for forty years followed the trade of carpenter. But he also made watercolor pictures depicting the life that went on in the Pennsylvania German town of York. We shall meet him from time to time in this volume.

"The Engine House in Main Street, fronting the market house, on John Hay Ser. Lot. This was the First Engine in town. I recollect it in the year 1799."

From watercolor paintings by Lewis Miller
*Courtesy*, The Historical Society of York County, York, Pa.

"Colonel George Spangler making Cherry Bounce in 1806. To a Barrel of Juice put in to it Six pound of sugar, and two gallon of whiskey and let the juice and sugar boil in a large kettle a half an hour and skim it."

## At Easton

in northeastern Pennsylvania, the Pennsylvania German craftsmen were making and using such conveniences as shown *below*.

Teapot, painted in red, green and yellow

Candlestick. Wrought-iron.

Mamele (baby-bottle). Tin

*Courtesy*, Landis Valley Museum, Lancaster, Pa.

## William Russell Birch, Painter and Engraver

born in England in 1755, came to America in 1794. Many of his drawings will be found in this volume.

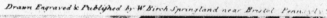

Mount Vernon, *Virginia, the Seat of the late* Gen.¹ G. Washington.

*Drawn Engraved & Published by* W.ᵣ *Birch Springland near Bristol Pennsylv.*ᵃ

Hampton *the Seat of* Gen.¹ Cha.ˢ Ridgley. *Maryland.*

*Drawn Engraved & Published by* W. *Birch Springland near Bristol Penn.*ᵃ

th illustrations above are through the *courtesy* of The Historical Society of Pennsylvania, Philadelphia

t is of interest to note that the artist inscribes both of the above as "Drawn Engraved & ublished by W. Birch, Springland near Bristol, Pennsylva."

## In the South

### View near Charleston, S. C., 1802

Charles Fraser, *A Charleston Sketchbook,*
1796-1806
*Courtesy,* The Carolina Art Association,
Charleston, S. C.

The windmill furnished power for sawing lumber. Water mills, operated by the tides, also were common.

### St. Andrew's Parish Church, 1800

The building was still standing, practically unchanged, in 1940, on the road from Charleston to Middleton Place

Charles Fraser, *A Charleston Sketchbook,*
1796-1806
*Courtesy,* The Carolina Art Association,
Charleston, S. C.

Eutaw Plantation House built in 1808, was typical of the plantation houses of lower South Carolina.

*Courtesy,* The Charleston Museum, Charleston, S. C.

## Catastrophes of 1811

On the westerly side of the Mississippi River, some 200 miles below St. Louis, as the river winds, in the area around New Madrid, occurred an earthquake which only the sparseness of the settlement kept from being a major disaster.

THE GREAT EARTHQUAKE AT NEW MADRID

"Then the houses crumbled, the trees waved together, the ground sunk; while ever and anon vivid flashes of lightning, gleaming through the troubled clouds of night, rendered the darkness doubly horrible"

Henry Howe, *Historical Collections of the Great West.* 1854

On December 26, a crowded theatre at Richmond, Va., burst into flames. There was but one main exit and as many people lost their lives by being trampled as did by the flames.

Henry Howe, *Historical Collections of Virginia.* 1849

## Far Separated but Converging Events

In 1810, John Jacob Astor, founder of the American Fur Company, decided to extend his operations to the Columbia River. The British fur traders moved to forestall him. On March 23, 1811, Astor's ship, the *Tonquin*, arrived at the mouth of the Columbia. When the British arrived in July, they found Astoria already established. For the moment the Americans had won.

ENTRANCE OF THE COLUMBIA RIVER.
*Ship Tonquin, crossing the bar. 25th March. 1811*

Gabriel Franchere, *Narrative of a Voyage to the Northwest Coast of America, 1811, 1812, 1813, 1814. 1854*

On May 16, 1811, the United States frigate *President*, in the Atlantic, off Cape Henry, gave a withering broadside to the British ship *Little Belt*—and the people of America approved.

*Courtesy*, Bailey Collection, The Mariners' Museum, Newport News, Va.

On Tippecanoe Creek, in Indiana Territory, the northwestern Indians, under the spell of The Prophet, the leadership of Tecumseh, and the encouragement of the British, on Nov. 7 1811, faced an American army under William Henry Harrison and were far from defeated.

### Tecumseh

Benson J. Lossing, *Pictorial Field Book of the War of 1812.* 1868

### The Prophet

McKenney and Hall, *History of the Indians of North America.* 1842

*Courtesy*, William L. Clements Library, Ann Arbor, Mich.

At Fort George, on the Canadian side of the Niagara River, British troops drilled

# 4
# WAR AND ITS AFTERMATH
## 1812-1816

## National Intelligencer.

[Vol. XII.] FIVE DOLLARS PER ANNUM    WASHINGTON CITY SATURDAY JUNE 20 1812    PAID IN ADVANCE. No 1825

### (By Authority:)

### AN ACT

*Declaring War between the United Kingdom of Great Britain and Ireland and the dependencies thereof and the United States of America and their Territories.*

BE it enacted by the Senate and House of Representatives of the United States of America in Congress assembled, That WAR be and the same is hereby declared to exist between the United Kingdom of Great Britain and Ireland and the dependencies thereof, and the United States of America and their territories; and that the President of the United States be and he is hereby authorised to use the whole land and naval force of the United States to carry the same into effect, and to issue to private armed vessels of the United States commissions or letters of marque and general reprisal, in such form as he shall think proper, and under the seal of the United States, against the vessels, goods, and effects of the government of the same United Kingdom of Great Britain and Ireland and of the subjects thereof.

H. CLAY,
*Speaker of the House of Representatives.*
WM. H. CRAWFORD,
*President of the Senate pro tempore.*
June 18, 1812.
APPROVED,    JAMES MADISON.

### WASHINGTON CITY.

*SATURDAY, JUNE 20.*

The veil is at length removed from the Secret Proceedings of Congress; and it appears that unqualified WAR is declared between the UNITED STATES and GREAT-BRITAIN. The measure must have been long anticipated, and therefore cannot excite surprize. Its adoption, however, stamps reality on what was before mere inference and conjecture.

It would be the height of presumption in us to obtrude on the public attention any remarks of ours in the same paper in which we present to it the eloquent and perspicuous Message of the Executive, and the equally admirable Report or Manifesto of the committee of Foreign Relations. The motives & object of the measure are therein sufficiently developed and explained. We will only say, that as the measure of War has been at length adopted from a conviction of its necessity almost to the existence of the nation, we offer our sincere prayers and ardent hopes for a vigorous prosecution and successful termination of the contest in which we are about to engage.

In another part of this paper will be found a statement of atrocious outrage committed on our commerce by French national vessels. The President has wisely abstained from suggesting the propriety of offensive measures against France, until late doubt shall become present certainty. If ample atonement be not made by France for these outrages, we trust in God she will be made to feel, by a vigorous retaliation of her flagrant injustice, the resentment of a rational and spirited people for affrontful and unwarrantable injuries committed on their rights and commerce.

From the length of the most important state papers we this day publish, we have not room for a detail of either the public or private proceedings of Congress, all which shall find their due place in our columns. We have

### BY THE
### PRESIDENT OF THE
### UNITED STATES OF AMERICA,
### A PROCLAMATION.

WHEREAS the Congress of the United States, by virtue of the Constituted Authority vested in them, have declared by their act, bearing date the eighteenth day of the present month, that War exists between the United Kingdom of Great Britain and Ireland, and the dependencies thereof, and the United States of America and

their territories; Now therefore, I, JAMES MADISON, President of the United States of America, do hereby proclaim the same to all whom it may concern: and I do specially enjoin on all persons holding offices, civil or military, under the authority of the United States, that they be vigilant and zealous, in discharging the duties respectively incident thereto: And I do moreover exhort all the good people of the United States, as they love their country; as they value the precious heritage derived from the virtue and valor of their fathers; as they feel the wrongs which have forced on them the last resort of injured nations; and as they consult the best means, under the blessing of Divine Providence, of abridging its calamities; that they exert themselves in preserving order, in promoting concord, in maintaining the authority and the efficacy of the laws, and in supporting and invigorating all the measures which may be adopted by the Constituted Authorities, for obtaining a speedy, a just, and an honorable peace.

IN TESTIMONY WHEREOF I have hereunto set my hand, and caused the seal of the United States to be affixed to these presents.

(SEAL.)

DONE at the City of Washington, the nineteenth day of June, one thousand eight hundred and twelve, and of the Independence of the United States the thirty-sixth.

(Signed) JAMES MADISON.
*By the President,*
(Signed) JAMES MUNROE,
*Secretary of State.*

At an election held on Tuesday, 16th inst. in the first ward, for a member of the board of common council, to fill the vacancy occasioned by the resignation of James Hoban Esq. resigned, it appears that William P. Gardner is duly elected. And on Wednesday, the 17th inst. Nicholas L. Queen was elected a member of the board of Alderman, for one year, from the first Monday of June inst. to fill the vacancy occasioned by the resignation of Daniel Rapine, appointed Mayor.

MARRIED

## The Attack on Canada

With war impending, Gen. William Hull, with a nondescript army from Ohio, was ordered to Detroit, where he arrived on July 5, 1812, three days after having been informed of the declaration of war.

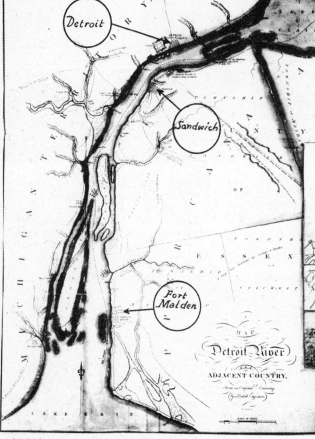

John Melish, *A Military and Topographical Atlas of the United States*. 1813

The British, across the Detroit River, had known of the state of war since June 30, and had also in their possession all Hull's papers which they had captured in a boat passing Fort Malden.

*Below,* Detroit in 1809

Courtesy, William L. Clements Library, Ann Arbor, Mich.

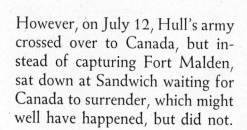

However, on July 12, Hull's army crossed over to Canada, but instead of capturing Fort Malden, sat down at Sandwich waiting for Canada to surrender, which might well have happened, but did not.

*Below,* Fort Malden, 1812

From a watercolor painting by Miss Catherine Reynolds
*Courtesy,* Mr. George F. Macdonald, Windsor, Canada

## The Tomahawk to the Rescue

While Hull waited at Sandwich, the English General Brock was acting. To the officers and partisan leaders of the Northwest went orders to rouse the Indians to the support of the British "White Father".

From a watercolor painting by Edward Walsh   *Courtesy, William L. Clements Library, Ann Arbor, Mich.*

Post St. Joseph

On July 17, from St. Joseph's Island, at the head of Lake Huron, a mixed force of Indians and British descended upon the strategic American post of Michilimackinac (see page 3) which discreetly surrendered. *Below* is a view of Michilimackinac.

H. R. Schoolcraft, *Information respecting Indian Tribes of the United States.* 1851-57

A month later Fort Dearborn, at Chicago, surrendered to the Indians—and a ghastly massacre ensued.

*Right,* Fort Dearborn

From a drawing made in 1808 by Capt. John Whistler, commanding at Fort Dearborn

Courtesy, The National Archives, Records of the War Department, Office of the Adjutant General, Washington, D. C.

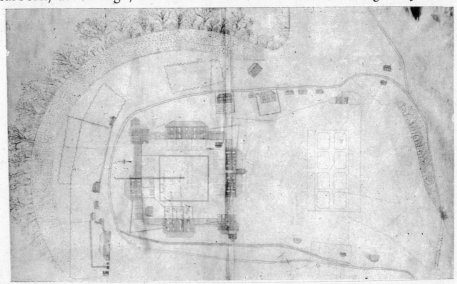

With the victorious Indian allies coming down the Lakes, and a British army approaching from the east, Hull retreated to Detroit, and on the same day that the Indians were scalping and killing at Chicago, he meekly surrendered Detroit to the British.

## Victory At Sea

Four days after the surrender of Detroit by Gen. William Hull, his nephew and adopted son, Capt. Isaac Hull, commanding the U.S.S. *Constitution*, overhauled the British frigate *Guerrière* in the Atlantic, and, in an engagement lasting thirty minutes, totally disabled and captured his opponent.

ISAAC HULL ESQ<sup>R</sup>

*of the United States Navy*

*Analectic Magazine*, March, 1813

*Below,* Constitution *and* Guerrière
*Courtesy,* The Historical Society of Pennsylvania, Philadelphia

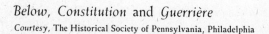

And while the country was still celebrating the victory of the *Constitution* over the *Guerrière*, Capt. Porter of the U.S.S. *Essex* sailed into Delaware Bay with the news of having met and captured the British sloop-of-war *Alert*.

*Opposite,* The Essex *captures the* Alert
From a watercolor drawing by Charles Turner Warren
*Courtesy,* Bailey Collection, The Mariners' Museum,
Newport News, Va.

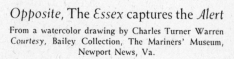

## Niagara

At the mouth of the Niagara River, where the waters of the Upper Lakes, after spilling over the Falls, flow placidly into Lake Ontario, stood, on the American side, Fort Niagara, and, on the Canadian side, Fort George.

Basil Hall, *Forty Etchings from Sketches made with the Camera Lucida in North America.* 1829
*Courtesy,* Peabody Institute, Baltimore, Md.

From a watercolor painting by Edward Walsh. 1804 *Courtesy,* William L. Clements Library, Ann Arbor, Mich.

Fort Niagara

From a watercolor painting by Edward Walsh. 1804 *Courtesy,* William L. Clements Library, Ann Arbor, Mich.

Fort George

## Another Failure

About midway between the Falls and the mouth of the river (just north of the end of the gorge down which the boiling waters rushed) stood, on the American side, the village of Lewiston. Across, on the Canadian side, was the village of Queenstown.

Here, in the dark hours of the morning of Oct. 13, 1812, Maj. Gen. Stephen Van Rensselaer, with some 3000 American troops, attempted a crossing into Canada. The troops that got across—about 1000—were, after a preliminary success, captured. Thus ended another attempted invasion of Canada.

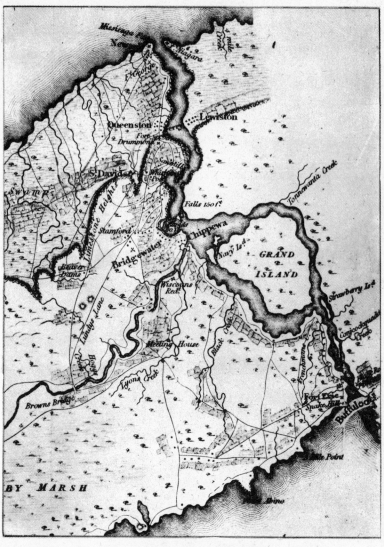

Francis Hall, *Travels in Canada and in the United States in 1816-1817.* 1818

The Niagara Frontier

The Port Folio,
August, 1814

*Queenstown, upper Canada*

## Out on the Atlantic

Off Halifax, the U. S. S. *Wasp* disabled and captured the British war-sloop *Frolic*, only herself to fall a prize to the British frigate *Poictiers*.

From a watercolor drawing by Charles Turner Warren
*Courtesy*, Bailey Collection, The Mariners' Museum, Newport News, Va.

The *Wasp* and *Frolic*

A week later (Oct. 25, 1812) Capt. Stephen Decatur, cruising in the vicinity of the Azores in the *United States*, fell in with the British frigate *Macedonian*. American gunnery gained a quick victory; the *Macedonian* was brought into Newport as a prize, and her flag was hung with those of the *Guerrière* and *Alert* (see page 128) in a Washington ballroom where tribute was being paid to the American Navy.

*Left*, Stephen Decatur
*Courtesy*, Bailey Collection, The Mariners' Museum, Newport News, Va.

From a painting by T. Birch
*Courtesy*, Bailey Collection, The Mariners' Museum, Newport News, Va.

The *United States* and *Macedonian*

## More Victories At Sea

On December 19, off the coast of Brazil, Commodore Bainbridge, in the U. S. S. *Constitution*, met the British ship *Java*, which put up a determined fight, but was so shot to pieces that she could only surrender. After the removal of the crew, the *Java* was blown up and sunk.

From a sketch by Lt. Buchanan
*Courtesy*, Bailey Collection, The Mariners' Museum, Newport News, Va.

*Constitution* and *Java*

A few weeks later (Feb. 24, 1813), the *Hornet*, a sloop of Bainbridge's squadron, commanded by James Lawrence, who a few weeks later was to immortalize the words, "Don't give up the ship", defeated and sunk the British brig *Peacock* off the coast of British Guiana.

HORNET AND PEACOCK.

Horace Kimball, *American Naval Battles*. 1831

This succession of victories over the British naval power caused great rejoicing in the United States—and corresponding dejection in England.

## Back On the Canadian Border

A fairly well organized plan of action developed during the Spring of 1813. On April 27, an American fleet appeared off York (later to be known as Toronto), the capital of Upper Canada. The town was captured; the military stores and shipping were destroyed; and, unfortunately, the Houses of Assembly were set on fire—an act that was publicly disavowed, but which was used by the

*Analectic Magazine,* April, 1819

British as an apology for their later burning of Washington (see page 145). Fort George, at the mouth of the Niagara River, was the next objective, and on May 27, it fell to a combined bombardment by the American fleet and an attack by a landing force.

*The Port Folio,* July, 1817.   Courtesy, The New-York Historical Society

But even as the Americans were taking Fort George, a British fleet from Kingston, on the Canadian shore at the eastern end of Lake Ontario, was on its way across the lake to attack the American naval depot at Sackett's Harbor, almost opposite. While the base was not actually captured, the shipping was severely crippled, leaving control of the lake in British hands.

*The Port Folio,* May, 1815

## "Don't Give Up the Ship"

On June 1, 1813, Capt. Broke, of the British frigate *Shannon*, standing off Boston, challenged Capt. James Lawrence, of the U.S.S. *Chesapeake*, then lying in Boston Harbor, to a fight. Lawrence sailed out, and the battle took place just out of sight of land. The roar of the cannon was plainly heard, then all was silence.

SHANNON & CHESAPEAKE GOING INTO ACTION. Nº I. JUNE 1ST 1813.

From a painting by Provo William Parry Wallis
*Courtesy*, Bailey Collection, The Mariners' Museum, Newport News, Va.

For two weeks there was uncertainty. Then came the report that the *Chesapeake* was a prize in Halifax Harbor, and that Capt. Lawrence had been buried there. The story proved all too true. The *Shannon* had outgunned and outmaneuvered the *Chesapeake*.

JAMES LAWRENCE ESQ.
*Late of the United States Navy*

*Analectic Magazine*, August, 1813

Lawrence had fallen mortally wounded. His last injunction had been, "Don't give up the ship"—but the ship had to be given up, and was led a captive into Halifax.

From a painting by Provo William Parry Wallis
*Courtesy*, Bailey Collection, The Mariners' Museum, Newport News, Va.

SHANNON & CHESAPEAKE GOING INTO HALIFAX. Nº 4.

## Raids and Counter-Raids

By the Spring of 1813, British warships were off the American coast in considerable strength.

An enemy flotilla sailed at will up and down Chesapeake Bay. On May 3, Havre de Grace, Md., at the head of the Bay, was burned and plundered.

From a caricature of 1813.
*Courtesy*, The Hambleton Collection, The Municipal Museum, Baltimore

*Left*, Havre de Grace being Burned and Plundered by Admiral Cockburn

Benson Lossing, *Pictorial Field-Book of the War of 1812.* (1868)

GENERAL VIEW OF CRANEY ISLAND.

An attack on Craney Island, near Hampton Roads, was defeated by Virginia militia, and Norfolk saved from capture.

ARGUS BURNING BRITISH VESSELS

Horace Kimball, *American Naval Battles.* 1831

At the same time, the U.S.S. *Argus* was burning and plundering British shipping in the Irish Channel.

## Blockaded

Slowly Britain's seapower swept American shipping from the Atlantic, and by the autumn of 1813, most of our warships were bottled up in port.

*The Naval Chronicle, 1814*

British Ships off Sandy Hook

New York Harbor was sealed up by British 74's (ships of the line carrying 74 guns) and frigates stationed off Sandy Hook.

In New York Harbor was Decatur with the *United States, Macedonian* and *Hornet*. He attempted to get to sea by running up Long Island Sound, but here again he found a British squadron awaiting him at Montauk Point, and was forced back to New London until the war ended.

*The Port Folio, February, 1814*

New London, 1813, with Decatur's Squadron in the Harbor

## An Echo of Tippecanoe

Before the battle of Tippecanoe (see page 124), Tecumseh had visited the Creek Indians (in what is now eastern Alabama) urging them to join in a great Indian confederacy. Tecumseh was now (1813) with the British in Canada, but his influence was still at work. The Creeks raised the tomahawk by the massacre, on August 30, 1813, of 500 Americans at Fort Mims on the Alabama River north of Mobile.

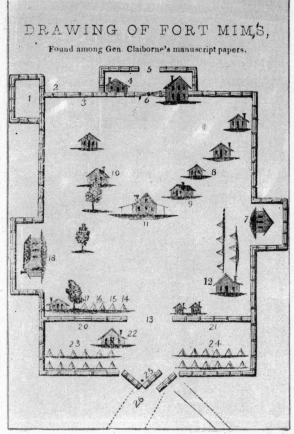

DRAWING OF FORT MIMS,

Found among Gen. Claiborne's manuscript papers.

A. J. Pickett, *History of Alabama.* (1851)

Push-Ma-Ta-Ha

*Courtesy,* Eames Collection, The New.York Public Library

Push-Ma-Ta-Ha of the Choctaw Indians (in present southwestern Mississippi) sided with the Americans.

And militia from Tennessee, under Andrew Jackson, marched against the Creek towns.

Amos Kendall, *Life of Andrew Jackson.* 1843

## The Tide Turns

A minor, but very stubbornly fought, engagement, between the U. S. brig *Enterprise* and the British brig *Boxer*, off the coast of Maine (Sept. 5, 1813), in which both commanders were killed, gave America a needed victory — and Longfellow inspiration for a stanza in the poem "My Lost Youth".

ENTERPRIZE AND BOXER.

Horace Kimball, *American Naval Battles.* 1831

But the event which brought a thrill to all America was Perry's victory over the British flotilla at Put-in-Bay on Lake Erie (Sept. 10). "We have met the enemy and they are ours, two ships, two brigs, one schooner, and one sloop", was Perry's laconic report of the battle.

BATTLE OF ERIE

*Naval Temple.* 1816

Eighteen days later the American squadron on Lake Ontario drove the British squadron into Kingston where it remained inactive

Action on Lake Ontario,
Sept. 28, 1813

From a watercolor drawing by Charles Turner Warren and/or his son Alfred William Warren
*Courtesy,* The Mariners' Museum, Newport News, Va.

## Tecumseh Falls

American control of the Lakes caused the British to evacuate Detroit and begin a hurried withdrawal eastward. The American army, under the command of Gen. William Henry Harrison, was fast in pursuit, which ended (Oct. 5, 1813) on the Thames River some fifty miles east of Detroit, in Upper Canada. The British were completely defeated, and Tecumseh, leader of the Indian allies, was killed.

DEATH of TECUMSEH

H. M. Brackenridge, *History of the Late War Between the United States and Great Britain.* 1817

With the West in its hands, the American army now streamed eastward, down the lakes, through the village of Buffalo and onward to the St. Lawrence, where things were not going so well.

Harrison's Troops Landing at Buffalo

*The Port Folio,* August, 1815

But with the Niagara region thus weakened, the British struck back. On Dec. 18 they surprised and captured Fort Niagara—and in retaliation for similar American outrages, burned Black Rock and Buffalo.

Fort Niagara

*The Port Folio,* April, 1814

## Privateers

While American warships were bottled up in port, American privateers still roamed the seas. Built for speed, carrying an unusual amount of canvas, they could cut a prize out of a convoy under the very nose of the British navy—and show their heels to pursuit. More than 1300 prizes are known to have been taken by privateers during the War of 1812. *Below* is the *America*, whose log shows a steady stream of captures from 1812 to 1814.

*Courtesy,* Francis B. Crowninshield and The Essex Institute, Salem, Mass.

Privateer *America*

## Astoria

The American Fur Company post, at the mouth of the Columbia River (see page 124), had, since late in 1812, been in the hands of the British, and had become known as Fort George.

Gabriel Franchere, *Narrative of a Voyage to the Northwest Coast of America,* 1811, 1812, 1813 and 1814. 1854

ASTORIA AS IT WAS IN 1813

## Horseshoe Bend

On March 27, 1814, on the banks of the Tallapoosa River (in present Alabama), Andrew Jackson broke the Creek warriors and forced Weatherford, their leader, to make his peace with the Great White Father at Washington.

Amos Kendall, *Life of Andrew Jackson.* 1843

Weatherford Surrenders to Jackson

ESSEX AND BRITISH FRIGATES IN THE HARBOUR OF VALPARAISO.

Horace Kimball, *American Naval Battles.* 1831

### The *Essex*

The day following the Battle of Horseshoe Bend, another famous battle was fought—on the water, off the western coast of South America. The *Essex*, which had long been preying on British shipping in the Pacific, was disabled and captured by two British warships.

## *Peacock* and *Epervier* Engagement

In February, 1814, the American war sloop *Peacock*, Master-Commandant Lewis Warrington, ran the blockade out of New York harbor, and on April 29 captured the British brig *Epervier* off the Florida coast, bringing her, a prize, into Savannah.

*Peacock* and *Epervier*
Courtesy, Bailey Collection, The Mariners'
Museum, Newport News, Va.

## The Southern Shore of Lake Ontario

was, in 1814, still largely unsettled. The site of the future city of Rochester, some distance south of the Lake and at the mouth of the Genesee River, was a slight clearing and a few houses around the water falls.

*Left*, Rochester in 1812
Henry O'Reilly, *Sketches of Rochester.* 1838

*Below*, Rochester in 1816
*Courtesy*, Rochester Historical Society, Rochester, N. Y.

Oswego, at the head of the old portage route, was the important place.

Here stood Fort Ontario guarding the American shipping and supplies. Just when the Americans were planning the capture of Kingston, across the lake, the British commander, Sir James Yeo, swooped down from Kingston and captured Oswego.

*Attack on Fort Oswego.*

*The Port Folio*, July, 1815

## Activity At Niagara

The summer of 1814 saw a determined effort of the Americans to clear the British out of the Niagara area.

Fort Erie, just across from Buffalo on the Canadian shore, was captured on July 3. The venerable Red Jacket, Seneca chief, aroused the Iroquois to aid their American brothers in the undertaking.

Courtesy, Stokes Collection, The New York Public Library
Fort Erie from Buffalo Creek

Red Jacket
Courtesy, Eames Collection, The New York Public Library

Two days later, at Chippewa Creek (see map on page 130), the Americans again pushed the British back

Chippewa Creek
From a watercolor by Edward Walsh
Courtesy, William L. Clements Library, Ann Arbor, Mich.

and on July 25, at the Battle of Niagara, or Lundy's Lane as it is often called, both sides claimed the victory.

The Port Folio, September, 1815

Battle of Niagara

## Fresh Water and Salt

In the narrow waters between Fort Erie and Buffalo, lay three American schooners. The British, with batteaux carried overland, on August 14, captured two of these, the *Ohio* and *Somers*, while the *Porcupine* escaped.

From a watercolor drawing by Charles Turner Warren and/or his son Alfred William Warren
*Courtesy,* The Mariners' Museum, Newport News, Va.

Boat Attack on *Ohio, Somers* and *Porcupine*

On the same day, far up on Lake Huron, the American brig *Niagara* attacked and destroyed the British schooner *Nancy.*

*Left,* The Attack on the *Nancy,* August 14, 1814

From a watercolor drawing by Charles Turner Warren and/or his son Alfred William Warren
*Courtesy,* The Mariners' Museum, Newport News, Va.

Off the coast of England, the American sloop *Wasp* (new), after sinking the British *Reindeer,* forced the *Avon* to strike and then, fleeing from a stronger British ship, was never heard of again.

*Right, Wasp* and *Avon*

From a watercolor drawing by Charles Turner Warren *Courtesy,* Bailey Collection, The Mariners' Museum, Newport News, Va.

## Washington Burned

In August, 1814, a British fleet sailed into the Chesapeake and landed an army which marched against the capital city. An easy victory for the enemy at Bladensburg, just northeast of Washington, placed the capital at the mercy of the British raiders.

*Courtesy, The New-York Historical Society, New York City*
Burning of Washington by the British, August 24, 1814

The capitol building, the Treasury and the departments of State and War buildings were burned, as were such naval supplies as could be reached.

Capitol after being burned by the British

Glenn Brown, *History of the United States Capital.* 1900

Nor even did the President's House escape. It, too, with all its furnishings was put to the torch along with a few private homes, and the office furniture of the *National Intelligencer.*

President's House after Fire

M. B. Smith, *First Forty Years of Washington Society.* 1906

## Plattsburg

Simultaneously with the attacks in the Chesapeake, the British, in the autumn of 1814, planned a move up the historic Lake Champlain waterway—the strategy of Burgoyne in 1777. Plattsburg, on the western shore of Lake Champlain, was the first objective, but what Sir George Prevost, the British Commander, saw when he arrived before that town, caused him to await the help of the British fleet coming up the Lake.

BATTLE OF PLATTSBURG.

*Naval Temple, 1816.*

## Macdonough Strikes

Opposed to the oncoming British fleet was an American flotilla of fourteen vessels under the intrepid Macdonough. The battle was joined by land and water on September 11. When the smoke cleared, the British fleet lay wrecked in the Bay and Prevost's army was on its way to Canada.

*Naval Action on Lake Champlain*

*Naval Temple, 1816.*

## North Point

After burning Washington, the British transports sailed up the Chesapeake to attack Baltimore. Again, the army was landed and, at North Point, east of Baltimore, defeated the Americans, though General Ross, the British commander, was killed.

BATTLE OF NORTH POINT, NEAR BALTIMORE,
September 12th 1814.

*Courtesy,* Maryland Historical Society, Baltimore, Md.

## Fort McHenry

Meanwhile, the British fleet was busy bombarding Fort McHenry which protected Baltimore on the water side. All night long the fort withstood the attack, and when "the dawn's early light" of September 14 showed the American flag still flying, the British fleet put out to sea.

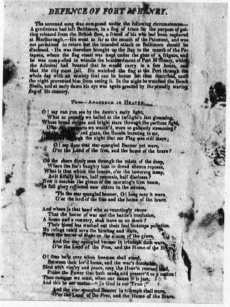

*Courtesy,* Walters Art Gallery, Baltimore, Md.

Broadside of the first printing of the
"Star Spangled Banner"

### O! SAY CAN YOU SEE

A young lawyer, Francis Scott Key, was so thrilled by the sight of the flag "still there" that he wrote on the back of an envelope the words of the "Star Spangled Banner", which, the following day, was printed as a handbill, and soon became our national anthem.

*Courtesy,* Stokes Collection, The New York Public Library

Bombardment of Fort McHenry

## New Orleans

The British troops in the Chesapeake went to Jamaica where they were joined to a formidable force under Sir Edward Pakenham, aimed at New Orleans and the gulf ports.

On December 10, the British armada was at the entrance to Lake Borgne, the back door of New Orleans. An American flotilla, which attempted to dispute the lake, was promptly destroyed, and the British landed below the city.

Battle of Lake Borgne, Dec. 14, 1814

From a watercolor drawing by Charles Turner Warren
*Courtesy*, Bailey Collection, The Mariners' Museum, Newport News, Va.

Amos Kendall, *Life of Andrew Jackson*. 1843
American troops floating down the Mississippi

In command of the American forces at New Orleans was Andrew Jackson. Down the Mississippi by boat, down the Natchez Trace from Tennessee, came reinforcements; from the swampy vastness of Barataria Bay came Lafitte and his pirates to help repel the British.

*Courtesy*, The New-York Historical Society, New York City
Battle of New Orleans

Slowly, Pakenham closed in. The decisive battle was fought on Jan. 8, 1815, and lasted less than half an hour, but within that time the British lost over 2000 men including Gen. Pakenham and most of his higher officers. New Orleans was saved.

## Peace

Fifteen days before the Battle of New Orleans, although in pre-cable days the news was not known, there had been signed, at Ghent, in Holland, a preliminary treaty of peace between Britain and the United States. The document reached America on Feb. 11, 1815, and was formally ratified on the 17th, President Madison signing it in one of the circular rooms of the Octagon (see page 80) on the table shown *opposite*.

*Courtesy,* Essex Institute,
Salem, Mass.

HORNET AND PENGUIN.

Horace Kimball, *American Naval Battles.*
1831

But three American warships had run the blockade from New York before news of the peace arrived. One of these, the *President*, commanded by Decatur, was promptly captured. Another, the *Hornet*, on March 23, defeated and sank the British brig, *Penguin*, in the South Atlantic. The *Peacock* reached the Indian Ocean safely, where she heard of the peace.

Still another American warship, the *Constitution*, at sea in the eastern Atlantic, on Feb. 20, captured the British frigate *Cyane* and sloop of war *Levant*.

From a watercolor drawing by Charles Turner Warren
*Courtesy,* Bailey Collection, The Mariners' Museum, Newport News, Va.

*Constitution, Cyane* and *Levant*

**United States Uniforms, 1812-1815**

General Staff and Infantry

General Staff and Line Officers,
Light Artillery

Artillery,
Infantry,
Rifle,
Dragoon,
Cadet

All illustrations on this page from *Uniforms of the Army of the United States, 1774-1889.* Issued by the U. S. Quartermaster General's Office, 1885

## A Reckoning With the Barbary States

The absence of American warships in the Mediterranean during the war with England encouraged Algiers to make unreasonable demands and to prey on our commerce.

U.S. SQADRON BEFORE THE CITY OF ALGIERS

*Naval Temple. 1816*

Immediately, upon the conclusion of peace in 1815, a strong fleet was sent to settle matters with the Barbary pirates. First capturing a part of the Algerian fleet, Decatur appeared before the city and forced a peace by which the payment of tribute was ended once and for all. Tunis and Tripoli were compelled to subscribe to the same terms, thus assuring future safety for American shipping in the Mediterranean.

*Naval Temple. 1816*

Triumphant Return of American Squadron from the Mediterranean, 1815

## Life Went On

At York, Pa., the corner stone of the German Lutheran Church was laid on July 2, 1812, and the consecration was held on May 1, 1814. We have the record and the picture from the hand of Lewis Miller, the carpenter and artist (see page 120).

*Courtesy, The Historical Society of York County, York, Pa.,*

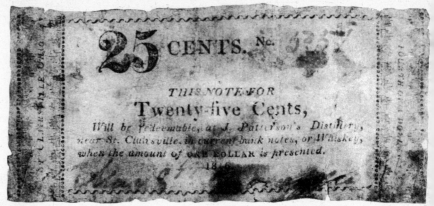

United States coins were almost non-existent, and all sorts of paper notes were in circulation, such as this 25-cent one issued by Patterson's Distillery.

*Courtesy, Chase Bank Collection of Moneys of the World, New York*

CHRISTOPHER TONGE

Nº 103 North Third Street

Between Arch & Race

PHILADELPHIA.

Manufacturer of Superior BLACKING

in Cakes, Balls & Liquid,

also of Water Colours, Poland Starch, extra fine Annatto, INK-POWDER, Writing and Durable Ink, Perfumery &c&c.

FANCY GOODS, Mahogany and Gilt frame LOOKING GLASSES, Brushes & Combs of every description together with all the most Approved PATENT MEDICINES, Wholesale & Retail on the most reasonable Terms.

But men blacked their boots and evidently had an interest in perfumery, looking glasses, brushes, combs and patent medicines.

*Courtesy, Historical Society of Pennsylvania, Philadelphia*

**Ladies' Gowns**

*At the Left*
is a dress and
petticoat of 1816

*Courtesy,* Essex Institute, Salem, Mass.

*Above* is the dress, hat and slippers worn by
Caira Robbins in 1812

## And Blooded Horses

In the south was the great stallion, Sir Archy
(foaled 1805), whose blood was to dominate
the American turf for years to come. *Right.*

From a watercolor by E. Troye after Alvan Fisher
Owned by Walter M. Jeffords, Glen Riddle, Pa.
*Courtesy,* The Jockey Club, New York

*Opposite,* is Virginian, a son of Sir Archy, foaled
in 1815

*Courtesy,* The Jockey Club, New York

WHITNEY'S ARMORY, NEAR NEW HAVEN, CT.

## Factories and Ferries

At Whitneyville, near New Haven, Conn., Eli Whitney, the inventor of the cotton gin (see page 61), was making muskets with interchangeable parts, a practice now universally followed in all mass production, but in 1812 a novelty.

Henry Howe, *Memoirs of American Mechanics.* 1846

On the East River, factories and shipping went peacefully on—and men fished from row boats.

*The Port Folio,*
March, 1813

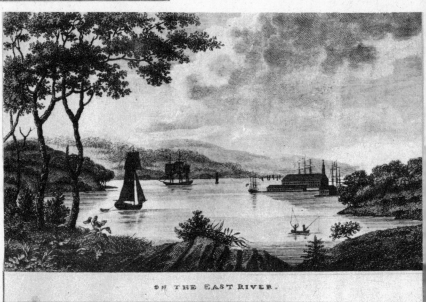

ON THE EAST RIVER.

*View on the Susquehannah.*

On the Susquehanna, ferries did duty where there were no bridges.

*The Port Folio,* December, 1815

## The Unreconcilables

Timothy Pickering, who had been Secretary of State under Washington, was representative of a powerful New England group which opposed the war with England, and even went so far as to advise separation from the Union.

Octavius Pickering, *Life of Timothy Pickering.* 1867

In Boston the first number of *The North-American Review* was published in 1815.

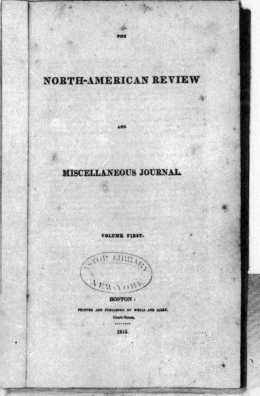

## Nantucket

an island off the New England coast, had been forced by the British fleet to declare itself neutral during the war.

The TOWN of SHERBURNE in the ISLAND of NANTUCKET

*The Port Folio,* January, 1811

## Steamboats

On the Hudson we see this craft propelled both, or perhaps either, by steam and sail.

*Catskill Mountains and the Steam Boat on the Hudson River.*

The Port Folio, November, 1813

At New York, on Oct. 29, 1814, the steam frigate *Fulton* was launched with appropriate ceremonies.

LAUNCH OF THE STEAM FRIGATE FULTON THE FIRST, AT NEW YORK, 29 OCT. 1814.

## America Again Looks Westward

Two months before the war opened in 1812, the Territory of Orleans, with some additions which made practically its present boundaries, was admitted as the State of Louisiana.

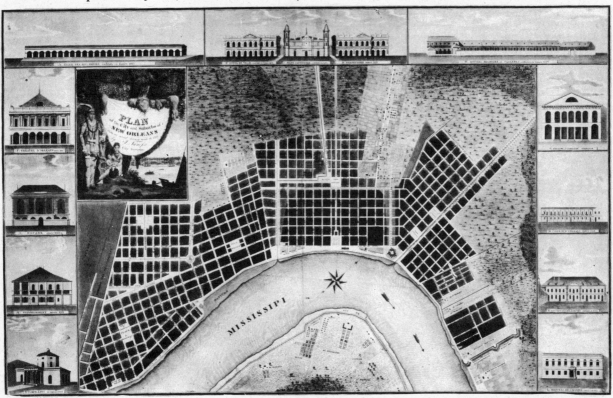

Courtesy, Stokes Collection, The New York Public Library

With the close of the war, a practical stalemate, and with seaboard trade at a low ebb, the population again turned its energies to developing the West. Indiana was admitted as a state in 1816.

Photo by Indiana Department of Conservation
Courtesy, The William Henry Smith Memorial Library of the Indiana State Historical Society, Indianapolis

*Above,* Hall of the House of Representatives, Corydon, Ind., State Capitol from 1816 until the latter part of 1824

*Log Tavern, Indiana*

A. Welby, *A Visit to North America.* 1821

# 5
# ERA OF GOOD FEELING
## 1817-1825

James Monroe took the oath of office as President of the United States on March 4, 1817—from the east portico of the Capitol, thus establishing a precedent in inauguration ceremonies.

James Monroe

From a painting by John Vanderlyn,
City Hall, New York

The public buildings in Washington, which had been burned by the British in 1814, were being repaired or rebuilt. In the view below, made in 1817, we see at the *left* the new Treasury building, while that in the *right center*, bearing the sign "Bank Metropolis", had formerly been the Indian King Tavern.

From a watercolor drawing by the Baroness Hyde de Neuville
*Courtesy*, Stokes Collection, The New York Public Library

F. Street, Washington. 1817

## Monroe Makes a Trip

Shortly after his inauguration, the President went on a tour of the country. He visited New York.

Broadway and City Hall, New York. 1819

He went down the Bay

New York Harbor from Brooklyn. 1820

and viewed the forts.

Governor's Island from Manhattan. About 1825

## West Point

From New York, the President went up the Hudson to West Point.

*J. Milbert, Itineraire Pittoresque du Fleuve Hudson. Atlas. 1828*

Military Academy—West Point. About 1817

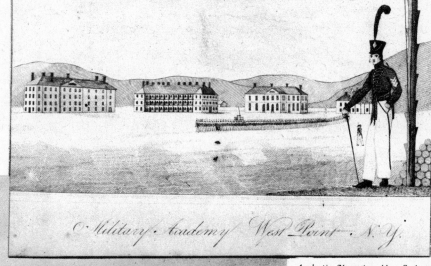

*Analectic Magazine, New Series,
Vol. 2, July to December, 1820*

Plain of West Point.
About 1817

*J. Milbert, Itineraire Pittoresque
du Fleuve Hudson. Atlas. 1828*

## At Providence

the President was given a great public reception.

North View of Providence. 1817

At Pawtucket he visited the spinning mills and saw the original spinning machine set up in 1790 (see page 61).

Pawtucket Falls. 1817

Both illustrations on this page are from J. Milbert, *Itineraire Pittoresque du Fleuve Hudson. Atlas.* 1828

## At Boston

The President received such an ovation that the *Centinel* gave the name "Era of Good Feeling" to the Monroe administration.

BOSTON.

*Analectic Magazine*, March, 1817

*J. Milbert, Itineraire Pittoresque du Fleuve Hudson. Atlas.* 1828

View of Boston and the South Boston Bridge. About 1817

From New England, the President turned westward, visiting Sackett's Harbor, Buffalo and Detroit before he returned to Washington.

*J. Milbert, Itineraire Pittoresque du Fleuve Hudson. Atlas.* 1828

Sackett's Harbor. About 1817

## "Clinton's Ditch"

Such was the derisive name applied to the dream of DeWitt Clinton—a canal to connect Lake Erie with the sea.

Excavation for the canal began on July 4, 1817.

Cadwallader D. Colden, *Memoir prepared (for the) Celebration of the Completion of the New York Canals. 1825*

## River Boats

on the Hudson were soon to find Albany an important transfer point.

From a drawing by Charles Alexandre Lesueur. 1823.   *Courtesy,* American Antiquarian Society, Worcester, Mass

Interior of river boat of the 1820's.

## Steamboats

The *Analectic Magazine* in 1818, showed the picture *opposite*, and said, "The following steam engine, constructed under the direction of Colonel Ogden of New Jersey, and intended for a steam-boat to ply to and from Norfolk in Virginia, seems calculated to give equal power, with diminished fuel, and dispensing with some of the apparatus commonly in use. The prodigious importance of steam engines seems now well understood, and any attempt to improve them deserves attention on part of the public."

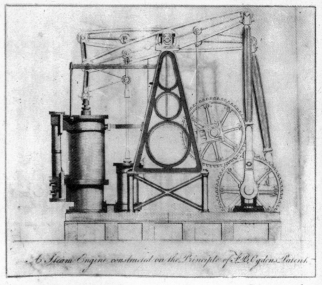

A Steam Engine constructed on the Principle of E. B. Ogdens Patent.

On May 22, 1819, the *Savannah*, a sailing ship with auxiliary steam power, left Savannah, Ga., and arrived at Liverpool 29 days later. Note the side wheel propeller.

THE STEAMSHIP SAVANNAH.
(From corrected drawing by C. B. Hudson, made under the direction of Capt. J. W. Collins, of the U. S. Commission of Fish and Fisheries.)

U. S. National Museum, *Annual Report*, 1889-90

## Gas for Lighting

was introduced in Peale's Museum in Philadelphia as early as 1816. In 1822, it was adopted for street lighting in Boston, and, the following year, the New York Gas-Light Company was incorporated.

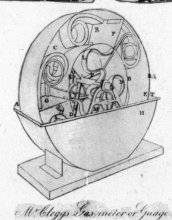

*Analectic Magazine,* October, 1816

M.ʳ Cleggs Gas meter or Guage.

## Agricultural Societies

Elkanah Watson, who had been a promoter of canals and stage roads in upper New York State, bought a large farm at Pittsfield, Mass., and engaged in scientific agriculture.

ELKANAH WATSON

Together with his neighbors, he organized the Berkshire Agricultural Society which actively promoted good farming and did much to popularize county agricultural fairs.

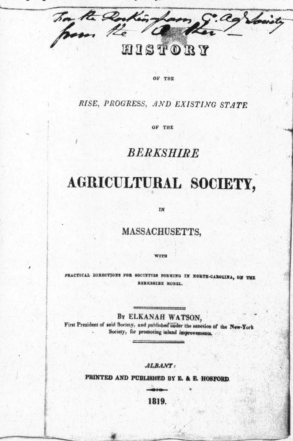

HISTORY

OF THE

RISE, PROGRESS, AND EXISTING STATE

OF THE

BERKSHIRE

AGRICULTURAL SOCIETY,

IN

MASSACHUSETTS,

WITH

PRACTICAL DIRECTIONS FOR SOCIETIES FORMING IN NORTH-CAROLINA, ON THE
BERKSHIRE MODEL.

By ELKANAH WATSON,
First President of said Society, and published under the sanction of the New-York
Society, for promoting inland improvements.

ALBANY:
PRINTED AND PUBLISHED BY E. & E. HOSFORD.

1819.

Country Fair. 1824

from a painting by John A. Woodside. Owned by Harry T. Peters and reproduced by his permission from a copy in the Metropolitan Museum of Art.

## Clocks

Eli Terry started as a clockmaker's apprentice in 1786. By 1807, he was sufficiently well established at Plymouth, Conn., to secure a contract for making 4000 wooden-works clocks at $4.00 each—and took in as a partner a young carpenter named Seth Thomas.

 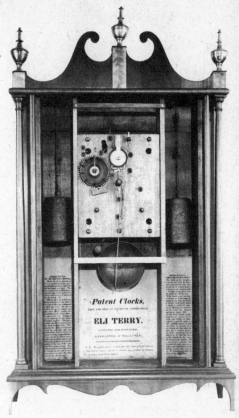

In 1814, Terry devised his "perfected wood clock" (shown *above*, closed and open, from a specimen owned by Paul G. Darrot, Southbury, Conn.). It was a shelf model, 31 inches high; dial made of wood with hand-painted decorations; black Arabic numerals and gold raised minute marks. The hands were made of pewter, and the case, known as the "pillar and scroll top case" was of mahogany.

Seth Thomas, who had by this time set up for himself, paid Terry $1000.00 for the right to manufacture this "pillar and scroll top case", wooden-works clock. *Right* is one of the Thomas models made between 1816 and 1818 (owned by Miss Natalie Van Vleck of Woodbury, Conn.).

*Left*, Watch owned by Timothy Pickering

Courtesy, Essex Institute, Salem, Mass.

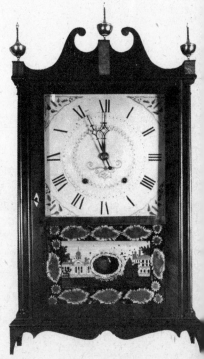

## Seth Thomas Clocks

Between 1816 and 1818, Seth Thomas (at Plymouth, Conn.) was making a 30-hour clock with some brass parts. He made the works only and peddled them on horseback.

The buyer then had a case made to suit his fancy. That shown at the *right* (closed and open) is made of native pine.

*Below* (closed and open) is a Seth Thomas clock made between 1825 and 1827. The case is of mahogany, 29 inches high. The dial is of wood with hand-painted decorations. The scene on the lower part of the door is hand-painted with an oval opening to show swing of pendulum. The works are of wood, the hands of steel and the pendulum ball of brass-covered lead.

Both clocks shown on this page are owned by Paul G. Darrot of Southbury, Conn.

**Silver**

Silver teaset by William B. Heyer, New York, made between 1810 and 1820

*Right*, Silver beaker by Robert Shepherd and William Boyd, Albany, 1814

*Left*, Silver caster by Isaac Hutton, Albany. Made between 1800 and 1825

All illustrations on this page are by the *courtesy* of The Metropolitan Museum of Art, New York City

## Silver and Pewter

*Opposite*, Silver porringer by William Moulton of New-buryport. Early 19th Century

Silver spoon by Gar-ret Eoff, New York. Early 19th Century

*Left*, Pewter porringer by Thomas Danforth Boardman and Sherman Boardman of Hart-ford. Early 19th Century

*Below*, Coffeepot by George Richardson, Boston. About 1820

## Wall Paintings

In many New England homes, panels or whole walls were decorated by itinerant painters, the scenes sometimes being of great historic value.

*Above,* is shown a panel originally over the fireplace in the Rufus Hitchcock house, Cheshire, Conn. Believed to have been painted by Sylvester Hall, otherwise unknown. It represents the Cheshire Village green between 1800 and 1825.

*Below,* is an ornamental panel painted with oils on a single piece of wood. It is from the Alexander King House, Suffield, Conn. The view is probably fanciful though the coach and figures are typical early 19th Century, at which period the painting was made.

Both illustrations on this page are from Edward B. Allen, *Early American Wall Paintings, 1710-1850.* 1926 *Courtesy,* Yale University Press, New Haven, Conn.

## A Great Race

In 1823, at the Union Course on Long Island, *American Eclipse* (foaled in 1814) was matched against *Henry* (foaled in 1819) for a purse of $20,000. *Henry*, the son of *Sir Archy*, was put forward by the Virginian, William R. Johnson (the Napoleon of the Turf), and one of the former owners of *Sir Archy* (see page 153).

The event came to be a sectional contest—the South (represented by *Henry*) against the North (represented by *American Eclipse*).

Painting by E. Troye, 1834
*American Eclipse*

Painting by E. Troye, 1834
*Henry*

*Henry* won the first heat, but the second and third went to the older horse. Thousands of people struggled for places of advantage at the race, and the result was the leading news of the day. More than $200,000 in bets were said to have changed hands.

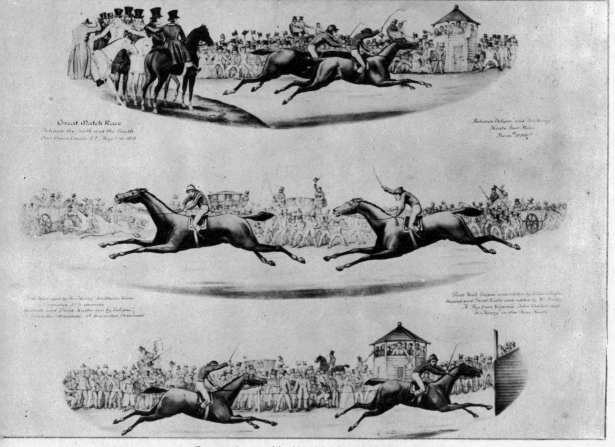

From a print owned by Mrs. John Osgood Blanchard
*Eclipse-Henry* Match Race

All illustrations shown on this page are through the *courtesy* of The Jockey Club, N. Y.

## In the Social Whirl

Young ladies of fashion, in 1817,
wore their hair as shown *below*.

J. B. M. D. Lafoy, *The Complete Coiffeur, etc.* 1817

Gay blades sped about on velocipedes.

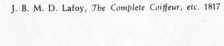

Analectic Magazine, June, 1819

Taking the water at the resorts, which grew up
around the various mineral
springs, was the thing
to do.

J. Milbert, *Itineraire Pittoresque du Fleuve
Hudson. Atlas.* 1828
*Above*, Saratoga Springs

*The Port Folio, June, 1817*    Bedford Springs, Pennsylvania

## An Artist is "Discovered"

*The Analectic Magazine* was the leading periodical of the day. In the early issue of 1820 it reproduced, in line engraving, a painting entitled "Country Wedding", by a young artist named John Lewis Krimmel.

*Analectic Magazine*, New Series, Vol. 1, January-June, 1820

Krimmel's original painting of the "Country Wedding" is now in the Pennsylvania Academy of Fine Arts.

This was followed, in the July-December issue, with a pair of Krimmel plates entitled "Going to Boarding School" and "Return from Boarding School."

*Right*, Going to Boarding School

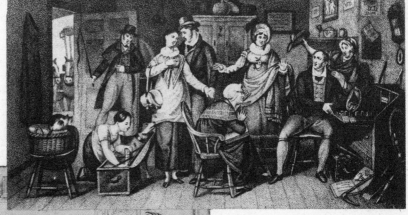

Young ladies attending boarding school may well have refrained from excess tears when the artist was accidentally drowned the following year.

*Left*, Return from Boarding School

## "Election Day at the State-House, About 1818"

Some two years before he was "discovered" by the *Analectic*, Krimmel made the picture shown *below*. Doubtless the State-House was in Philadelphia—and the details speak for themselves.

*Courtesy*, The Historical Society of Pennsylvania, Philadelphia

## Lithography

It was the *Analectic*, too, that introduced lithography to the American public. In the issue for July, 1819, appeared the picture shown *below*.

Bass Otis was the artist. The drawing was made on a stone from Munich, presented to the American Philosophical Society.

## Authors and Books

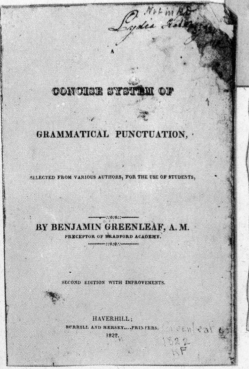

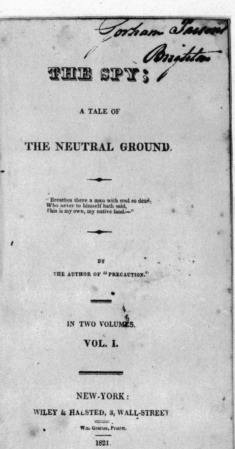

Washington Irving, who, since the publication of *Knickerbocker's History of New York* (see page 108), had been restlessly dallying at many things, including a year's editorship of *The Analectic Magazine*, wrote and published in 1819 *The Sketch Book*, which instantly established the author in the field of letters

Another young American, James Fenimore Cooper, made a name for himself with the publication in 1821 of a novel entitled *The Spy*.

Benjamin Greenleaf, who graduated from Dartmouth in 1813, and the following year became Preceptor of Bradford Academy, was, in 1822, publishing the Second, and improved, Edition of a textbook on *Grammatical Punctuation*.

*Thanatopsis.*

Not that from life, and all its woes
The hand of death shall set me free;
Not that this head, shall then repose
In the low vale most peacefully.

Ah, when I touch time's farthest brink,
A kinder solace must attend;
It chills my very soul, to think
On that dread hour when life must end.

In vain the flatt'ring verse may breathe,
Of ease from pain, and rest from strife,

In the *North American Review*, September, 1817, appeared a poem entitled "Thanatopsis," written by William Cullen Bryant, born in 1794.

## At the Park Theatre

in New York, on Nov. 7, 1822, Charles Mathews and Miss Johnston appeared in Moncrieff's farce "Monsieur Tonson."

From an original watercolor by John Searle
*Courtesy*, The New-York Historical Society, New York City

## Theatre, Orphan Asylum and Prison

*Left* is the New Theatre, in Chestnut Street, Philadelphia, from a drawing published in 1823 by William Birch.

*Courtesy,* The Historical Society of Pennsylvania, Philadelphia

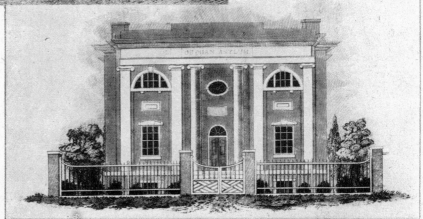

According to *The Port Folio* of July, 1819, the building at the *right* is The Female Orphan Asylum of Norfolk, Va.

*Courtesy,* The Historical Society of Pennsylvania, Philadelphia

The age of humanitarianism was coming in. *Above* is the prison at Pittsburgh, Pa., 1824

## New England and Lake Champlain

FALLS on CONNECTICUT RIVER, at GILL, Mass.

*The Port Folio,* December, 1818

VIEW OF WINDHAM, CONN. IN 1815.

*Courtesy,* The New-York Historical Society, New York City

VIEW of the RUINS of TICONDEROGA FORTS on LAKE CHAMPLAIN.

*Analectic Magazine,* April, 1818

**Albany and Down the Hudson**

Albany about 1823

Albany about 1823. House of Dutch Governors

View of Hudson and the Catskill Mountains

All views on this page are from J. Milbert, *Itineraire Pittoresque du Fleuve Hudson. Atlas*. 1828

## New York City and Brooklyn

J. Milbert, *Itineraire Pittoresque du Fleuve Hudson. Atlas.* 1828
Provost Street and Chapel, New York

J. Milbert, *Itineraire Pittoresque du Fleuve Hudson. Atlas.* 1828
Pierpont's Distillery on Long Island

Brooklyn, 1816-17.
From a painting by
Francis Guy

Courtesy, Brooklyn Museum,
Brooklyn, New York

## New Jersey and Pennsylvania

Count de Survilliers was otherwise Joseph Bonaparte, brother of Napoleon and sometime King of Spain.

*Analectic Magazine*, New Series, Vol. I, January-June, 1820

VIEW NEAR BORDENTON, from the GARDENS of the COUNT DE SURVILLIERS

*Bridge at Columbia, Pennsylvania*

A. Welby, *A Visit to North America . . .* 1821

In 1812, Harrisburg became the permanent capital of Pennsylvania, and in 1820 a capitol building was being erected.

STATE CAPITOL AT HARRISBURG, PENNSYLVANIA.

*Analectic Magazine*, New Series, Vol. II, July-December, 1820

## In the Pennsylvania Dutch Country

*Courtesy,* Landis Valley Museum, Lancaster, Pa.

Sleigh. About 1820

*Courtesy,* Landis Valley Museum, Lancaster, Pa.

Homemade Hay Rake

*Courtesy,* Landis Valley Museum, Lancaster, Pa.

Waffle Irons

## And in the Pennsylvania Mountains

*Place of Worship & Burial Ground, at Ligonier Town, Pennsylvania.*

A. Welby, *A Visit to North America* . . . 1821

## Washington

The Capitol, burned by the British in 1814, was being restored under the direction of Benjamin H. Latrobe (see page 81). The wings were now joined and surmounted by a low dome designed by Charles Bulfinch (see page 79).

*Analectic Magazine,* March, 1820

A back View of the CAPITOL.
Washington.

From a painting by Samuel F. B. Morse
*Courtesy*, Corcoran Gallery of Art, Washington, D. C.

The Old House of Representatives, 1821-23

*Courtesy*, Stokes Collection, The New York Public Library

Baroness Hyde de Neuville, wife of the French Consul General, painted the picture *above* in 1820-21. The central building is the President's House; *left foreground* is the State Department; *left background* is the Treasury Department; *right foreground* is the War Department; and *right background* is the Navy Department.

## Duelling

In the 1820's, gentlemen commonly settled their differences by a challenge and a duel. One of the famous duelling grounds was near Bladensburg, Md., just east of Washington. Here, in 1820, Stephen Decatur and James Barron met, with fatal results for the former.

Benson J. Lossing, *Pictorial Field-Book of the War of 1812.* 1868

Duelling Ground near Bladensburg

## Norfolk in 1819

In the picture *below*, painted by J. Shaw, engraved by J. Hill, and published in 1821, we see Norfolk, Va., in the distance, while at the *left* is a glimpse of the Gosport Navy Yard with the 74-gun *Delaware* on the stocks.

Courtesy, Stokes Collection, The New York Public Library

**Charleston, S. C., 1817-23**

The City of CHARLESTON, So. Carolina.

The tall steeple, *left center*, is St. Michael's Church. In the *foreground* is the Cooper River, with Castle Pinckney at the *right*.

At *right*, wrought-iron gate, put up in 1823, St. John's Lutheran Church, at Charleston.

Albert H. Sonn, *Early American Wrought Iron*. 1928

**Savannah, Ga.**

On Jan. 11, 1820, this city suffered a severe fire. The original painting, in color, of which the view *opposite* is a copy, shows the lurid sky and billowing smoke.

Painted by J. Shaw. Engraved by J. Hill

## McIntosh of the Creeks

McKenney and Hall, *History of the Indians of North America.* 1842

The State of Georgia wished the Creek Indians removed from their long established homes on the Chattahoochee. The Creeks did not wish to go. In February, 1825, at Indian Springs, McIntosh, *left*, a Creek Chief friendly to the Whites, signed a treaty of cession—and within a few weeks was killed by the opposing faction of his Nation. (McIntosh was the son of Capt. William McIntosh, of the British Army, and an unknown Indian woman.)

## Two New States

In 1817, the old Mississippi Territory was divided to make the states of Mississippi (admitted, 1817) and of Alabama (admitted, 1819).

From a Plan and View of the City of Mobile. By James M. Goodwin and G. Haire. Made in 1824
*Courtesy,* Library of Congress, Division of Maps and Charts, Washington, D. C.

Mobile Harbor and City. 1824

UNITED STATES HOTEL.

FIRE PROOF BUILDING.
For Pressing & Storing of Cotton A.D. 1825

From a Plan and View of the City of Mobile. By James M. Goodwin and G. Haire. Made in 1824
*Courtesy,* Library of Congress, Division of Maps and Charts, Washington, D. C.

## Florida

South of Georgia and Alabama Territory, lay Spanish Florida—weakly held, a refuge for runaway slaves, and wanted by the United States. By a treaty signed at Washington in February, 1819, Florida was acquired, and the boundary between the United States and Spanish Territory —from the Gulf of Mexico to the Pacific Ocean—was settled, for the time.

Castillo de San Marcos

Begun by the Spaniards in 1672, the Castillo de San Marcos at St. Augustine, Fla., is the oldest existing masonry fortification in the United States.

Northwest Bastion and Watch Tower Castillo de San Marcos

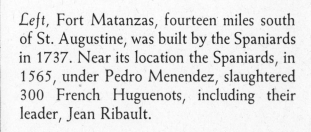

*Left*, Fort Matanzas, fourteen miles south of St. Augustine, was built by the Spaniards in 1737. Near its location the Spaniards, in 1565, under Pedro Menendez, slaughtered 300 French Huguenots, including their leader, Jean Ribault.

All illustrations on this page are through the *courtesy* of the National Park Service, St. Augustine, Fla.

## The Westward Rush

Courtesy, Buffalo Historical Society

By stage, by wagon, by horseback and afoot,
people and families pushed west

The second decade of the 19th Century saw a renewal of the westward migration so great that it filled the roads and depopulated eastern farms and towns.

P. Stansbury, *A Pedestrian Tour in North America.* 1822

Emigrant camps were to be seen along the roads and in wooded fields.

Henry Howe, *Historical Collections of the Great West.* 1854

Hard times in Europe and an active interest in America brought thousands more from across the sea.

Sketches of America.

A
NARRATIVE OF A JOURNEY
OF FIVE THOUSAND MILES
THROUGH
THE EASTERN AND WESTERN STATES
OF
AMERICA;
CONTAINED IN EIGHT REPORTS
ADDRESSED TO THE
THIRTY-NINE ENGLISH FAMILIES
BY WHOM THE AUTHOR WAS DEPUTED, IN JUNE 1817, TO ASCERTAIN
WHETHER ANY AND WHAT PART OF THE UNITED STATES WOULD
BE SUITABLE FOR THEIR RESIDENCE.
WITH
REMARKS ON
MR. BIRKBECK'S "NOTES" AND "LETTERS."

BY HENRY BRADSHAW FEARON.

SECOND EDITION.

LONDON:
PRINTED FOR LONGMAN, HURST, REES, ORME, AND BROWN,
PATERNOSTER-ROW.
1818.

OBSERVATIONS
ON
EMIGRATION
TO
British America,
AND THE
UNITED STATES;
Written expressly
FOR THE USE OF PERSONS ABOUT TO EMIGRATE TO
THOSE COUNTRIES.

By ROBERT HOLDITCH, Esq.
Member of the Royal College of Surgeons.

Ad societatem, et communitatem humani generis nati sumus; itaque semper aliquid
ad communem utilitatem debemus afferre.    CICERO.

PLYMOUTH-DOCK:
Printed for the Author, and sold by W. BYERS, (Cobourg-Office
109, Fore-street; and may be had of all other Booksellers.

## The Cumberland Road

from Cumberland, Md., over the mountains to Wheeling on the Ohio River, was open by 1818 —and over it rolled thousands of vehicles, many those of homeseekers. It was our first "national" road, built by the Federal government.

View of Fort Cumberland Maryland

A. Welby, *A Visit to North America . . .*
1821

The Road crossed the Youghiogheny River on Great Crossings Bridge (finished July 4, 1818), a few miles east of the spot where in 1754 Washington built Fort Necessity. In fact, the Cumberland Road closely followed the old Braddock Road.

T. B. Searight, *The Old Pike.* 1894
*Courtesy,* Uniontown Free Public Library,
Uniontown, Pa.
Great Crossings Bridge

The White Swan Tavern, at Uniontown, Pa., was a famous stopping place on the Road.

White Swan Tavern
T. B. Searight, *The Old Pike.* 1894
*Courtesy,* Uniontown Free Public Library,
Uniontown, Pa.

## Cumberland Road (Continued)

T. B. Searight, *The Old Pike.* 1894
*Courtesy,* Uniontown Free Public Library, Uniontown, Pa.

Toll House, five miles west of Uniontown, Pa.

In time, under state supervision, tolls were required on some sections of the Road, and toll houses, such as that shown at the *left,* were erected along the route.

Milestones, set by the roadside, informed the traveller of his location.

T. B. Searight, *The Old Pike.* 1894
*Courtesy,* Uniontown Free Public Library, Uniontown, Pa.

Henry Howe, *Historical Collections of Virginia.* 1849

Wheeling. Viewed from the Ohio Side

The Island appears in the *middle left,* and, coming down the hill in the *background,* may be seen the Cumberland Road, or National Road as it later came to be called.

## Down the Ohio

At Wheeling (or Pittsburgh) most of the immigrants took to the Ohio River, floating down in flatboats or keelboats.

*Right*, Flatboat on the Ohio

William A. Croft, *Pioneers in the Settlement of America.* 1876

*Opposite*, Keelboat on the Ohio. From a drawing by Charles A. Lesueur. 1826

*Courtesy*, American Antiquarian Society, Worcester, Mass.

*Opposite*. Interior of a flatboat on the Ohio. From a drawing by Charles A. Lesueur. 1826

*Courtesy*, American Antiquarian Society, Worcester, Mass.

## On Down the Ohio

*Maysville on the Ohio Kentucky*

On the left bank of the river was Maysville, Ky.

A Welby, *A Visit to North America* . . . 1821

Often the flatboaters tied up to the bank to do the family wash and chop some wood.

From a drawing by Charles A. Lesueur.
1828
*Courtesy,* American Antiquarian Society,
Worcester, Mass.

Some settled in Kentucky, but many kept on down the river.

*Frankfort Kentucky*

A. Welby, *A Visit to North America* . . . 1821

## Still Onward, Down the Ohio

At the Falls of the Ohio, where it was often necessary to unload and carry, there stood on the right bank the village of Clarksville, Indiana, and on the left bank the village of Louisville, Ky.

*View of the Rapids of the Ohio and of Louisville taken from the village of Clarksville.*

Victor Collot, *Voyage dans l'Amerique. Atlas.* 1826

Here the migration began to spread out and seek homes—mostly on the Indiana side. Some twenty miles up the Wabash River, in Indiana, was a German Separatist Community known as the Harmony Society or Rappists. In 1825 they sold out to Robert Owen, an English philanthropist, who established, here on the banks of the Wabash, "The New Harmony Community of Equality" (see page 226).

Church at Harmony

A. Welby, *A Visit to North America . . . 1821*

Courtesy, American Antiquarian Society, Worcester, Mass.

Shawneetown. 1830

Just beyond the mouth of the Wabash, was Shawneetown, Ill.—and from this point onward, the migration spread widely into the rich new lands of Illinois.

## Illinois

Along the eastern side of the Mississippi, from the mouth of the Illinois River southward to the entrance of the Ohio, was old French country. Here stood the village of Kaskaskia, founded by the Jesuits in about 1703.

Kaskaskia

Wild, *Valley of the Mississippi.* 1841
Courtesy, Illinois State Historical Library,
Springfield

When Illinois was admitted as a state in 1818, Kaskaskia was made the capital, but on the removal of the seat of the Government to Vandalia in 1820, Kaskaskia sank back into a decay which ended some 60 years later when the Mississippi changed its course to occupy the site of the town.

State House at Vandalia

Courtesy, The Chicago Historical Society

Older by far than Kaskaskia, was the silent city a few miles east of presentday St. Louis. The great central mound, sometimes known as Monk's Mound, is the largest known work of the mound builders. It occupies some sixteen acres, is over 100 feet high and, with the city of East St. Louis creeping up to its base, remains a mystery.

Cahokia Mounds

Wild, *Valley of the Mississippi.* 1841
Courtesy, Illinois State Historical Society,
Springfield

## Mr. and Mrs. George Flower

George Flower
*Courtesy,* Chicago Historical Society

Typical of the settlers in Illinois was George Flower, a well-to-do English tenant farmer, who came to America in 1816 in search of land which he could own. He travelled about the country extensively and was finally attracted to Illinois by good land at low prices. Crossing the Wabash from Indiana near New Harmony, Flower and his party of prospective English emigrants first saw "the prairie", which fascinated them.

*Courtesy,* The Illinois State Historical Library, Springfield
The Flower Home. Built in 1819-20

Putting together what money they had, the Englishmen bought or "entered" some 3000 acres of land in what came to be known as English Settlement (in Edwards County, Ill.).

Flower then returned to England and arranged for a mass migration to the new lands. Whole families, with cows, hogs and sheep came over in a chartered ship in 1818. By the end of the year there were 200 English farmers on the Settlement. And the Flower home, built the following year, was said to be the finest residence west of the Alleghenies.

Mrs. George Flower
*Courtesy,* The Chicago Historical Society

## Chicago in 1820

was little more than a frontier post. Fort Dearborn, destroyed by the Indians in 1812 (see page 127), had been re-established in 1816 and is shown on the left of the River in the picture below. Opposite the Fort is the house of John Kinzie, "the father of Chicago."

*Courtesy*, The Chicago Historical Society

Chicago in 1820
(Note that the view is from the Lake, with Chicago River and its branches in the background)

## Detroit in 1820

was not only a flourishing city, but was enjoying steamship service by the *Walk-in-the-Water*, built at Buffalo and launched in 1818.

From a painting made in 1820 by George W. Whistler
*Courtesy*, Pike Collection, Chicago Historical Society

Detroit in 1820. *Walk-in-the-Water* in foreground

## Anti-Slavery Agitation

was finding a new weapon in books and pamphlets.

A

PORTRAITURE

OF

**DOMESTIC SLAVERY,**

IN THE

UNITED STATES:

WITH

REFLECTIONS ON THE PRACTICABILITY OF RESTORING THE
MORAL RIGHTS OF THE SLAVE, WITHOUT IMPAIRING
THE LEGAL PRIVILEGES OF THE POSSESSOR;

AND

A PROJECT OF A COLONIAL ASYLUM

FOR FREE PERSONS OF COLOUR:

INCLUDING

MEMOIRS OF FACTS ON THE INTERIOR TRAFFIC IN SLAVES,

AND ON

**KIDNAPPING.**

ILLUSTRATED WITH ENGRAVINGS.

BY JESSE TORREY, JUN. PHYSICIAN;
Author of a Series of Essays on Morals and the Diffusion of Knowledge.

PHILADELPHIA:
PUBLISHED BY THE AUTHOR.
JOHN BIOREN, PRINTER.
1817.

Kidnapping or Negro stealing, a profession too often engaged in by unscrupulous persons, came in for a great amount of heated attention.

KIDNAPPING.

Jesse Torrey, Jr., *A Portraiture of Domestic
Slavery in the United States.* 1817

Barbarity committed on a free African, who was found on the ensuing morning, by the side of the road, dead!

Jesse Torrey, Jr., *A Portraiture of Domestic
Slavery in the United States.* 1817

## Missouri

part of the Louisiana Purchase (see page 93), was largely settled from the slave states. Typical perhaps was the case of Moses Austin who, while it was still Spanish Territory, received a grant of Mine á Burton (present Potosi, Mo.), where he produced lead with slave labor.

POTOSI
*alias Mine á Burton.*

H. R. Schoolcraft, *A View of the Lead Mines of Missouri.* 1819

Herculaneum, on the Mississippi, northeast of Potosi, was also an early lead-mining area.

From a drawing by Charles A. Lesueur. 1826
*Courtesy,* American Antiquarian Society, Worcester, Mass.

Herculaneum

By the famous Missouri Compromise of 1820, Missouri was admitted as a slave state in 1821.

## The Great American Desert

Beyond Missouri, westward toward the mountains, lay a little-known country. In 1819-20, Maj. Stephen Long led an exploring expedition into this region. Encamping on the western side of the Missouri, northerly of presentday Omaha, Long held councils with the Missouri and Pawnee tribes.

Major Long. Holding a Council with the Oto (Missouri) Indians. 1819

Council with the Pawnee near Council Bluffs, 1819

Both illustrations on this page are from Edwin James, *Account of An Expedition from Pittsburgh to the Rocky Mountains performed in the Years 1819, 1820.* 1823

## The Foothills of the Rockies

From Council Bluffs, Major Long marched west, striking the Platte River a little above Grand Island. Following the main Platte to its fork, he turned southwestward on the South Platte.

Soon the Rocky Mountains came into view at a distance. One of the prominent peaks which he saw has since borne the name of Longs Peak.

He explored the chasm from which the South Platte issues from the mountains.

Still along the eastern edge of the mountains he continued south to the Arkansas River, which he descended a distance and again turned south to a river which he thought was the Red and which he followed eastward only to discover that it was the Canadian, a southern tributary of the Arkansas.

Kiowa Encampment. 1820

All illustrations on this page are from Edwin James, *Account of an Expedition from Pittsburgh to the Rocky Mountains performed in the Years 1819, 1820. 1823*

## The Useless Pacific Coast

It will be recalled that in the War of 1812, the British took possession of Astoria at the mouth of the Columbia River (see pages 124 and 140). In 1818, J. B. Prevost went, as U. S. Commissioner, to accept the formal return of the post from the British. On his way home, he stopped at Monterey, in Spanish California, and wrote a long report.

Photo by Lee
*Courtesy*, Farm Security Administration, Washington, D. C.

Pacific Ocean. Monterey, Calif.

One of the things that bothered Prevost was a Russian fort (Ross) recently established some fifty miles north of San Francisco Bay.

FORT ROSS IN THE FORTIES
(From the original sketch made by G. M. Waseurtz af Sandels—one of the "King's Orphans"
—in 1843. From the MS. in the collection of the Society of California Pioneers.)

*Courtesy*, The Society of California Pioneers, San Francisco

But Congress did not consider the Far West worth getting excited about.

## The Red River of the North

Three years after the exploring expedition to the West (see pages 199 and 200), Maj. Long was sent on another mission—this time to the North.

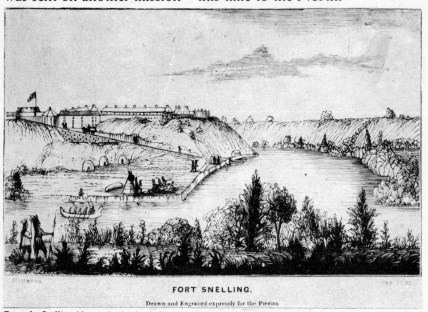

**FORT SNELLING.**

Drawn and Engraved expressly for the Pierian

From the Snelling Manuscript in the E. E. Ayer Collection of the Newberry Library, Chicago.

Fort Snelling in the 1820's

Starting from Fort Snelling, established in 1819, at the junction of the Minnesota and Mississippi rivers, he went up the Minnesota and *down* the Red (which flows north), to the 49th parallel. By a Convention between the United States and Great Britain, in 1818, this parallel, as far as the Rocky Mountains, had been established as the International Boundary.

Pembina, the post of an English colony founded by Lord Selkirk on the Red River, was found to be just south of the boundary, and thus within the United States.

From a drawing by Rindisbacher

*Courtesy*, Public Archives of Canada, Research and Publicity Division, Ottawa

Pembina. 1822

## The Monroe Doctrine

Extension of colonization by Russia on the Pacific Coast (see page 201), and, more especially, possible conquests by European powers of the newly formed nations in South and Central America, led President Monroe, in 1823, to declare that "the American continents, by the free and independent condition which they have assumed and maintained, are henceforth not to be considered as subjects for future colonization by any European Powers."

*Proclamas y Discursos del Libertador. 1939*

Carabobo, the decisive battle in the struggle for independence in northern South America

Simon Bolivar, South American Liberator

*Cartas del Libertador. 1929*

The thin line of authority back of the Monroe Doctrine.

From a contemporary watercolor in the possession of the Misses Macomb, Washington, D. C.
*Courtesy,* Office of Records and Library, Navy Department, Washington, D. C.

U. S. Squadron (*North Carolina,* Line of Battleship, *Constitution,* Frigate, *Brandywine,* Frigate, *Erie,* Sloop-of-War, *Ontario,* Sloop-of-War) Parting from Port Mahon, Island of Minorca in Mediterranean, 1825.

## Arkansas Territory

consisting of not only the later state of that name, but also of present southern Oklahoma, was organized in 1819. In that year, Thomas Nuttall, the botanist, visited the territory and left us pictures of the Cadron Settlement (above Little Rock on the Arkansas River), where land speculators were selling town lots; and of the Mamelle, a physical landmark of the area.

Cadron Settlement. 1819

Thomas Nuttall, *Journal of Travels in the Arkansas Territory during the Year 1819.* 1821

Mamelle

Thomas Nuttall, *Journal of Travels in the Arkansas Territory during the Year 1819.* 1821

## And Texas

At Nacogdoches, in eastern Texas (Mexican), stood the Old Stone Fort, built about 1779. Past here, in 1821, went Stephen Austin, the son of Moses Austin (see page 198). While

young Stephen had been speculating in Arkansas land, his father Moses Austin had secured from the Mexican government the privilege of founding a colony in Texas. Moses Austin now lay dead in Missouri and on the shoulders of the son descended the responsibility of being the Father of Texas.

Old Stone Fort at Nacogdoches

*Courtesy, Nacogdoches Historical Society, Texas*

## The Santa Fe Trail

Under the Spanish regime, trade with Santa Fe, on the Rio Grande, was closed to outsiders, but when Mexico achieved independence, the American trader was welcomed.

Beginning in 1821, great caravans, organized at Franklin or Independence, on the Missouri River, went annually down the Santa Fe Trail.

MARCH OF THE CARAVAN

INDIAN ALARM ON THE CIMARRON RIVER.

Across country to the big bend of the Arkansas River, then over the upper Cimarron and Canadian rivers, went the seven-hundred-mile-long Trail.

ARRIVAL OF THE CARAVAN AT SANTA FÉ.

A dip around the southern end of the Sangre de Cristo mountains brought the traders into Santa Fe.

All illustrations on this page are from Josiah Gregg, *Commerce of the Prairies.* 1844

## Lafayette's Visit

In 1824, President Monroe invited Lafayette to visit the United States.

His arrival, at New York, on Aug. 16, was the occasion for a tremendous welcome.

From a portrait painted in 1825 by Samuel F. B. Morse
*Courtesy*, The New York Public Library

Marquis de Lafayette

LAFAYETTE'S ARRIVAL AT NEW YORK. 1824.

*Courtesy*, Stokes Collection, The New York Public Library

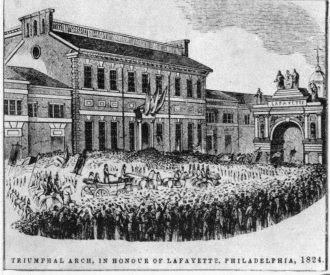

TRIUMPHAL ARCH, IN HONOUR OF LAFAYETTE, PHILADELPHIA, 1824.

*Pictorial Life of Gen. Lafayette. 1847*

After a tour of New England, Lafayette visited Philadelphia, Baltimore and other cities, receiving an ovation everywhere.

*Opposite,* from the hand of our old friend, Lewis Miller (see page 120), we see Lafayette being proudly driven through York, Pa., by John Coons in his own open barouche and with his best team of gray horses.

*Courtesy*, Historical Society of York County, York, Pa.

# 6

# FROM THE LAKES TO THE SEA

## 1825-1829

### John Quincy Adams

in 1824, was one of four candidates, including Andrew Jackson, for the Presidency. Jackson received 99 votes, Adams 84, Crawford 41 and Clay 37. Thus none of the candidates received a majority, and, under the terms of the Constitution, the election was thrown into the House of Representatives. Clay turned his support to Adams and the latter was elected. On March 4, 1825, he took the oath of office as sixth President of the United States, his father, John Adams, having been the second.

John Quincy Adams
Stuart and Sully Portrait
*Courtesy*, Fogg Art Museum, Harvard University, Cambridge, Mass.

When the new President was inaugurated, the Capitol had developed into the building shown *opposite*.

*Courtesy*, Stokes Collection, The New York Public Library

And the President's House was a vastly more comfortable home than that occupied by the President's father and mother a quarter of a century earlier (see page 84).

*Courtesy*, Stokes Collection, The New York Public Library

## The Erie Canal

begun in 1817 (see page 163), was completed in 1825. Extending from the straggling town of Buffalo, on Lake Erie, to Albany, on the Hudson, it opened a water route from the Lakes to the Atlantic Ocean.

BUFFALO FROM THE LIGHT HOUSE.

Basil Hall, *Forty Etchings from Sketches made with the Camera Lucida in North America.* 1829
*Courtesy,* Peabody Institute, Baltimore, Md.

BUFFALO ON LAKE ERIE

Cadwallader D. Colden, *Memoir Prepared for the Celebration of the Completion of the New York Canals.* 1825

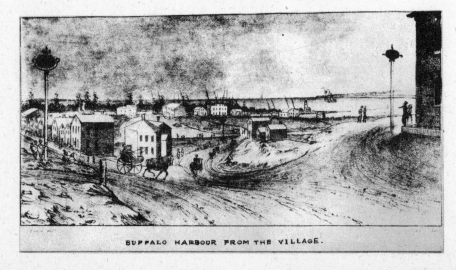

BUFFALO HARBOUR FROM THE VILLAGE.

Cadwallader D. Colden, *Memoir Prepared for the Celebration of the Completion of the New York Canals.* 1825

## The Erie Canal (Continued)

*Opposite* is an engraving, made in 1825 by George Catlin, of the Eagle Tavern in Buffalo.

*Below* is a sketch of the western end of the canal as seen by Basil Hall shortly after its opening.

Basil Hall, *Forty Etchings from Sketches made with the Camera Lucida in North America.* 1829
Courtesy, Peabody Institute, Baltimore, Md.

Courtesy, The Buffalo Historical Society, Buffalo, N. Y.

WESTERN END OF THE GREAT ERIE CANAL

From Buffalo, the course of the Canal was northerly to a place which came to be known as Lockport, where, by deep cuts and a series of locks, the Canal was carried through one of its most difficult stretches.

DEEP CUTTING LOCKPORT.

Cadwallader D. Colden, *Memoir Prepared for the Celebration of the Completion of the New York Canals.* 1825

ENTRANCE TO THE HARBOUR, LOCKPORT.

Cadwallader D. Colden, *Memoir Prepared for the Celebration of the Completion of the New York Canals.* 1825

## The Erie Canal (Continued)

From Lockport the canal turned northeasterly and then easterly, crossing the Genesee River at Rochester—now assured of future greatness.

VIEW OF THE AQUEDUCT BRIDGE AT ROCHESTER

Cadwallader D. Colden, *Memoir Prepared for the Celebration of the Completion of the New York Canals.* 1825

Crossing of the Genesee River at Rochester as seen by A. Duttenhofer, a German tourist, in 1826

A. Duttenhofer, *Bereitung der Vereinigten Staates von Nordamerika.* 1835

THE VILLAGE OF ROCHESTER

The view *opposite* was made by Basil Hall in 1827 and appeared two years later in his *Forty Etchings from Sketches made with the Camera Lucida in North America.*

Courtesy, Peabody Institute, Baltimore, Md.

## The Erie Canal (Continued)

On easterly went the Canal, on the southern side of the Mohawk, through villages where cities were to spring into being, to Rome, Little Falls and Schenectady.

VIEW OF THE AQUEDUCT BRIDGE AT LITTLE FALLS

*Cadwallader D. Colden, Memoir Prepared for the Celebration of the Completion of the New York Canals. 1825*

*A. Duttenhofer, Bereitung der Vereinigten Staates von Nordamerika. 1835*

Some five miles east of Schenectady the Canal crossed the Mohawk River on sixteen great piers, and, within a few miles, re-crossed by an aqueduct 1988 feet in length resting on twenty-six piers.

Opposite Troy, the Champlain Canal, coming down from the north, joined the Erie, and both headed for Albany and an outlet into the Hudson.

*Cadwallader D. Colden, Memoir Prepared for the Celebration of the Completion of the New York Canals. 1825*

VIEW OF THE JUNCTION OF THE NORTHERN AND WESTERN CANALS.

## The Erie Canal (Continued)

At Albany—363 miles by its course from Buffalo—the Canal entered the Hudson, with deep water to the open sea.

ENTRANCE OF THE CANAL INTO THE HUDSON AT ALBANY

Cadwallader D. Colden, *Memoir Prepared for the Celebration of the Completion of the New York Canals. 1825*

*Courtesy, Stokes Collection, The New York Public Library*

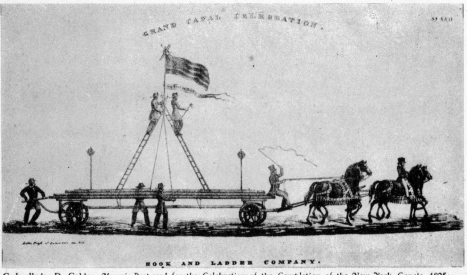

GRAND CANAL CELEBRATION.

HOOK AND LADDER COMPANY.

**Cadwallader D. Colden,** *Memoir Prepared for the Celebration of the Completion of the New York Canals. 1825*

## The Erie Canal Celebration

The dream of a century had come true. The East and the West were connected by a continuous waterway. The event was to be celebrated—and fittingly. On an October day in 1825, a bedecked canal boat, the *Seneca Chief*, with DeWitt Clinton and other notables aboard, led the procession eastward from Buffalo—past Lockport, past Rochester, past Rome, into the Hudson at Albany, down the great river in tow of one of Fulton's new steamboats—to New York, where a kegful of Lake Erie water was poured into the Atlantic.

Fleet in New York Harbor falling into line for the celebration of the opening of the Canal

The booming of cannon announced the progress of the procession. In New York Harbor the fleet fell into line with roaring guns. Fire companies and tradesmen paraded. At night, the City Hall burst into a "Magnificent and Extraordinary" display of fire works. The Atlantic and the Lakes were married. Freight rates between New York and Buffalo promptly dropped from $100.00 to $8.00 per ton.

Cadwallader D. Colden. *Memoir Prepared for the Celebration of the Completion of the New York Canals.* 1825

## New York City

was still a leisurely place with plenty of room on the streets for a dog fight.

*Courtesy, Stokes Collection, The New York Public Library*

Broadway. 1826

From a painting by C. Burton
*Courtesy, The New-York Historical Society, New York City*

Grace and Trinity Churches. About 1830

Water was peddled in horse-drawn barrels on wheels, like ice of a later generation, and ladies wore hats which were modelled on, or supplied the model for, sunbonnets.

From a sketch by W. G.
Wall. 1826
*Courtesy, Stokes Collection, The New York Public Library*

## Wall Street

The Delaware and Hudson Canal Co. had an office down the street from the United States' Branch Bank. And elderly ladies sold flowers or apples on the street corners.

UNITED STATES' BRANCH BANK.

WALL STREET.

F. Henry, draper and tailor, had his store beside the Phoenix Bank—and a gentleman in a top hat could sit down on the curb and rest.

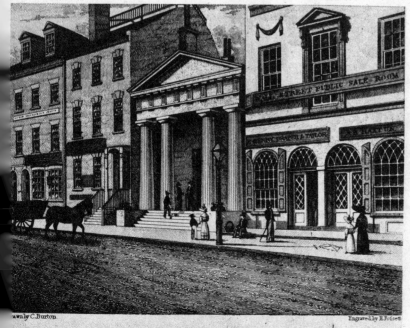

PHENIX BANK, WALL ST

NEW YORK.

Both illustrations on this page are through the courtesy of The New-York Historical Society, New York City

## Broadway and Trinity Church

From a watercolor painting by J. W. Hill. 1830

The view *above* shows Broadway looking south from Liberty Street. Grace Church may be seen in the background.

## City Hall and Park Row

From a watercolor painting by J. W. Hill. 1830

Note the fire engines, and, again, the water wagon

Both illustrations on this page are through the *courtesy* of the Stokes Collection, The New York Public Library

## The *Lady Clinton*

was one of two "safety barges" put into operation by the Fulton Company to meet competition on the Hudson River. It was a floating palace towed by a steamboat, and was "safe" because if the boiler of the steamboat blew up, the passengers would not be so closely involved. Thomas L. McKenney, who went up the river in the *Lady Clinton* in June, 1826, said, "It certainly exceeds every thing I have ever yet seen in all that enters into the composition of safety and comfort."

Thomas L. McKenney, *Sketches of a Tour to the Lakes.* 1827

Troy was, by 1829, a thriving factory city.

VIEW OF TROY

David Hosack, *Memoirs of DeWitt Clinton.* 1829

While the falls at the mouth of the Mohawk River were—thanks to the Erie Canal—an asset to industry rather than a deterrent.

A. Duttenhofer, *Bereitung der Vereinigten Staates von Nordamerika.* 1835.

Cohoes Falls

## Westward Across New York State

The long bridge across Lake Cayuga was one of the minor wonders of the 1820's.

BRIDGE ACROSS LAKE CAYUGA.

Basil Hall, *Forty Etchings from Sketches made with the Camera Lucida in North America.* 1829
Courtesy, Peabody Institute, Baltimore, Md.

Within four years of the opening of the Erie Canal, Buffalo was beginning to take on the appearance of a city.

Courtesy, Buffalo Historical Society,
Buffalo, N. Y.

To Capt. Basil Hall, visiting America in 1827-1828, the bridge across the rapids at Niagara was well worth a picture.

BUFFALO IN 1829.

Basil Hall, *Forty Etchings from Sketches made with the Camera Lucida in North America.* 1829
Courtesy, Peabody Institute, Baltimore, Md.

## The Blackstone Canal

completed in 1828, was a proper illustration for an advertisement by J. P. Kettell & Co., manufacturers of men's hats.

*Courtesy, American Antiquarian Society, Worcester, Mass.*

## Tunnels

became necessary in the case of canals in the mountainous country. The first tunnel built in the United States was for the Schuylkill Canal and was 400 feet long. The second tunnel (shown *below*) was for the Union Canal and was 729 feet in length.

Theodore B. Klein, *The Canals of Pennsylvania.* 1901

End of Union Canal Tunnel

## In Philadelphia

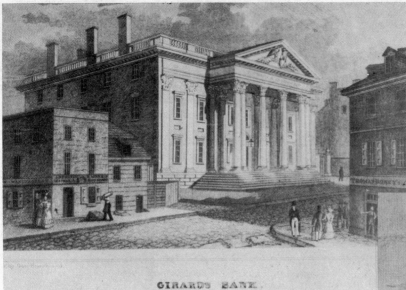

GIRARD'S BANK

Stephen Girard, who, in 1810, had bought the building and assets of the expiring First Bank of the United States, was busy making the fortune that was to create Girard College (see page 256).

(see page 256)

*Courtesy, The Historical Society of Pennsylvania, Philadelphia*

*James Mease, Picture of Philadelphia. 1831*

Brass Foundry

*Courtesy, The Historical Society of Pennsylvania, Philadelphia*

Christ Church

On Fourth Street were the buildings of the Old Academy, nucleus of the University of Pennsylvania.

*Courtesy, The Historical Society of Pennsylvania, Philadelphia*

Old Academy Buildings. About 1830

## Fashions of the Day

## American Stage Coach

Capt. Hall, whose travels about the United States gave him ample knowledge of the construction of stage coaches, not only drew but captioned the vehicle *opposite* as an American stage coach.

## Robert Mills, Architect

Born in Charleston, S. C., in 1781, Mills, while on his way north to study architecture, passed through Richmond, V·a., in 1800 and was fascinated by the newly completed state capitol (see page 81).

Subsequent association with Thomas Jefferson and with Latrobe sharpened Mills' interest in the Grecian Revival style of architecture. This is reflected in the Court House at Camden, S. C., *left*, built in 1826 from Mills' design.

*Courtesy,* National Park Service, Chicago

Also in 1826, the Fire-Proof Building (Record Office), *right*, at Charleston, S.C., was completed from designs by Mills.

*Courtesy,* The Charleston Museum, Charleston, S. C.

*Left.* A view of the interior of the Fire-Proof Building —said to be the first fire-proof building to be constructed in America.

*Courtesy,* The Charleston Museum, Charleston, S. C.

**Down South**

VILLAGE OF RICEBOROUGH IN THE STATE OF GEORGIA

Slave Driver

Backwoodsman

SWAMP PLANTATION ON THE BANKS OF THE ALATAMAHA

All illustrations on this page are from Basil Hall, *Forty Etchings from Sketches made with the Camera Lucida in North America.* 1829

## Pittsburgh

In due time Duttenhofer, whom we left making pictures of the Erie Canal, arrived at Pittsburgh—leaving us the picture below.

PITTSBURG am OHIO.

A. Duttenhofer, *Bereitung der Vereinigten Staates von Nordamerika.* 1835

Pittsburgh in 1826

A few months earlier, in December, 1825, there had assembled at Pittsburgh, a group of scientists, scholars and visionaries, who, in a keelboat named the *Philanthropist*, started down the Ohio River. Charles A. Lesueur, the artist and one of the group, left us a picture record of the trip.

The *Philanthropist* at Pittsburgh

Lesueur's sketches turned up at the Museum of Natural History, Havre, France. Photographic copies of these sketches were subsequently made and presented to the American Antiquarian Society, Worcester, Mass., by whose *courtesy* they are here reproduced.

Supper aboard the *Philanthropist* at Pittsburgh, Dec. 8, 1825

## Down the Ohio on a Keelboat

Somewhere between Pittsburgh and Steubenville, the *Philanthropist* had to tie up to a tree until a floating bridge was opened.

At Steubenville we see the *Philanthropist* berthed opposite the ferry, while passengers are approaching by foot and, seemingly, by cowback.

Next came Wheeling, where the *Philanthropist* appears to be tied up at the Island—beside a steamboat.

## Down the Ohio on a Keelboat *(Continued)*

By January 17 or 18, the *Philanthropist* had reached Cincinnati—which held interesting sights for the passengers, including women and children.

The destination of the party was New Harmony, on the Wabash River, where Robert Owen, the English philanthropist and a member of the party, was founding one of those idealistic communities so popular during this period—and destined to the usual failure. However, Lesueur spent the next twelve years of his life at New Harmony.

## With Lesueur on the Ohio and Mississippi

*Left.* An undignified debarkation from a river boat.

*Right.* A sugar camp visited by Lesueur between the Ohio River and New Harmony.

Several times Lesueur floated down the Mississippi on flatboats to New Orleans and returned on the river steamers.

St. Genevieve on the Mississippi

Steamer on which Lesueur came up the Mississippi in 1828

## The Lower Mississippi in the 1820's

*Opposite* is Vicksburg as Lesueur saw it. Note the floatboat tied up at the bank.

*Courtesy, American Antiquarian Society, Worcester, Mass.*

Also at New Orleans in this period was the English artist, Basil Hall. *Below* is his view of the river front.

THE MISSISSIPPI AT NEW ORLEANS

Basil Hall, *Forty Etchings from Sketches made with the Camera Lucida in North America.* 1829
*Courtesy, Peabody Institute, Baltimore, Md.*

In one of the mouths of the Mississippi was the Balize, where pilots—who knew the tortuous course of the river—were picked up or dropped by the sea-going vessels.

THE BALIZE AT THE MOUTH OF THE MISSISSIPPI.

Basil Hall, *Forty Etchings from Sketches made with the Camera Lucida in North America.* 1829
*Courtesy, Peabody Institute, Baltimore, Md.*

## Three Publications

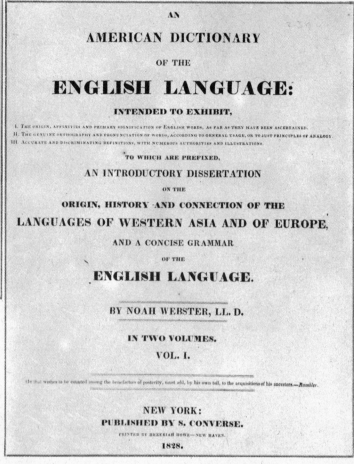

In 1827 appeared the first number of the *Youth's Companion* under the editorship of Nathaniel Willis and destined to continue for over a century.

The following year, Noah Webster, who, twenty-two years earlier (see page 108) had published his *Compendious Dictionary*, brought out *An American Dictionary of the English Language*. The name Webster was to become synonymous with the word "dictionary."

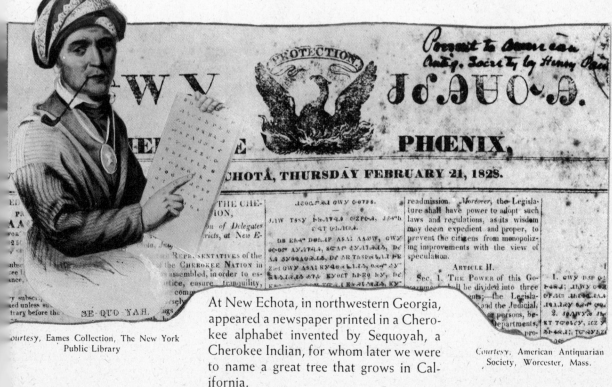

*Courtesy, Eames Collection, The New York Public Library*

At New Echota, in northwestern Georgia, appeared a newspaper printed in a Cherokee alphabet invented by Sequoyah, a Cherokee Indian, for whom later we were to name a great tree that grows in California.

*Courtesy, American Antiquarian Society, Worcester, Mass.*

## At Prairie du Chien, 1825

Here, where the Wisconsin River enters the Mississippi, an ancient meeting place of the Indians, was held a memorable "Treaty" between the northern and western tribes and the Commissioners of the United States.

From a painting made in 1829 by Seth Eastman
*Smithsonian Miscellaneous Collections*, Vol. 87, No. 3 (1932-33)

Fort Crawford, built at Prairie du Chien in 1816

Down from the North came the wild Chippewas. Present was J. O. Lewis, the painter who made from life the picture shown *below*.

THE PIPE DANCE        and        THE TOMAHAWK DANCE

of the Chippeway tribe.

J. O. Lewis, *Aboriginal Portfolio*. 1835
Courtesy, Illinois State Historical Library, Springfield

## Prairie du Chien *(Continued)*

Outside the walls of the fort a council ground was set up—where the Sioux from the west met in peace their deadly foe, the Chippewa. Here too were Sauk and Fox, Potawatomie and Winnebago.

From a painting made by J. O. Lewis at the treaty ground

Present in all his regalia was Keokuk of the Sauk, later to replace Black Hawk (see page 278) and to have a city named in his honor. Lewis made the portrait *opposite*.

KEE-O-KUCK or THE WATCHING FOX

The present Chief of the Sauk tribe and Successor to Black Hawk.

## In the Chippewa Country

The year following the "treaty" at Prairie du Chien, Gov. Cass of Michigan Territory met with the Chippewa in their own country—at Fond du Lac, at the western end of Lake Superior, where the American Fur Company had a post.

Thomas L. McKenney, *Sketches of a Tour to the Lakes.* 1827

J. O. Lewis, *Aboriginal Portfolio.* 1836
*Courtesy,* The Illinois State Historical Library, Springfield

J. O. Lewis was also present at this "treaty" and made the *above* sketch, among others.

American Fur Cos buildings, Fond du Lac. *(Back view)*

Thomas L. McKenney, *Sketches of a Tour to the Lakes.* 1827

*Below* we see the Commissioners arriving at the treaty ground in a typical Lake Superior canoe.

Thomas L. McKenney, *Sketches of a Tour to the Lakes.* 1827

## The Treaty at Fond du Lac

A great "talk" was held under waving flags. The Chippewa agreed to meet with the Winnebago and Menominee on Green Bay the following year.

Thomas L. McKenney, *Sketches of a Tour to the Lakes.* 1827

The Council at Fond du Lac

Thomas L. McKenney, *Sketches of a Tour to the Lakes.* 1827

Chippewa Pipe Dance

The Indians put on a pipe dance; presents were distributed; and in 1827 Indians and Commissioners met again near Green Bay at a place bearing the odd name of

**Butte des Morts
(Hill of the Dead)**

J. O. Lewis, *Aboriginal Portfolio.* 1835
Courtesy, Illinois State Historical Library, Springfield

The Commissioners arriving at Butte des Morts

From the Butte, which was a prehistoric Indian burial mound, subsequent excavations brought forth a vast number of objects, such as the hornstone knife shown *opposite.*

From the Charles Koehn Collection,
Courtesy, Oshkosh Museum, Oshkosh, Wisconsin

## Peace

Paul Kane, *Wanderings of an Artist among the Indians of North America.* 1859

Wisconsin was an Indian's paradise. By torchlight they speared fish on the Fox River.

From canoes they gathered wild rice in the sluggish currents.

George Catlin, *Letters and Notes on the Manners, Customs, and Condition of the North American Indians.* 1841

## And War

McKenney and Hall, *History of the Indians of North America.* 1849-50

Red Bird (shown *above*, standing) surrendered, was put in irons, and died of a broken spirit within half a year.

But even as the treaty at the Butte des Morts was progressing, Red Bird, chief of the Winnebagos, struck. It was a senseless uprising, instantly put down, but a white man's fort soon arose in the Winnebago country, which within a decade knew the Winnebago no more.

FORT WINNEBAGO IN 1831.

J. A. Kinzie, *Wau-Bun,* 1857

# 7

# WHEN JACKSON WAS PRESIDENT

## 1829-1837

The elections of 1828 gave Andrew Jackson the honor which the House had denied him four years earlier (see page 207). The electoral vote stood 178 for Jackson and 83 for John Quincy Adams.

Andrew Jackson
Painted from life by Asher B. Durand in 1835
*Courtesy*, The New-York Historical Society, New York City

Political success, however, was ashes in the heart of "Old Hickory," as, in the late winter of 1829, he journeyed to Washington. Buried in the garden of The Hermitage at Nashville lay his beloved Rachel, who had died six weeks after the election.

*Harper's New Monthly Magazine*, January, 1855
The Hermitage. Home of Andrew Jackson

*Courtesy*, The Historical Society of Pennsylvania, Philadelphia
The President's House. Washington. 1831

And the President's House was a lonely abode for the Hero of New Orleans.

## The City of Washington

Washington from beyond the Navy Yard. 1833

*Left*
West Front of the
Capitol in the 1830's

Glenn Brown, *History of the United States Capital.*
1900

*Right*, Department of State.
1831

## Coming of the Railroad

Hardly had the canals proved their value when a new method of transportation gripped the public mind—the "rail" road. In 1828, construction was begun on two pioneer lines, the Baltimore & Ohio and the Charleston & Hamburg (or "South Carolina" as it was more generally called). Horse-power and sails were experimented with on the "South Carolina" Railroad in 1829 and 1830.

W. H. Brown, *History of the First Locomotives in America.* 1871
Courtesy, Engineering Societies Library, New York

W. H. Brown, *History of the First Locomotives in America.* 1871
Courtesy, Engineering Societies Library, New York

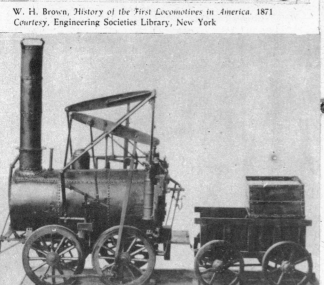

In 1829 the Delaware & Hudson Canal Co. imported a steam locomotive, the "Stourbridge Lion" from England and found that it worked.

*Left,* The "Stourbridge Lion"
Courtesy, The Delaware and Hudson Railroad, Albany

At the same time, Peter Cooper, at the Canton Iron Works in Baltimore, "knocked together" for the Baltimore & Ohio, the first locomotive made in America—the "Tom Thumb." It pulled a load of forty people at ten miles an hour.

W. H. Brown, *The History of the First Locomotives in America.* 1871
*Above* we see the "Tom Thumb" (on Aug. 28, 1830) racing with a fast horse—and beating it; but unfortunately something happened a few minutes later.

## Locomotives

In January, 1831, the Baltimore & Ohio offered a prize of $4000.00 for the best locomotive—burning coal or coke, and drawing fifteen tons at fifteen miles per hour—delivered before June 1, 1831. Phineas Davis, of York, Pa., won the prize with his "York", which weighed only 3½ tons. Davis also won a job with the B. & O., designing locomotives.

The "York"

*Courtesy, Baltimore and Ohio Railroad, Baltimore, Md.*

The West Point Foundry Shops in New York had by this time gone into the production of locomotives, and, late in 1830, delivered to the South Carolina Railroad "The Best Friend of Charleston", which we see (*below*) making its first trip on Jan. 15, 1831.

W. H. Brown, *The History of the First Locomotives in America.* 1874
*Courtesy,* The New-York Historical Society, New York City

A few weeks later the "West Point", from the same foundry, was pulling both freight and an excursion party on the South Carolina Railroad.

W. H. Brown, *The History of the First Locomotives in America.* 1874
*Courtesy,* The New-York Historical Society, New York City

The "West Point," March 5, 1831

## The Mohawk & Hudson

In 1831 the Mohawk & Hudson Railroad opened between Albany and Schenectady, in New York. For it, the West Point Foundry had built the "DeWitt Clinton", a dimensional drawing of which is shown *below*.

*Courtesy,* Transportation Library, University of Michigan, Ann Arbor

The picture *below*, depicting the formal opening trip, in 1831, of the "DeWitt Clinton" over the Mohawk & Hudson, is from a painting made many years later by Edward L. Henry (1841-1919). But so painstaking in his research and so exact in his portrayal was Henry, that the picture may be received as authentic. It is said that Henry's pictures were "accurate to the last chair and the most minute button".

Courtesy, The New York Central System

## More Railroads

The "John Bull" locomotive, *below*, built in England in 1831, was operated on the Camden & Amboy Railroad, now a part of the Pennsylvania Railroad System.

*Courtesy*, Pennsylvania Railroad, Philadelphia

In 1832, M. W. Baldwin completed his first locomotive, "Old Ironsides"—shown *below*.

*Courtesy*, The Baldwin Locomotive Works, Philadelphia, Pa.

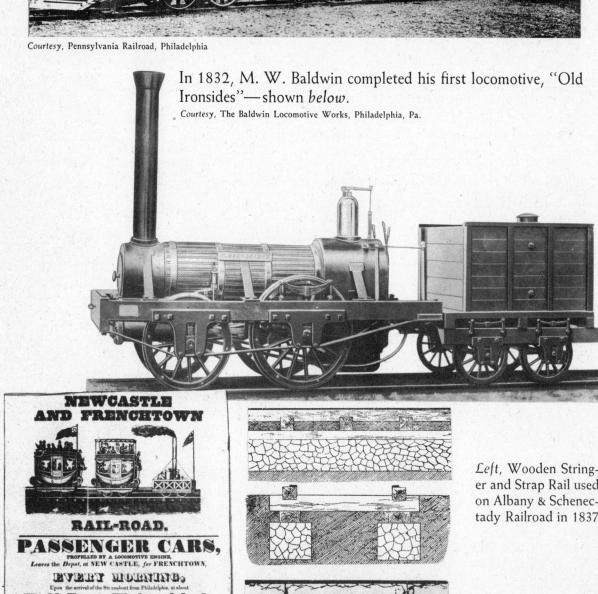

*Courtesy*, American Antiquarian Society, Worcester, Mass.

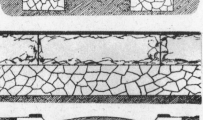

*Left*, Wooden Stringer and Strap Rail used on Albany & Schenectady Railroad in 1837

*Left*, Stone Stringer and Strap Rail used on B. & O. Railroad in 1833

*Courtesy*, United States National Museum, Washington, D. C.

## Canals

had, however, a long period of successful operation still ahead of them.

Courtesy, Northampton County Historical and Genealogical Society, Easton, Pa.

Easton, Pa. About 1831

According to Alvin F. Harlow, in *Old Towpaths*, we see in the picture *above* the Morris Canal in the foreground and the Lehigh Canal and Delaware division across the river.

*Right*, Reading, Pa. (1834) where the Schuylkill and the Union canals joined.

Courtesy, Stokes Collection, The New York Public Library

*Left*, The James River and Kanawha Canal (1833), at Richmond, Va. Begun in 1785, it got as far as Buchanan, Va. (125 miles up the river from Richmond) by 1851 and ended there. Nonetheless, it contributed greatly to the growth and prosperity of Richmond.

From an engraving by W. J. Bennett after a painting by G. Cooke
Courtesy, Stokes Collection, The New York Public Library

## The Erie Canal

which we saw opened in 1825 (pages 208-213) continued as the great, busy waterway to the West, through which floated a vast commerce and travel.

Courtesy, Stokes Collection, The New York Public Library

The Erie Canal, 1830-31

*Left*
Lockport, on the Erie Canal,
in the 1830's

Nathaniel Parker Willis, *American Scenery.* 1840

*Right*
The Erie Canal, near Little
Falls, in the 1830's

Nathaniel Parker Willis, *American Scenery.* 1840

## The Inclined Plane

Pennsylvania, seeing its western trade endangered by the Erie Canal, undertook a system of state financed canals. But one obstacle these canals could not surmount was the Allegheny range of mountains.

*Courtesy*, The Pennsylvania Railroad, Philadelphia

Sectional canal boat crossing the Allegheny Mountains on an inclined plane. The Portage Railroad

The situation was met by a Portage Railroad completed in 1834. At Hollidaysburg, on the eastern side of the mountains, the canal boats were loaded on a sort of flat car, pulled up the mountain on an "inclined plane", and lowered down the west side of the mountain to Johnstown, where the boats were again launched into the canal and pursued their way to Pittsburgh.

*Opposite*, Stone blocks took the place of cross-ties on the Portage Railroad

*Courtesy*, The Pennsylvania Railroad, Philadelphia

Maximilian, *Travels in the Interior of North America*. 1843

The view *above* shows an inclined plane which brought the coal from the mines at Mauch Chunk, Pa., to the Lehigh Canal which connected with tidewater.

## Clipper Ships

brought new speed into ocean commerce. Long, slim, with a great height of canvas, they out-distanced all competitors. The *Ann McKim*, built at Baltimore in 1832, was the first real clipper.

The Clipper Ship "ANN McKIM"
The First Clipper Ship ever Constructed - 1832    From a drawing by Capt. McCann

*Courtesy*, Peabody Museum of Salem, Mass.

## Whaling

provided oil for lamps and spermaceti for candles. From New Bedford and other New England ports, hundreds of whaling ships visited the Pacific during the 1830's.

From a rare engraving by J. Hill, after a painting by T. Birch
*Courtesy*, Weeks Whaling Museum, Stonington, Conn.

A Shoal of Sperm Whales off Hawaii. 1833

## The Tariff, Nullification and States' Rights

In 1828, John C. Calhoun had issued his *Exposition*, in which he proposed nullification as an answer to a tariff detrimental to the South. This brought up for discussion in Congress the whole question of States' Rights, in which Daniel Webster, of Massachusetts, in a series of debates with Robert Y. Hayne, of South Carolina, defended the "federal union" point of view. But in 1832 South Carolina acted by passing an Ordinance of Nullification against the offending tariff. President Jackson countered with a threat of using the Army to enforce collection, but Congress smoothed over the difficulty, and the right of nullification remained an unsettled issue.

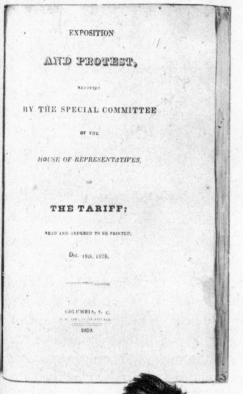

United States Magazine and Democratic Review. 1838

New England Magazine, August, 1834
Daniel Webster

Courtesy, The South Carolina Historical Society, Charleston, S. C.

## The Bank of The United States

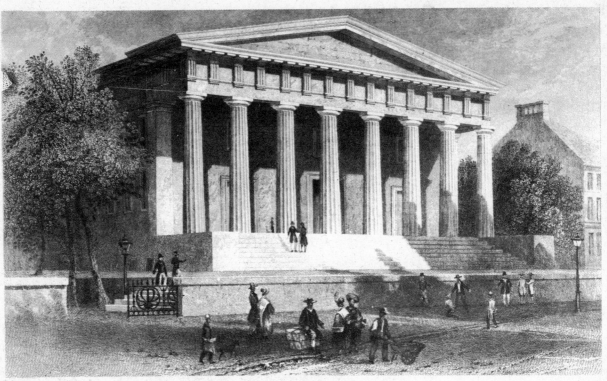

Nathaniel Parker Willis, *American Scenery*. 1840

Bank of the United States. Philadelphia

The charter of the first Bank of the United States (see page 45) expired in 1811. After five years of unsatisfactory state banking, a Second Bank of the United States had been chartered in 1816 for a period of twenty years. In 1823, Nicholas Biddle became President of the Bank, which was efficiently managed and gave good service. However, President Jackson became convinced that the Bank opposed his administration and in 1833 withdrew the government deposits. Upon the expiration of the charter in 1836, Jackson's opposition to a renewal ended the existence of the Bank.

*Courtesy, Chase Bank Collection of Moneys of the World*

Note of the Second Bank of the United States

*Nicholas Biddle, 250th Anniversary, 1681-1931*

## Farm Implements

The increasing production of small grain brought into being machines to reap and thresh it. Somewhat simultaneously in the early 1830's, reapers were made, demonstrated and patented by Cyrus H. McCormick, of Virginia, and by Obed Hussey, of Ohio. Both reapers worked successfully and, within a few years, both had a wide use. A bitter rivalry naturally developed, but in time the McCormick machine, by taking advantage of improvements, won the field.

*Courtesy,* The International Harvester Company, Chicago

The original McCormick Reaper, which was perfected by Cyrus McCormick and first publicly demonstrated at the McCormick farm in Virginia in 1831.

By 1835, a threshing machine, invented by David Flagg, was in general use in western New York. Joseph Pope, of Maine, had a competing machine.

Flagg's Threshing Machine and
Horse Power

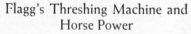

Thomas G. Fessenden, *The Complete Farmer and Rural Economist.* 1835

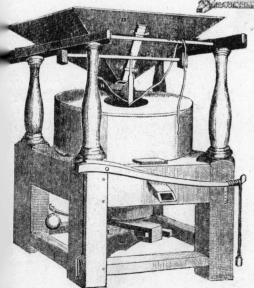

*The Farmers' Register.* 1834
A Farmyard of 1834

*Left,* Hotchkiss' Patent Grist Mill. 1833

*Mechanics' Magazine, and Register of Inventions and Improvements.* March, 1833

## Textile Manufacturing

As we have seen (page 61) Samuel Slater began the use of power-driven spinning machines at Pawtucket as early as 1790. By the time of Slater's death in 1835, the industry had grown to large proportions.

Pawtucket in 1835

CARDING, DRAWING, ROVING and SPINNING.
As introduced by S. Slater 1790.

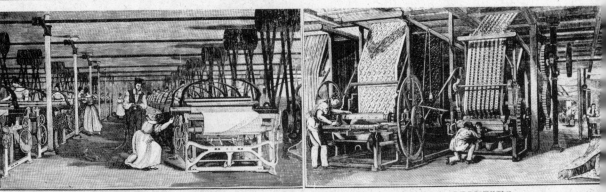

POWER LOOM WEAVING.                    CALICO PRINTING.

All illustrations on this page are from George S. White, *Memoir of Samuel Slater: The Father of American Manufactures.* 1836

## Textile Manufacturing (Continued)

In addition to his mills at Pawtucket, Slater had a yarn spinning mill at Webster, Mass.

*Right*
View of Webster, Mass. 1836

George S. White, *Memoir of Samuel Slater: The Father of American Manufactures.* 1836

But Slater was not the only manufacturer of textiles. At Comlyville, Pa., was the Calico Print Mill shown *below.*

COMLY VILLE near FRANKFORD_ Philadelphia C°
Nº 5. OF THE LADY'S BOOK.
Published by L. A. Godey & Co. 112 Chesnut Street Philadelphia

*Godey's Lady's Book.* 1830

*Opposite* is a close-up view of the factory shown *above. Godey's Lady's Book* for January, 1831 (from whence the picture is taken), states that there were several other factories in the village, making bed ticking, cords, etc.

## Printing Machinery

Robert Hoe had started in the business of making printing type and presses in 1805. By 1833, the year of his death, the Hoe presses had an established place in the printing industry.

ROBERT HOE & CO'S MANUFACTURING ESTABLISHMENT,
Nos 29 & 31 Gold Street New York.

One of Hoe's great contributions was the improvement and manufacture of the cylinder press. Copied from one made by Napier of England, but with many improvements, the Hoe cylinder press quickly replaced many used in this country.

*Left,* Rutt's Printing Machine, made by Napier (Hoe's Improvement)

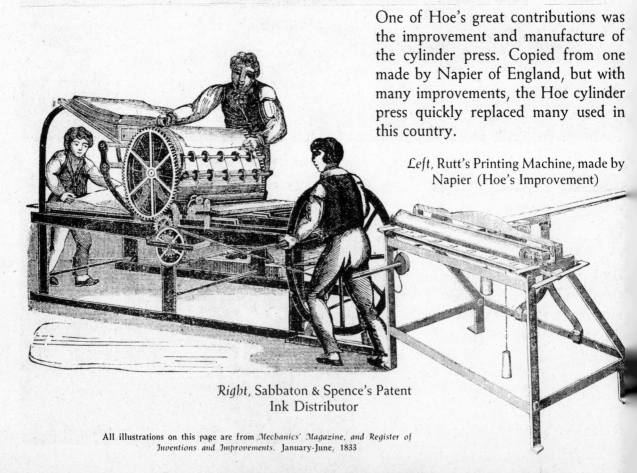

*Right,* Sabbaton & Spence's Patent Ink Distributor

All illustrations on this page are from *Mechanics' Magazine, and Register of Inventions and Improvements.* January-June, 1833

## Ladies' Styles

In 1830 had appeared the first issue of Godey's *The Lady's Book*, which for half a century was the supreme authority on fashions, etiquette and home economics.

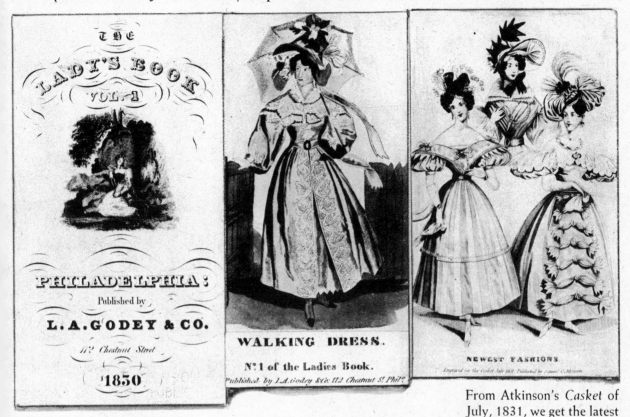

From Atkinson's *Casket* of July, 1831, we get the latest in evening dresses (right and left *above*) and morning dress (center *above*)

But down in Natchez, on the Mississippi, some of the girls had their own standards of etiquette —and smoked cigars during the dance.

From a drawing by Charles Alexandre Lesueur
*Courtesy*, American Antiquarian Society, Worcester, Mass.

Natchez Ballroom. 1830

## Shipwrecks

occurred along our eastern coast and passengers were cast adrift in open boats.

*Melancholy Shipwreck. 1834*

### Some Were Saved

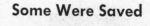

" Power Supreme,
O Everlasting King to thee I kneel,
To thee I lift my voice."

*Melancholy Shipwreck. 1834*

On the Mississippi River boats, games of chance attracted both professional and amateur.

*The Theatrical Apprenticeship and Anecdotical Recollections of Sol Smith. 1847*

" And what else!" asked every body.  " Another Ace!"—Four Aces!"

In 1831 at York, Pa., a farmer tried to sell some underweight butter. The Marketmaster seized the whole basketful as a forfeit, and the butcher told the farmer, "If you got more of lightweight butter at home you better grease your wagon with it."

*Right.* From a drawing by Lewis Miller.
*Courtesy.* The Historical Society of York County, York, Pa.

## Ithiel Town, Architect,

made his first reputation through building Center Church on the New Haven (Conn.) Green. In 1820, he was granted a patent for a truss bridge. By the 1830's "Ithiel Town Bridges" were being built all over the country. In fact, many of our old covered bridges are "Ithiel Town's."

Courtesy, Mrs. Charles W. Whittlesey, New Haven, Conn.

Gage Bridge, near Bellows Falls, Vt. Ithiel Town Truss. Built 1835

*Opposite*, Logan Bridge across the Wabash River. Ithiel Town Plan. Completed in 1837.

From a painting by George Winter
Courtesy, The William Henry Smith Memorial Library of The Indiana Historical Society, Indianapolis

The first Indiana state capitol at Indianapolis, completed in 1835, was designed by Ithiel Town. The building was 200 feet long by 100 feet wide, and cost $60,000.

Indiana State Capitol. 1835

Courtesy, The William Henry Smith Memorial Library of The Indiana Historical Society, Indianapolis

## Fire!

In 1832 there was a bad fire in Boston.

*Courtesy, H. V. Smith Collection, New York City*

Boston Fire. 1832

*Below*
Pewter Lamp for "Burning Fluids," made by Allen Porter, of Westbrook, Conn., between 1830-38.

*Courtesy, Metropolitan Museum of Art, New York City*

On December 16 and 17, 1835, there was a great fire in New York. *Below*, we view it as seen from the top of the Bank of North America, corner of Wall and William streets.

*Courtesy, Eno Collection, The New York Public Library*

## Penitentiaries

The 1820's and 1830's witnessed a movement for prison reform. Instead of the indiscriminate crowding of prisoners into a common room, a solitary cell system was developed.

EASTERN PENITENTIARY OF PENNSYLVANIA.

*First and Second Reports of the Inspection of the Eastern State Penitentiary of Pennsylvania. 1831*

In separate cells, on either side of corridors which extended like spokes of a wheel, from a central hub, the inmates spent their years of confinement in various types of labor, and saw no one except the prison attendants or authorities.

*First and Second Reports of the Inspection of the Eastern State Penitentiary of Pennsylvania. 1831*

*Nathaniel Parker Willis, American Scenery. 1840*

Sing Sing Prison. New York

## Philadelphia

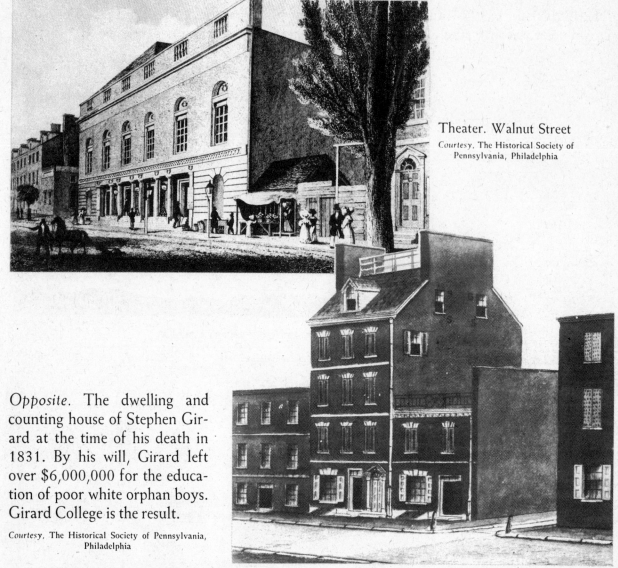

Theater. Walnut Street
*Courtesy*, The Historical Society of
Pennsylvania, Philadelphia

*Opposite*. The dwelling and counting house of Stephen Girard at the time of his death in 1831. By his will, Girard left over $6,000,000 for the education of poor white orphan boys. Girard College is the result.

*Courtesy*, The Historical Society of Pennsylvania, Philadelphia

Built by Thomas U. Walter in 1833, Girard College is regarded as one of the finest examples of the early 19th century vogue for Grecian architecture.

*Courtesy*, Stokes Collection, The New York Public Library

Girard College for Orphans

**New York City**

St. Paul's Church and the
Broadway Stages. 1831

*Right.* Washington Hotel,
Broadway, 1831. Drawn
by C. Burton

*Left.* Bowling Green, 1830.
This was then still a fashionable residence section of
the City. Drawn by
C. Burton

All illustrations on this page are through the
*courtesy* of The New-York Historical Society,
New York City

**New York City** (Continued)

BROADWAY, NEW-YORK.

*Courtesy, Eno Collection, The New York Public Library*

About 1834

*Courtesy, The New-York Historical Society, New York City*

*Left.* City Hotel. Broadway. About 1833.
Drawn by C. Burton

*Below.* Holt's New Hotel, between Water, Fulton and Pearl streets. On the second floor was a dining room 100 feet long, and a "Public Ordinary" to which resorted "many of the most respectable and influential men of the city."

*Mechanics' Magazine, and Register of Inventions and Improvements.*
January-June, 1833

**New York City** (*Continued*)

Drawn by C. Burton
*Courtesy,* The New-York Historical Society, New York City

The Bowery Theatre. 1830

*Right.* The Merchants' Exchange, at the corner of Wall and Hanover streets. The basement (in 1833) was occupied by the Post Office. In the dome was the Exchange Telegraph by which messages (through signals) could be sent to or received from the lower harbor in a few minutes time.

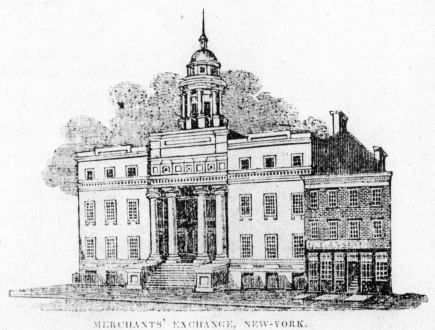

MERCHANTS' EXCHANGE, NEW-YORK.

*Mechanics' Magazine, and Register of Inventions and Improvements.* January-June, 1833

## New York City (Continued)

VIEW OF THE BAY AND HARBOUR OF NEW-YORK, FROM THE BATTERY.

Especially engraved for the *New York Mirror.* 1830

*Right.* No. 1 Park Row. 1830

Drawn by C. Burton
*Courtesy,* The New-York Historical Society, New York City

*Left.* Steamboat Landing. Foot of Courtlandt Street. About 1830

Drawn by C. Burton
*Courtesy,* The New-York Historical Society, New York City

**New York City** (*Continued*)

From a watercolor drawing by Alexander Jackson Davis

Interior of the John C. Stevens House. College Place and Murray Street. About 1830

ST GEORGE'S CHURCH, BEEKMAN ST         CLINTON HALL, BEEKMAN ST

All illustrations shown on this page are through the *courtesy* of The New-York Historical Society, New York City

**New York City** (*Continued*)

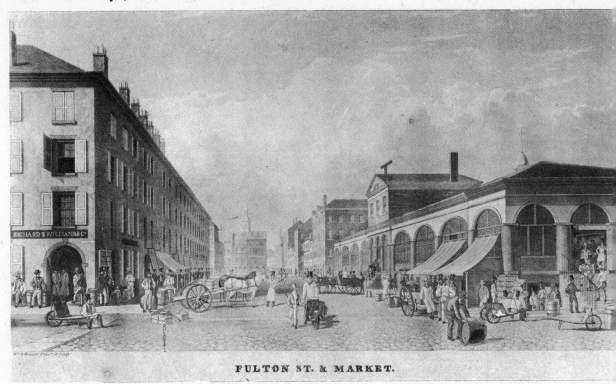

FULTON ST. & MARKET.

*Courtesy*, Stokes Collection, The New York Public Library

### The Brooklyn Ferry
Nathaniel Parker Willis, *American Scenery.*
1840

*Courtesy*, Eno Collection, The New York Public Library

New York from Brooklyn, 1836-39

## The Circus

Prior to 1800, circuses were more or less stationary, but by the 1830's there were many "rolling" shows—travelling about the country.

*Opposite*, is the earliest-known circus poster, measuring approximately 3 by 6 feet. It states that the circus will be at Easton (Pa.?) on Sept. 8, 1831, for one day only.

The second oldest-known circus poster, shown *opposite*, measures 6½ by 9½ feet. It tells us that the menagerie will be exhibited at Clinton on Friday the 12th day of June, 1835. Admittance 25 cents, children half price.

Both illustrations on this page are shown through the *courtesy* of the American Antiquarian Society, Worcester, Mass.

**Up the Hudson**

*Courtesy*, The Historical Society of Pennsylvania, Philadelphia

The Military Academy at West Point, 1831

Newburgh, N. Y. About 1830

J. H. Hinton, *History and Topography of the United States*. 1834

Summer resorts, such as those at Saratoga Springs, were becoming increasingly popular as wealth and means of transportation developed.

Piazza of Congress Hall, Saratoga Springs. About 1830

J. H. Hinton, *History and Topography of the United States*. 1834

## Northeastern Pennsylvania

Nathaniel Parker Willis, *American Scenery.* 1840

Descent into the Valley of Wyoming, a name applied to this section of Pennsylvania long before the area of the State of Wyoming had been trod by the feet of white men. The village in the distance is presumably Wilkes-Barre.

Judge Hollenback's House in Wyoming Valley. About 1835.

George Peck, *Wyoming, Its History, Stirring Incidents and Romantic Adventures.* 1860

The Myers House, Wyoming Valley. About 1835

George Peck, *Wyoming, Its History, Stirring Incidents and Romantic Adventures.* 1860

## The Frontier

North and west the frontier pushed onward—always the clearing, always the log house.

*Courtesy*, The Historical Society of Pennsylvania, Philadelphia

Conway, N. H. About 1831

COMMENCING A SETTLEMENT IN THE WILDERNESS

*The Genesee Farmer,* January, 1851

From an old print in the possession of Mr. Ferdinand W. Roebling. Reprinted from Schuyler, *The Roeblings,* through the courtesy of the Princeton University Press.

Saxonburg, near Pittsburgh, where in the 1830's a settlement was started by colonists from Germany.

## Westward on the National Road

From Wheeling, the Cumberland Road (see pages 189-190), now more generally known as the National Road, was pushed westward over the hills of southeastern Ohio to Zanesville and Columbus—with Vandalia, Ill., as its goal.

At Hendrysburg, Ohio, some twenty-five miles west of Wheeling, was the famous Crooked Bridge.

Two or three miles west of Zanesville was the Headley Inn.

Near Columbus was a toll house and gate.

All illustrations on this page are shown through the *courtesy* of The Ohio State Archaeological and Historical Society, Columbus

## Down the Ohio

Steamboats had by now become common on the Ohio River. *Below* is the river as viewed by Bodmer, a Swiss artist who accompanied Maximilian of Wied to America in 1832.

Maximilian, *Travels in the Interior of North America.* 1843

But flatboats still held sway for downstream transportation. *Left*, we get a view of men sitting or sleeping around a fireplace in a flatboat cabin—as Lesueur (see page 224) went down the Ohio at about the same time.

From a watercolor drawing by Charles Alexandre Lesueur
*Courtesy*, American Antiquarian Society, Worcester, Mass.

## A Barbecue

In 1832 Lesueur attended, on the Wabash River, one of those events so dear to the hearts of the frontiers-men—a barbecue.

From a watercolor drawing by Charles Alexandre Lesueur
*Courtesy*, American Antiquarian Society, Worcester, Mass.

## The Toledo War

The State of Ohio and the Territory of Michigan had long been at odds over a strip of land claimed by both—and including the City of Toledo.

*Courtesy, The Western Reserve Historical Society, Cleveland, Ohio*

A view of Cleveland "from Buffalo Road (Euclid Avenue) east of the court house." 1833

By 1835, the controversy had reached the stage of brawls, and armed forces were being collected by both sides.

*Courtesy, Stokes Collection, The New York Public Library*

Detroit from the Canada Shore. 1836

In 1836 Congress offered Michigan the Upper Peninsula in lieu of the disputed strip. Michigan accepted and in 1837 was admitted as a state.

## The South

Nathaniel Parker Willis, *American Scenery*. 1840

Harpers Ferry. Looking across and down the Potomac, with the Shenandoah coming in on right middle.

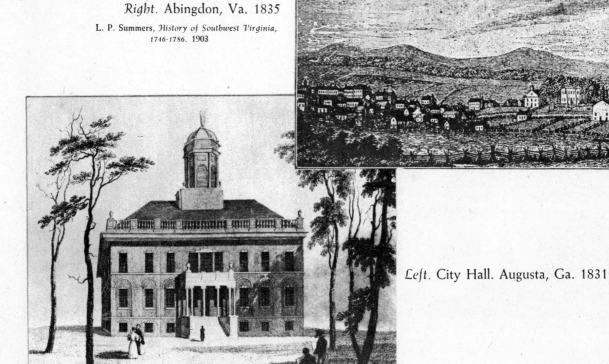

*Right*. Abingdon, Va. 1835

L. P. Summers, *History of Southwest Virginia,*
*1746-1786*. 1903

*Left*. City Hall. Augusta, Ga. 1831

Courtesy, The Historical Society of Pennsylvania, Philadelphia

## Removal of the Cherokee

For centuries, northwestern Georgia had been Cherokee country. These Indians had made great advances in the arts of civilization and loved their homeland, the possession of which had been guaranteed to them by the United States Government. But the Georgians wanted the land, and President Jackson sided with the Georgians. John Ross, a Cherokee chief, was leader of the faction of the tribe opposed to the cession of their lands, but to no avail.

John Ross
McKenney and Hall, *History of the Indians of North America.* 1849-50

The "John Ross House," near Chattanooga. Residence of one of the old Cherokee Landholders.

Edward King, *The Southern States of North America.* 1875

Another chief, Major Ridge, was prevailed upon to sign a treaty with the Government (at New Echota, Ga., Dec. 29, 1835) by which the Cherokee ceded all their lands east of the Mississippi in return for land in Indian Territory and southeastern Kansas. Within the next few years the Cherokee were removed from Georgia to their new home. Hardly were they there before Ridge fell to the avenging bullets of his infuriated fellow tribesmen. Ross lived on until 1866.

Major Ridge
McKenney and Hall, *History of the Indians of North America.* 1842

## The Etowah Mounds

Within the territory ceded by the Cherokee in 1835 (see page 271) were the famous Etowah Mounds—on the Etowah River some twenty miles east of present Rome, Ga. Surrounded by a moat from the river are six mounds, the largest being second only to the Cahokia Mound in size (see page 194), and is estimated as being 60 to 70 feet high and covering almost three acres.

*Courtesy,* Department of Mines, Mining and Geology, State Division of Conservation, Atlanta, Ga.

Large Mound of the Etowah Group

Exploration and excavation, by amateurs as well as by experts have brought forth from the mounds a vast number of interesting and artistic objects.

*Left.* Pottery water bottle, decorated with symbols of the sun.

Warren King Moorehead, *Exploration of the Etowah Site in Georgia.* 1932

*Right.* Embossed copper plate from Temple Mound, Etowah Group. (Bureau of Ethnology.) Note the resemblance to Mexican or Mayan designs.

The most recent scientific exploration of the Etowah Group was that conducted from 1925 to 1927 by Warren K. Moorehead for the Department of Archaeology of Phillips Academy. Dr. Moorehead ventured a theory for the Mound Builders, namely that a band of Indians came from Eastern Yucatan to Cuba, spreading into Florida and the Mississippi Valley, and carrying their mound building culture with them.

Warren King Moorehead, *Exploration of the Etowah Site in Georgia.* 1932

*Above.* Monolithic axe discovered with a skeleton

## Florida and the Seminoles

In 1823, shortly after the acquisition of Florida (see page 187), the Government made a treaty with the Florida Indians, mostly Seminole, restricting them to an area in the central part of the peninsula north of the Everglades.

**ST. JOHN'S RIVER & VOLUSIA on the RIGHT BANK.**

John Lee Williams, *The Territory of Florida*. 1837

But in the 1830's the plan of "Indian removal" was in full swing, and by the treaties of Payne's Landing (1832) and Fort Gibson (1833) the Seminole were forced to cede all their lands in Florida in return for land in Indian Territory (now Oklahoma). Osceola, a Seminole leader, is reported to have plunged his dagger instead of a pen into the treaty of cession.

From a painting by Seth Eastman
*Smithsonian Miscellaneous Collections*,
Vol. 87, No. 3 (1932-33)

*Above.* The village of Chitto Tustenuggee (otherwise known as Sam Jones), a Seminole chief in lower Florida

Welch, *A Narrative of the Early Days and Remembrance of Oceola Nikkanochee—A Young Seminole Indian*. 1841

OCEOLA'S MODE OF SIGNING THE TREATY

## The Seminole War

Osceola's action (see preceding page) resulted in his arrest by the military, but he was soon released, and used his freedom to organize an opposition that, if not war, at least kept the army very busy. So troublesome were Osceola and his followers that, when in 1837 they appeared under a flag of truce, he was seized and imprisoned.

*Left*, Osceola
*Courtesy*, Eames Collection, The New York Public Library

*Below*. Fort Mellon, Lake Monroe, Florida Territory

John Lee Williams, *The Territory of Florida*. 1837

It was well into the 1840's before the Seminole were cleared out of Florida. The sketch *opposite* made by George Catlin during the Seminole War indicates that not all the Seminole were within the treaty area even at that time.

Seminole Indians drying fish on Santa Rosa Island near Pensacola, Fla.

George Catlin, *Letters and Notes on the Manners, Customs, and Condition of the North American Indians*. 1841

## Along the Lower Mississippi

With cotton planters pushing into the new and fertile
lands along the Mississippi,
Natchez became a center
of wealth and of aristo-
cratic southern homes.

Natchez on the Hill. From the
Old Fort. About 1835

Courtesy, Department of Archives and
History, State of Mississippi, Jackson

North of Natchez was
Memphis, trade center for
western Tennessee and
eastern Arkansas.

*Left* is a view of Memphis
made by Lesueur (see page
224) about 1829

Courtesy, American Antiquarian Society,
Worcester, Mass.

Part of Memphis

Farther up the river, New
Madrid (*Right*) was failing to
realize its early promise,

From a watercolor drawing by Charles
Alexandre Lesueur
Courtesy, American Antiquarian Society,
Worcester, Mass.

while St. Louis, near the
junction of the Missouri
with the Mississippi, was
becoming the metropolis of
the middle stretch of the
river.

View of St. Louis. About 1837

From a painting by J. C. Wild
Courtesy, Pike Collection, The Chicago
Historical Society

## Comanche, Kiowa and Pawnee Picts

Back of the new "Indian Territory" to which the Government was removing the Cherokee and other tribes (see pages 271 and 274) was the hunting range of the wild plains tribes, who proceeded to make life miserable for the newcomers as well as for the whites who ventured into the region.

To impress these wild Indians with the power of the United States, a regiment of Dragoons under Col. Henry Dodge proceeded from Fort Gibson (in the then far-flung Arkansas Territory) southwesterly into the plains country. George Catlin, the artist, went along and has left us the pictures here shown.

Col. Dodge meeting the Comanche. Between the Washita and Red Rivers. 1834

Comanche Village

The expedition first visited the Comanche encampment and then went to what Catlin calls the Pawnee Pict village on the Red River. Some of the Indian leaders returned with Col. Dodge to Fort Gibson where treaties of friendship were completed—and soon broken.

Pawnee Pict Village

All illustrations shown on this page are from George Catlin, *Letters and Notes on the Manners, Customs, and Condition of the North American Indians.* 1841

## In the Land of the Sauk and Fox

By a "treaty" made in 1804 with a few leaders of the Sauk and Fox Indians, the Government acquired an area bounded, in general, by the Mississippi, Wisconsin, Rock and Illinois rivers (northwestern Illinois and southwestern Wisconsin). By the 1830's this country was filling up with white settlers. Peoria, on the old French portage route, was incorporated as a town in 1835.

Courtesy, Illinois State Historical Library, Springfield

The suppression of the Winnebago in 1827 (see page 234) brought a rush of lead miners into southwestern Wisconsin—still a part of Michigan Territory.

Cassville (Wis.). 1829

Henry Lewis, Das Illustrirte Mississippithal. 1854-57, but probably based on Seth Eastman's picture of 1829

## Chicago

was still mostly Fort Dearborn, but on Aug. 4, 1830, the Illinois and Michigan Canal Commissioners, who were planning a navigable connection between the Lakes and the Gulf, published a plat showing the "Town of Chicago."

Courtesy, Pike Collection, The Chicago Historical Society

Chicago. 1831

## Black Hawk's War

Among the Sauk and Fox was one chief who did not recognize the cession of 1804 (see preceding page). This was Black Hawk, who, from his new home on the western side of the Mississippi, insisted upon raising corn at his old home near Rock Island—where white squatters also wished to raise corn. In 1832 Black Hawk crossed into Illinois with several hundred followers—and a war was on.

Black Hawk

J. O. Lewis, *The Aboriginal Portfolio.* November, 1835
Courtesy, Illinois State Historical Library, Springfield

WAR DANCE OF THE SAUKS AND FOXES.

Courtesy, Eames Collection, The New York Public Library

The Army pursued the Indians up the Rock River and across southern Wisconsin where they headed back toward the Mississippi.

At the mouth of the Bad Axe River (emptying into the Mississippi some forty miles above the mouth of the Wisconsin) the Army caught up with the fleeing Indians, and a massacre ensued.

Battle of Bad Axe. 1832

Henry Lewis, *Das Illustrirte Mississippithal.*
1854-57

## Up the Missouri River

lay the country from which came most of the furs in the 1830's. Up this river, for the previous forty years, had gone from St. Louis, bateaux loaded with supplies for the Indian trade; and back down it to St. Louis had come bateaux loaded with packs of furs.

Maximilian, *Travels in the Interior of North America.* 1843

The *Yellowstone* on the Missouri River

In 1832 the steamboat *Yellowstone* started on a memorable voyage up the Missouri—memorable in that for the first time a steamboat reached the mouth of the Yellowstone River. Among the passengers was the artist, George Catlin, who made many of the pictures here shown, while others were made by the Swiss artist, Charles Bodmer, who went up the river with Maximilian, Prince of Wied, the following year.

Just above the mouth of the Platte River, the steamer stopped at Bellevue, a small trading post of the American Fur Company. *Right.*

Maximilian, *Travels in the Interior of North America.*
1843

Some three hundred miles farther up, the *Yellowstone* came to another American Fur Company post, which was being rebuilt and which, in honor of Pierre Chouteau, a member of the Company and also aboard the *Yellowstone*, was named Fort Pierre.

*Left.* Fort Pierre.

George Catlin, *Letters and Notes on the Manners, Customs, and Condition of the North American Indians* 1841

## The Sioux

Fort Pierre was in the heart of the Sioux country. Here Catlin saw these Indians hunting the buffalo: whose meat furnished them with food; whose hides made their lodges and their clothing; and whose excess hides were traded for white man's goods, including whiskey.

George Catlin, *Letters and Notes on the Manners, Customs, and Condition of the North American Indians*. 1841

H. R. Schoolcraft, *Information respecting Indian Tribes of the United States*. 1851-57

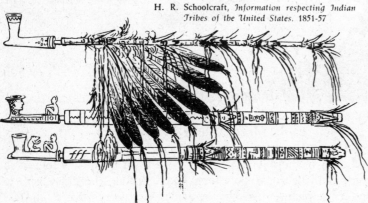

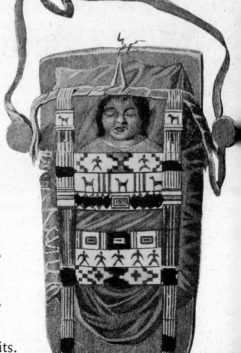

George Catlin, *Letters and Notes on the Manners, Customs, and Condition of the North American Indians*. 1841

He smoked their pipes and observed their domestic habits.

Maximilian, *Travels in the Interior of North America*. 1843

Bodmer (see page 279) made the above sketch of a Sioux funeral in 1833.

## To the Mouth of the Yellowstone River

Two hundred and fifty miles on up the Missouri, the steamboat *Yellowstone* (on the trip of 1832) came to another American Fur Company post, then or shortly after called Fort Clark, located about opposite the winter encampment of the Lewis and Clark Expedition of 1804-05.

Maximilian, *Travels in the Interior of North America.* 1843

Fort Clark. As seen by Bodmer in February, 1834

Maximilian, *Travels in the Interior of North America.* 1843

Fort Union, 1833

At the mouth of the Yellowstone River, the steamboat *Yellowstone* ended its upward trip of 1832. There stood Fort Union, the most important and most pretentious of the many American Fur Company posts. There, as did almost everyone else who went into the region, Catlin stopped for a visit. His purpose in ascending the Missouri was to paint the living Indians. One of his first subjects at Fort Union was a Blackfoot medicine man doing his "medicine" over a fellow tribesman who was dying from a bullet wound.

*Left.* Blackfoot Medicine Man

George Catlin, *Letters and Notes on the Manners, Customs, and Condition of the North American Indians.* 1841

## Catlin Portrays Indian Life

To Fort Union came all the surrounding tribes—enemies on the range, at peace at the Fort.
The presence of a band of Crow Indians gave the artist an opportunity of sketching their mode
of travel and of setting up their lodges.

Crows on the March

Note, *above*, the dogs as well as
the ponies dragging lodge poles
(the Indian travois) : And, *opposite*, the buffalo meat hung up
to dry while the squaws scraped
the skins.

Crow Lodges

From Fort Union, Catlin descended
the Missouri to the Mandan Village
near Fort Clark. Among these Indians he lived for some time, study-
ing their way of life and transferring
it to canvas.

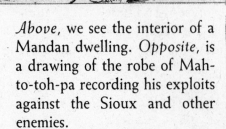

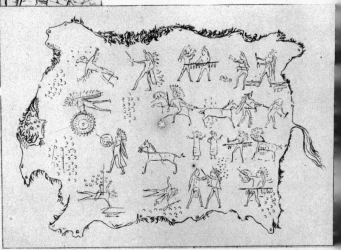

*Above*, we see the interior of a
Mandan dwelling. *Opposite*, is
a drawing of the robe of Mah-
to-toh-pa recording his exploits
against the Sioux and other
enemies.

All illustrations shown on this page are from George
Catlin, *Letters and Notes on the Manners, Customs,
and Condition of the North American Indians.* 1841

## Mandan and Minataree

*Left.* From Catlin's brush we see a Mandan "Rain Maker," mounted on one of their typical circular lodges—with the people standing about—commanding the rain to come.

*Right.* Voluntary torture endured by the Mandan youth to prove their courage. Catlin was allowed to witness this and similar ceremonies.

From the Mandan Village, Catlin went back up the river a few miles to the Minataree Village — shown *left* — on the west bank of the Missouri.

*Right* is a Minataree Turkish Bath. The "bather" sat in a tent over heated stones on which water was thrown to make steam. The process ended by the bather jumping into the river.

All illustrations shown on this page are from George Catlin, *Letters and Notes on the Manners, Customs, and Condition of the North American Indians.* 1841

## The Northern Buffalo Range

Far to the west, on the upper waters of the Missouri, were the Blackfeet Indians, one of the strongest and most aggressive of the tribes or confederations.

Maximilian, *Travels in the Interior of North America.* 1843

Blackfoot Encampment. Near Fort Mackenzie

The Blackfeet competed with the Crow Indians for the buffalo in the Big Horn and Tongue river valleys south of the Yellowstone River. Elk and other game were hunted for the skins as well as food, but the buffalo was the source of life for these Indians.

Elk

William E. Webb, *Buffalo Land.* 1874

McKenney and Hall. *History of the Indian Tribes of North America.* 1842

## Trapping Country

Up and down the Rocky Mountains every stream had become a trapping ground for parties operating independently or under the direction of the American Fur Company (with posts on the eastern side of the mountains), or of the Hudson's Bay Company (with posts over the mountains).

*Opposite*, we see two trappers setting and baiting their traps for beaver— from the brush of A. J. Miller, an artist who visited the West in 1837.

*Courtesy*, The Walters Art Gallery, Baltimore, Md.

In 1834, a fur trading post was built on the Laramie River near its entrance into the North Platte River. This post soon came to be known as Fort Laramie, and in 1836 passed into the hands of the far reaching American Fur Company.

William E. Webb, *Buffalo Land.* 1874

*Opposite*, is a view of the interior of Fort Laramie— made in 1837 by A. J. Miller.

*Courtesy*, The Walters Art Gallery, Baltimore, Md. ·

## Over the Great Divide

Just west of the Continental Divide, where the Snake River starts its long journey to the Pacific, was Jackson's Hole, a favorite hunting ground of the trappers.

Courtesy, U. S. Department of the Interior, National Park Service

Jackson's Hole

And, far on to the West, near where the Snake River joins the Columbia (in the present state of Washington) stood Fort Walla Walla, a fur trading post owned by the Hudson's Bay Company, a British monopoly, supplied with trade goods from London, and shipping its furs to London—partly by ships at the mouth of the Columbia.

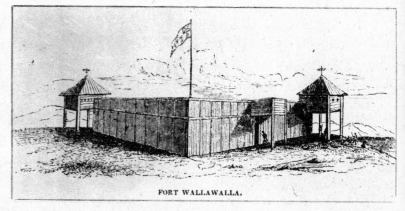

FORT WALLAWALLA.

Charles Wilkes, U. S. Exploring Expedition. 1844

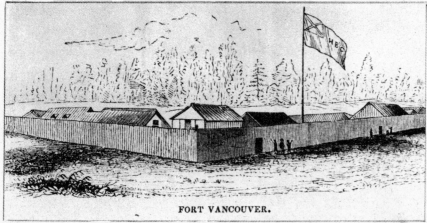

FORT VANCOUVER.

Charles Wilkes, U. S. Exploring Expedition. 1844

Fort Vancouver (at present Vancouver, Wash.), was the western headquarters of the Hudson's Bay Company.

It should be recalled that at this time the Oregon Country was occupied jointly by the United States and Great Britain. Not until 1846 was the boundary drawn.

## California

was still a part of Mexico, separated from the trapping country described in the preceding pages by a vast stretch of almost impassable deserts. Great Salt Lake was vaguely known to exist, but did not attract the wandering trappers.

California Mode of Catching Cattle

In 1833, Capt. Bonneville, whose exploits have been vividly recorded by Washington Irving, sent a party under Joseph Walker to explore Great Salt Lake. Walker spent little time on the Lake but crossed the Sierras into the Valley of California and spent the winter at Monterey.

Monterey, Calif. About 1834

From a book on California, by an Englishman named Alex. Forbes, who was in California at about the time Walker was there, and whose illustrations were undoubtedly made by an artist on the ground, we get some views of the region as Walker and his party saw it.

San Carlos Mission,
California. About 1834

All illustrations shown on this page are from Alex. Forbes, *California: A History of Upper and Lower California.* 1839

## Back in the East

the railroad was pushing steadily westward.

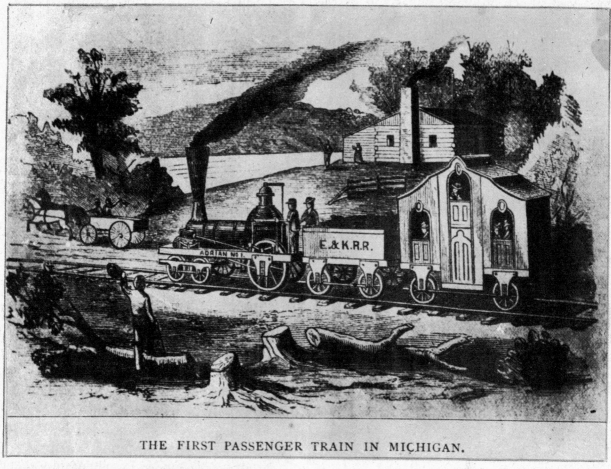

THE FIRST PASSENGER TRAIN IN MICHIGAN.

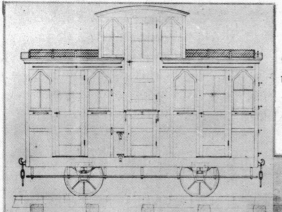

*Opposite.* Scaled plan of the first passenger car on the Erie & Kalamazoo Railroad.

From Detroit to Pontiac, Mich., ran the Detroit & Pontiac Railroad in 1835. *Opposite* we see the depot and Rail-Road Hotel.

All illustrations on this page are through the *courtesy* of the Transportation Library, University of Michigan, Ann Arbor

## Railroads

Construction on the Boston & Lowell, the first New England railroad, had started in 1831. *Below* we see the first train on this line (1835), being pulled by a locomotive made in England by George Stephenson.

*Courtesy, Boston and Maine Railroad, Boston, Mass.*

*Left.* Viaduct on the Washington division of the Baltimore & Ohio Railroad. About 1836.

From a painting by William Henry Bartlett
Nathaniel Parker Willis, *American Scenery.*
1840

By 1836 the railroad had been built west from Schenectady, N. Y., to Utica.

*Opposite* we see a train roaring through Little Falls—paralleling the Erie Canal, finished eleven years earlier (see pages 208-213).

From a painting by William Henry Bartlett    Nathaniel Parker Willis, *American Scenery.* 1840

## Railroad Fares and Locomotives

**SOUTH-CAROLINA RAIL-ROAD,**

*Between Charleston and Hamburg, S. C. opposite Augusta. (Geo.)*

### RATES OF PASSAGE.

| From Charleston to | Miles | $ Cts. | From Hamburg to | Miles | $ Cts. |
|---|---|---|---|---|---|
| Woodstock, | 15 | 50 | Aiken, | 16 | 75 |
| Summerville, | 21 | 75 | Blackville, | 46 | 2 25 |
| Inabnet's, | 32½ | 1 62½ | Midway, | 64 | 3 25 |
| Branchville, | 62 | 3 00 | Branchville, | 74 | 3 75 |
| Midway, | 72 | 3 50 | Inabnet's, | 103½ | 5 12½ |
| Blackville, | 90 | 4 50 | Summerville, | 115 | 6 00 |
| Aiken, | 120 | 6 00 | Woodstock, | 121 | 6 25 |
| Hamburg, | 136 | 6 75 | Charleston, | 136 | 6 75 |

And from one intermediate Station to *another*, FIVE CENTS per MILE. *Children under 12 years and Coloured Persons, half price*

*Regulations for the Passenger Carriage.*

1st. All baggage at owner's risk—75 lbs. allowed. 2d...
not admitted, unless having the care of children, withou...
...of all the Passengers. 3d Passengers not allowed to...
...king prohibited. 5th. No...

*Miller's Planters' and Merchants' Almanac for the Year 1836. 1835*

*Right.* Baldwin Locomotive No. 125, built in 1839, but similar in design and construction to the "E. L. Miller," Mr. Baldwin's second locomotive, completed Feb. 18, 1834.

*Courtesy,* The Baldwin Locomotive Works, Philadelphia

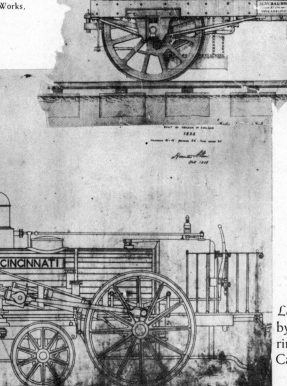

*Left.* Locomotive built in 1835 by C. Tayleur & Co., of Warrington, England, for the South Carolina Railroad.

*Courtesy,* Southern Railway Company, Washington, D. C.

**Railroad Timetable**

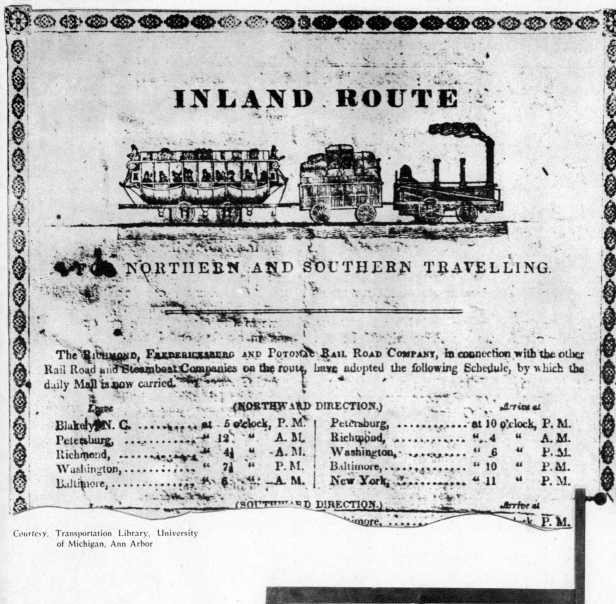

# INLAND ROUTE

## NORTHERN AND SOUTHERN TRAVELLING.

The RICHMOND, FREDERICKSBURG AND POTOMAC RAIL ROAD COMPANY, in connection with the other Rail Road and Steamboat Companies on the route, have adopted the following Schedule, by which the daily Mail is now carried.

| Leave | (NORTHWARD DIRECTION.) | | Arrive at |
|---|---|---|---|
| Blakely, N. C. ......... at 5 o'clock, P. M. | | Petersburg, ......... at 10 o'clock, P. M. |
| Petersburg, ......... " 12 " A. M. | | Richmond, ......... " 4 " A. M. |
| Richmond, ......... " 4½ " A. M. | | Washington, ......... " 6 " P. M. |
| Washington, ......... " 7½ " P. M. | | Baltimore, ......... " 10 " P. M. |
| Baltimore, ......... " 6 " A. M. | | New York, ......... " 11 " P. M. |

(SOUTHWARD DIRECTION.)                        Arrive at
            ...imore. ......... ...k P. M.

Courtesy, Transportation Library, University
of Michigan, Ann Arbor

## And the Telegraph

Even as the railroads reached ever farther, the invention which was to make their schedules possible was being worked out. In 1837, after five years of experimentation, Samuel F. B. Morse, an artist, filed at the Patent Office a caveat for a magnetic telegraph. *Opposite* is a view of his sending and receiving instruments of 1837.

Courtesy, Smithsonian Institution,
Washington, D. C.

## Texas

In the fifteen years since Stephen Austin went into Texas (see page 204) he had built up a prosperous colony between the Brazos and Colorado rivers. Other Americans had developed similar colonies. Thousands of families had poured in from the United States. In 1836 the inevitable conflict between Latin and Anglo-Saxon came to a head. Texas declared her independence of Mexico and war broke out. At first all went well for the Texans—and then Mexico struck in force. At the Alamo (in San Antonio) some one hundred and eighty Texans, including James Bowie of the Bowie Knife fame, were killed.

From a painting by Seth Eastman
*Smithsonian Miscellaneous Collections*, Vol. 87, No. 3 (1932-33)

Slowly across Texas, toward the Sabine, the Texans retreated—with Sam Houston as their leader.

*Right*, Houston dictating orders during retreat across Texas

C. E. Lester, *Life of Sam Houston*. 1860

On the San Jacinto River, forty miles above Galveston, the Mexican army under Santa Anna, President of Mexico, caught up with the Texans. In the battle that followed, the Mexicans were routed and Santa Anna was captured. The independence of Texas was established.

The Battle of San Jacinto, April 21, 1836
C. E. Lester, *Life of Sam Houston*. 1860

# 8
# FINANCIAL PANIC AND WESTWARD EXPANSION

## 1837-1845

### Martin Van Buren

who was Jackson's choice as a successor, was duly elected President in 1836, and on March 4, 1837, became the eighth President of the United States.

*Left*, Martin Van Buren

Engraving by A. L. Dick from a miniature by Mrs. Bogardus
*United States Magazine and Democratic Review.* November, 1841

*Below* we see the City of Washington in 1837. In the center foreground appears the Washington Canal, extending from the Potomac toward the Capitol.

Courtesy, Stokes Collection, The New York Public Library

## THE GLOBE.

### CITY OF WASHINGTON.

#### MONDAY MORNING, APRIL 10, 1837.

##### THE PANIC AND PRESSURE IN NEW YORK.

WALL STREET.—The boasted relief of Mr. Biddle last week turns out to be the reverse. As soon ... was discovered, stocks took a down-...

THE MONEY MARKET IN BOSTON.—The Boston advocate of Wednesday says: The temporary and deceitful fall in the money market has changed in a white squall. Yesterday was a hard day in state street, two per cent. a month was paid on post notes and blue books having six months to run, and the advices from New York were by no means flattering, as the specie drafts for the quarterly payments for the surplus had straitened the banks...

Hardly was Van Buren inaugurated before the unsound economic condition of the country, aggravated by President Jackson's action in refusing a new charter to the Bank of the United States (see page 246), developed into a full-fledged financial panic.

## THE WEEKLY HERALD.

VOL. I.                NEW YORK, SATURDAY EVENING, MAY 6, 1837.

During the week the great commercial and social revolution has been going onward with terrible rapidity. In New York nearly *seventy* large houses have suspended payment—and out of the city, probably one hundred other failures have taken place, all over the country, of merchants, manufacturers, bankers, brokers, and what not. The whole country is in one whirlpool of agitation. A Committee has gone to Washington to wait on the President—a meeting of Congress is called for. The legislature is still in session, but it talks—acts not.

In this city bankruptcy has swept away our best and most pious citizens. The sinner and the saint are equally brought down. No respect is paid to long prayers—or builders of churches. Arthur Tappan, John W. Leavitt, and a whole batch of christ...

## A Panic

NEW YORK  MERCHANTS' EXCHANGE.

*Courtesy, Eno Collection, The New York Public Library*

With the failure of mercantile establishments, banks could not meet the demand for gold and silver coins, and soon specie payments were suspended.

*Courtesy, Chase Bank Collection of Moneys of the World, New York*

There being no coins available for paying wages or debts, business institutions and even municipalities began issuing private notes which circulated like money.

*Courtesy, Chase Bank Collection of Moneys of the World, New York*

## Industry

The financial depression quickly extended to the industries of the country—

**Coal Mines**

View of the great Coal Seam on the Monongahela at Brownsville, Pennsylvania.

Charles Lyell, *Travels in North America, 1841-1842.* 1845

**Salt Works**

The view *opposite* is in present West Virginia, which was, at the time of the picture, a part of Virginia.

*View of the Salt-Works on the Kanawha.*

Henry Howe, *Historical Collections of Virginia.* 1849

**Lead Mines**

Courtesy, Chicago Historical Society, Ill.

Lead-Bearing Rocks and Furnace near Galena, Ill.

## Transatlantic Steamships

In the midst of the economic disruption, there occurred an event of great economic significance. On April 22, 1838, the British steamer *Sirius* arrived at New York from London—the first ship propelled wholly by steam to reach the United States from Europe. It had crossed the Atlantic in 16½ days.

THE BRITISH STEAMER SIRIUS

The following day, another steamship from England, the *Great Western*, arrived in New York Harbor.

The Arrival of the *Great Western* at New York, April 23, 1838

With the arrival at New York in 1839 of the *British Queen*, built expressly for such service, transatlantic steam transportation became an established fact.

*Left*, The *British Queen* Arriving at New York, July 28, 1839

Bay of New York from the Battery. 1838

## Whaling

From Nantucket, New Bedford, Sag Harbor and other ports, whaling ships went forth in search of whale oil and whale bone. Often these ships were out as long as four or five years on a single voyage. By 1846, there were more than 700 American whaling ships at sea, and New Bedford was the whaling capital of the world.

*Courtesy, Allan Forbes, Esq.*

### Capturing a Sperm Whale

The view *above* is from a painting by William Page made from a sketch by C. B. Hulsart, who lost an arm in the Pacific fisheries while aboard a ship out of New London.

*Right*. Whaling scene in the California Lagoons

Charles M. Scàmmon, *The Marine Mammals of the North-Western Coast of North America*. 1874

*Below*.
Sperm Whale

Charles M. Scammon, *The Marine Mammals of the North-Western Coast of North America*. 1874

*Opposite*.
Heavy draft whaler being carried over the shoal at entrance to Nantucket.

*Courtesy, Captain John A. Cook*

## Railroads, Inclined Planes and Canals

View of North Queen Street, Philadelphia. 1843

*Opposite.*
Inclined plane near
Philadelphia. 1840.

*Opposite.*
View of Northumberland
with the Pennsylvania State
Canal in the foreground.
1842.

## Bridges, Waterpower and Rafts

*Below* is shown the Tonnewanta Railroad Bridge across the Erie Canal at Rochester, N. Y., in 1837. Note the locomotive and coach entering the bridge; and the canal boat being towed along below.

Henry O'Reilly, *Sketches of Rochester.* 1838

*Opposite.* View of the falls of the Genesee River at Rochester, N. Y., about 1838. The falls provided the water power that contributed greatly to Rochester's rapid growth and economic importance.

From an engraving by J. Cousen, from a sketch by W. H. Bartlett
*Courtesy,* Rochester Historical Society, N. Y.

*Opposite.* Rafts descending the Susquehanna River and canal boats being towed in the canal beside the river.

Nathaniel P. Willis, *American Scenery.* 1840

## Railroads and Stages

*Opposite.* Pen sketch of Main Street, Branchville, S. C., looking toward the South Carolina Railroad. The artist is not known, but the time represented is probably the 1840's.

Courtesy, Southern Railway Company, Washington, D. C.

*Opposite* is another view of Branchville, looking toward Charleston— made by the same artist as above.

Courtesy, Southern Railway Company, Washington, D. C.

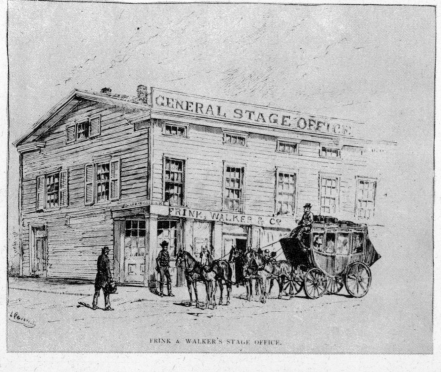

In Illinois and adjoining states the Frink & Walker Company operated a line of stagecoaches.

A. T. Andreas, *History of Chicago.* 1884

## State Agricultural Fairs

From the first county fairs (see page 165) had grown great state fairs. *Opposite* we have a view of the New York State Cattle Show held at Poughkeepsie in 1844.

*The Farmer's Museum*, October, 1844
Courtesy, New York State Library, Albany

*Right* is a plan of the Poughkeepsie fair grounds. The four buildings in the center are (G) Floral Hall, (H) Ladies' Home, (I) Manufacturer's Lodge, (K) Farmer's Hall.

*The Farmer's Museum*, October, 1844
Courtesy, New York State Library, Albany

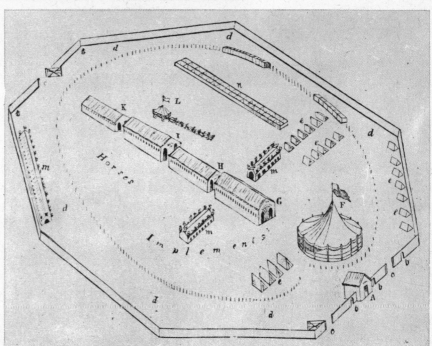

*The American Agriculturist*, June, 1843

Durham Bull, "Archer." The property of Col. J. M. Sherwood of Auburn, N. Y.

*Right.* Durham Heifer, "Esterville." The property of E. P. Prentice of Mount Hope, N. Y.

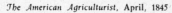

*The American Agriculturist*, April, 1845

## Better Livestock, More Grain, Improved Plows

Cotswold Sheep. Property of Messrs. Corning and Sotham, Albany, N. Y.

*The American Agriculturist, April, 1843*

Berkshire Hog bred at Herkimer, N. Y. It weighed 721 net when butchered.

*The American Agriculturist, June, 1845*

*The American Agriculturist, April, 1843*

Hereford Cow, "Matchless" (Imported). Property of Messrs. Corning and Sotham, Albany, N. Y.

Corn

*The American Agriculturist, May, 1845*

About 1837 a young blacksmith named John Deere opened a shop at Grand Detour, Ill. He soon found that the plows brought from the East did not work well in prairie soil. Deere made a plow with a steel mouldboard so shaped that it "scoured" itself in the rich soil of the west. A new name was being added in the field of invention and industry (see page 354).

*The American Agriculturist, April, 1845*

Wheat

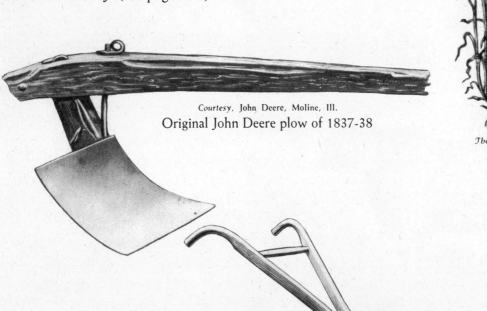

*Courtesy, John Deere, Moline, Ill.*
Original John Deere plow of 1837-38

Reconstruction of original John Deere plow
*Courtesy, John Deere, Moline, Ill.*

## Mr. Colt's Revolving Pistols, Shotguns and Rifles

In February, 1836, Samuel Colt, then twenty-two years old, received a patent for a revolving firearm. The following month he formed the Patent Arms Company and opened a factory in an unused section of a silk mill at Paterson, N. J.

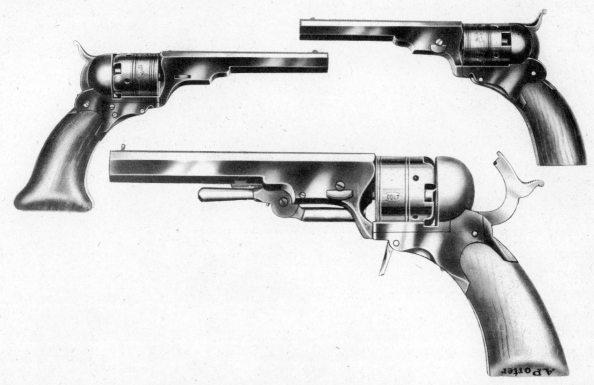

There he manufactured the famous Paterson Revolving Pistols shown *above*. They were of .34 caliber and fired five shots. At the same time, he made revolving rifles and shotguns as shown *below*.

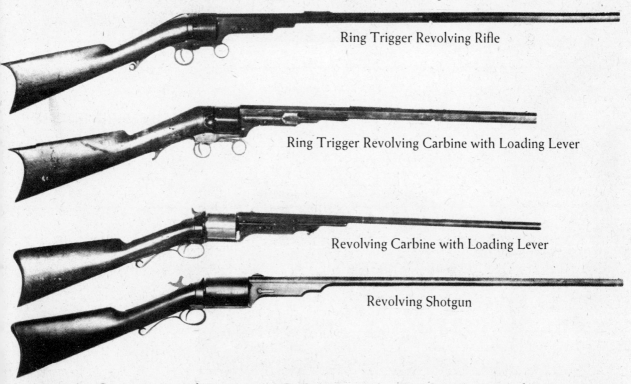

Ring Trigger Revolving Rifle

Ring Trigger Revolving Carbine with Loading Lever

Revolving Carbine with Loading Lever

Revolving Shotgun

In 1841 the Government, after a test at Carlisle Barracks, Pa., bought 160 of the revolving carbines at $45.00 each.

All illustrations shown on this page are through the *courtesy* of the Colt's Patent Fire Arms Manufacturing Company, Hartford, Conn.

## Boston in 1837

THE NATIONAL LANCERS with the REVIEWING OFFICERS on BOSTON COMMON.

*Courtesy*, Stokes Collection, The New York Public Library

*Opposite.*

## New York Harbor in 1838

showing the Narrows from Fort Hamilton.

Nathaniel P. Willis, *American Scenery.*
1840

*Left.*

## Philadelphia in 1838

MARKET STREET,
from Front St.
PHILADELPHIA.

*Courtesy*, The Historical Society of Pennsylvania, Philadelphia

## Northampton, Mass., in 1840

*Below* we see a typical New England village in the 1840's. Note the churches and homes surrounding the green—viewed from the porch of the inn.

Nathaniel P. Willis, *American Scenery.* 1840

*Left.*

### The Palisades—Hudson River—in 1837

Nathaniel P. Willis, *American Scenery.* 1840

## Troy, N. Y. in 1838

Stimulated by the Erie Canal and the railroads, Troy was definitely becoming an important manufacturing city.

*Courtesy,* Eno Collection, The New York Public Library

## "Tippecanoe and Tyler Too!"

As a challenge to the strong executive power wielded by Jackson and Van Buren, a new political party came into being—the Whigs.

*Courtesy*, The Municipal Museum of the City of Baltimore, Md.

National Convention of Whig Young Men, Baltimore, May 4, 1840

For President the Whig Party nominated William Henry Harrison, hero of the Battle of Tippecanoe (see page 124), and for Vice-President, John Tyler of Virginia. The campaign was conducted by the Whigs on an emotional basis. Log cabins (see one on wheels in picture *above*) and hard cider, both connecting Harrison with the "Common Man," held spectacular places in the appeal for votes.

From a portrait by J. R. Lambdin

William Henry Harrison

*United States Magazine and Democratic Review.*
November, 1842

John Tyler

## The Inauguration of Harrison

The Whigs won, and *below* we see the inauguration on the east portico of the Capitol, March 4, 1841.

*Courtesy*, Stokes Collection, The New York Public Library

Exactly a month after his inauguration, President Harrison died, worn out from the strain of the election, and John Tyler became President.

Southwest View of Capitol.
About 1840

Glenn Brown, *History of the United States Capital.* 1900

## Styles of 1837

Left. From *Godey's Lady's Book*, January, 1837

Below. From *The Casket*, April, 1837

Below. From *Godey's Lady's Book*, October, 1837

## Styles of the 1840's

*Above.* From *Godey's Lady's Book*, July, 1840

*Right.* Silk dress. About 1845
Courtesy, Essex Institute, Salem, Mass.

Courtesy, The New-York Historical Society, New York City
*Above.* From *Graham's Magazine*,
November, 1843

*Right.* Silk dress. About 1840-45
Courtesy, Essex Institute, Salem, Mass.

## The Daguerreotype and the Silhouette

The daguerreotype was the first successful permanent photograph. It took its name from one of its inventors, L. J. M. Daguerre, a Frenchman. The process was purchased by the government of France, and, in 1839, given to the world. It was quickly introduced into the United States where for a period of years it practically superseded the work of the portrait painters.

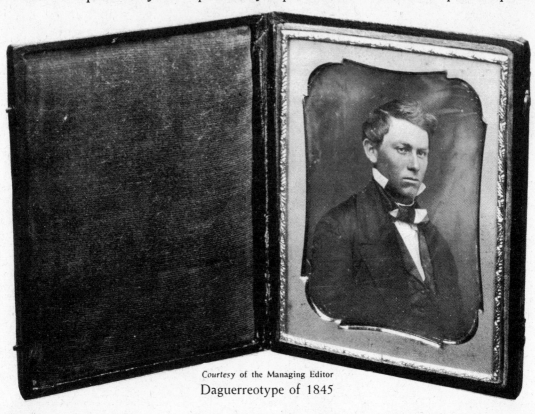

*Courtesy* of the Managing Editor
Daguerreotype of 1845

The silhouettes shown below are of the type known as "hollow cuts," which is to say that the outline was cut from white paper which was then placed over a black cloth background. In the portraits here shown the artist added to the lady's frills with a pen and with the same instrument gave the man some hair and certain decorations about the cravat.

*Courtesy,* Betty and Ralph Sollitt, Westport, Conn.

## The Coast Survey

authorized in 1807 (see page 103), devoted most of its early years to supplying scientific data to mariners, but in 1839 there appeared the first of a magnificent series of charts mapping every detail of our coast line.

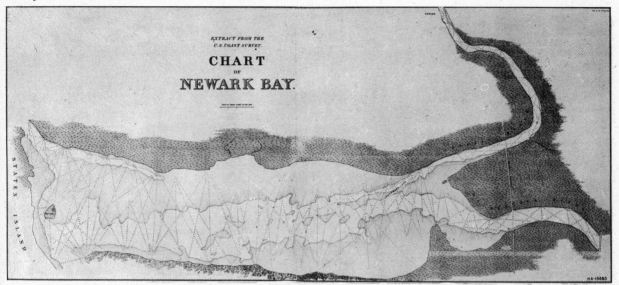

*Courtesy,* U. S. Coast and Geodetic Survey, Washington, D. C.

Chart of Newark Bay, N. J. First Survey Chart published by the Coast Survey. 1839

## Water Supply

With the growth of cities, the old method of securing water from wells or wagons (see page 214) became inadequate. In 1842 New York City completed the Croton Dam from which water was piped a distance of 40 miles to an artificial reservoir located where The New York Public Library now stands.

## CROTON WATER CELEBRATION 1842

*Courtesy,* Eno Collection, The New York Public Library

## The Magnetic Telegraph

The sending of messages by signal stations placed within sight of each other had long been in operation. And as we have seen (see page 291), Samuel F. B. Morse had patented a magnetic telegraph in 1837.

Nathaniel P. Willis, *American Scenery*. 1840

A signal telegraph station on New York Bay in 1838

For seven years Morse experimented with and perfected his instrument. Meanwhile (in 1843), Congress appropriated $30,000.00 for an experimental telegraph line from Washington to Baltimore.

On May 24, 1844, the line was formally opened, and Morse, at the Washington end, ticked off on the instrument (shown *below*) the famous message, "What hath God wrought!"

MORSE MAKING HIS OWN INSTRUMENT.

Samuel Irenaeus Prime, *The Life of Samuel F. B. Morse*. 1875

Courtesy, College of Engineering, Cornell University, Ithaca, N. Y.

Morse Telegraph Instrument of 1844

## Currier & Ives

On Monday evening, Jan. 13, 1840, the steamboat *Lexington* burned in Long Island Sound with an appalling loss of life.

*Awful Conflagration of the Steam Boat*
# LEXINGTON.
*Long Island Sound, on Monday Eve.ᵍ Jan.ʸ 13ᵗʰ 1840: by which melancholy occurrence,* over **120 PERSONS PERISHED.**
*Pub.ᵈ at Sun Office.*

Courtesy, The Print Room, The New York Public Library

Three days later, while the public concern was still at fever pitch, there appeared on the streets of New York a sheet entitled *The Extra Sun*, bearing the picture shown *above* together with a brief statement of the tragedy and a list of the missing persons. News boys hawked the *Extra* throughout the city. Copies went all over the country. This picture was issued by N. Currier and established the fame of the prints which later came to be known by the name of Currier & Ives.

*United States Magazine and Democratic Review*, July, 1843

THE NEWS BOY.

## The Gambling Instinct

was, unfortunately, deeply ingrained in the human make-up. Men sat about grog shops and played cards.

THE CARD PLAYERS.

*United States Magazine and Democratic Review.* November, 1843

Cock fighting was a common pastime, particularly in the South and West—and it too was accompanied by much betting.

*George P. Putnam, The Game Fowl, for the Pit or the Spit.* 1877

Cock Fighting

**Police**

CORNER LOUNGERS.

*United States Magazine and Democratic Review.* August, 1843

Young fellows lounged about the streets or spent their time "whittling." Order was enforced by constables or sheriffs, but in general it was left to the people themselves to maintain the peace or not maintain it.

Not until 1844 did New York City have a regular police department, and for some years thereafter the police wore no uniforms or other distinguishing marks than a star-shaped badge pinned to their coats.

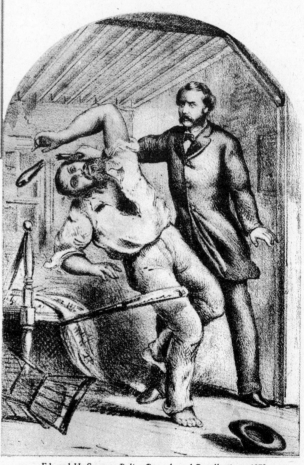

Edward H. Savage, *Police Records and Recollections.* 1873

*Above* we see a policeman of the 1840's making an arrest.

*Opposite* is the badge of Chief of Police Matsell, appointed by the Mayor of New York in 1845.

A. E. Costello, *Our Police Protectors.* 1885

## Virginia in the 1840's

View of the Harbor of NORFOLK and PORTSMOUTH, from Fort Norfolk.

LIFE IN EASTERN VIRGINIA.
The Home of the Planter.

William and Mary College, Williamsburg.

UNIVERSITY OF VIRGINIA, AT CHARLOTTESVILLE.

All illustrations on this page are from Henry Howe, *Historical Collections of Virginia.* 1849

## The Slave Trade

Although Congress had, in 1808, legally put a stop to the importation of slaves, thousands of Negroes were smuggled into Charleston and other southern ports.

*Charleston, South Carolina.*

J. S. Buckingham, *The Slave States of America.* 1842

Meanwhile a large domestic slave trade developed. Dealers in the Upper South bought and assembled surplus slaves which in coffles (groups chained together or otherwise restrained) were marched to the markets in the cotton states, where they brought high prices.

G. W. Featherstonhaugh, *Excursion through the Slave States from Washington on the Potomac to the Frontier of Mexico.* 1844

*Above* and *Opposite.* Coffles of slaves being moved to southern markets.

J. S. Buckingham, *The Slave States of America.* 1842

## The Cotton States

The invention of the cotton gin (see page 61), and the growth of cotton manufacturing, created a vastly increased demand for raw cotton at steadily mounting prices.

PICKING COTTON ON A SOUTHERN PLANTATION.

George A. Sala, *America Revisited.* 1883

The result was increased production of cotton and an increased need for slave labor. From South Carolina and Georgia, cotton planters moved westward into Alabama, Mississippi and Louisiana.

*Right.* View of cotton being pressed into bales for market.

George A. Sala, *America Revisited.* 1883

*Opposite.* Slaves loading a ship with cotton, by torchlight, on the Alabama River in the 1840's.

J. S. Buckingham, *The Slave States of America.* 1842

**Georgia and Alabama**

J. S. Buckingham, *The Slave States of America*, 1842

*Above*. Court House, Medical College and Church at Augusta, Ga. About 1840

*Courtesy, The New-York Historical Society, New York City*
Mobile Harbor in 1842

This vast array of shipping was largely based upon production of cotton in the hinterland.

## New Orleans

The settlement of the country along the Mississippi naturally made New Orleans a great shipping port. *Below* is a view of the river front from opposite the city.

VIEW OF NEW ORLEANS, LOUISIANA, FROM ABOVE THE MIDDLE FERRY

From a colored aquatint, published in 1841, after a painting by William J. Bennett, in the
Macpherson Collection

H. I. Chappelle, *The Baltimore Clipper.* 1930
*Courtesy,* The Macpherson Collection, Marine Research Society, Salem, Mass.

*Opposite.* Auction of estates, pictures and slaves in the Rotunda at New Orleans. About 1840.

J. S. Buckingham, *The Slave States of America.* 1842

## In the Backwoods and Mountains

FELLING TIMBER — WINTER.

Eli Bowen, *The Pictorial Sketch Book of Pennsylvania.* 1854

*Opposite.* A view in western Pennsylvania where settlement was still pushing into the country back of the valleys.

In the mountains of western Virginia, frontier conditions were to persist long after the West was filled up.

Henry Howe, *Historical Collections of Virginia.* 1849

LIFE IN WESTERN VIRGINIA.
The Home of the Mountaineer.

*Left.* A backwoods sawmill and cabins.

From a painting by W. H. Bartlett.
   J. S. Buckingham, *East and West States of America.* 1842

The camp meeting was still the great social and emotional event in the frontier community.

Henry Howe, *Historical Collections of the Great West.* 1852

A CAMP MEETING.

## Ohio

By the 1840's, Ohio was a thriving commonwealth with a population greater than many of the older states.

Courtesy, Stokes Collection, The New York Public Library

*Above.* A view of the river front at Cincinnati in 1838

From a painting by S. Heine.   *Courtesy,* The Western Reserve Historical Society, Cleveland, Ohio

Cleveland. The southwestern corner of the Public Square in 1839

## Indiana,

lying just west of Ohio, was developing into a well-settled state.

PRAIRIE SCENE, INDIANA.

FORDING THE WABASH

From Virginia, North Carolina, Kentucky, Pennsylvania and Ohio came a steady stream of population. The broad prairies were surveyed into farms. Villages grew up. Churches and schools came into being.

In 1840 the Potawatomi Indians who had resided on reservations in Indiana were moved to the west.

Potawatomi Indians on the Wabash River

All pictures on this page are from paintings by George Winter
Courtesy, The William Henry Smith Memorial Library of The Indiana Historical Society, Indianapolis

## Ohio and Indiana Canals

In 1825 the State of Ohio authorized the building of two state canals, connecting the Ohio River and Lake Erie. *Below* we have a view of the Miami & Erie running from Cincinnati through Dayton to Toledo—opened in 1843.

*Ladies' Repository. December, 1842*

The Miami and Erie Canal. 1842

Indiana in 1836 passed a bill carrying appropriations of $13,000,000.00—a sixth of the state's wealth—for canal construction. *Below* we have a view of one these projects, the White Water Canal, as it appeared in 1841—running in front of the North Bend residence of William Henry Harrison (see page 306). The river shown in the foreground is the Ohio.

*Ladies' Repository. July, 1841*

## Into the Mississippi

In the neck of land lying between the junction of the Ohio River with the Mississippi, there came into being in 1837 the town of Cairo, Ill.

J. C. Wild, *Valley of the Mississippi.* 1841.    *Courtesy,* Illinois State Historical Library, Springfield

Cairo, Ill. About 1840

The river front at St. Louis was, by 1840, lined with steamboats loading and unloading freight.

From a lithograph by J. C. Wild.    *Courtesy,* The New-York Historical Society, New York City

Front Street, St. Louis. 1840

Jefferson Barracks, on the Mississippi ten miles south of St. Louis, had been established in 1826.
*Opposite* is a view as it appeared in 1840.

J. C. Wild, *Valley of the Mississippi.* 1841
*Courtesy,* Illinois State Historical Library, Springfield

JEFFERSON BARRACKS.

*Copyright secured according to Act of Congress.*

## On the Great River

From the headwaters and tributaries of the Mississippi, came the produce of the trapping and hunting country, and of the frontier. From the Missouri River came the fur traders—singly in their loaded canoes or in great fleets of Mackinac boats from Fort Union (see page 281) and other posts of the American Fur Company.

From a painting by George Caleb Bingham.
*Courtesy,* The Metropolitan Museum of Art, New York City

Fur Trader descending the Missouri

On the left bank of the Missouri, a few miles above its junction with the Mississippi, stood the village of St. Charles.

J. C. Wild, *Valley of the Mississippi.* 1841
*Courtesy,* Illinois State Historical Library, Springfield

VIEW OF ST. CHARLES.

Flatboats, carrying grain and other products of the upper country, mixed with steamboats on the Mississippi.

The Jolly Flatboatmen

From a painting by George Caleb Bingham.
*Courtesy,* St. Louis Mercantile Library Association, and the City Art Museum, St. Louis, Mo.

## On the Upper Mississippi

Fort Snelling, at the junction of the Minnesota River with the Mississippi, was headquarters for the Sioux Agency and also protected the American Fur Company post at Mendota, across the Minnesota River.

From a painting by Paul Kane
*Courtesy*, Royal Ontario Museum of Archaeology, Toronto, Canada

Fort Snelling. About 1845

## The Mormon Capital

In 1839, the Mormons purchased a site on the Illinois side of the Mississippi, two hundred miles above St. Louis, and there built the city of Nauvoo, designed to be the capital of the faith. By 1845 it had a population of 12,000. The Temple, begun in 1844, was 86 feet wide by 127 feet long, and with a steeple 70 feet high—in all costing about one million dollars to erect.

*Courtesy*, LeRoi C. Snow, Salt Lake City, Utah

Mormon Temple at Nauvoo

*Opposite.*
Nauvoo, as seen by Henry Lewis, the panorama artist, in 1848.

Henry Lewis, *Das Illustrirte Mississippi-thal.* 1854-57

## The Santa Fe Trade

Josiah Gregg, whom we met earlier (see page 205) going down the Santa Fe Trail from Independence to the Great Bend of the Arkansas River and thence to Santa Fe, tried a new route in 1839. Starting from Van Buren, Ark., he followed the Canadian River across the present state of Oklahoma and brought his caravan safely into Santa Fe.

CAMP COMANCHE.

*Opposite.* A view of one of Gregg's encampments. An escort of U. S. Dragoons accompanied him to the 100th meridian, the boundary between the United States and the Republic of Texas.

Josiah Gregg, *Commerce of the Prairies.* 1844

*Opposite.* A prairie dog "town" encountered on the trip.

'DOG TOWN,' OR SETTLEMENT OF PRAIRIE DOGS.

Josiah Gregg, *Commerce of the Prairies.* 1844

To the southward, emigrants to Texas had their troubles with the wild plains Indians.

EMIGRANTS ATTACKED BY THE COMANCHES

H. R. Schoolcraft, *Information respecting Indian Tribes of the United States.* 1851-57

## The Republic of Texas

As we have seen (page 292), Texas achieved its independence in 1836. *Below* is a picture of the Executive Mansion of the Republic of Texas at Houston in 1837.

Courtesy, The Mirabeau B. Lamar Library, University of Texas, Austin

Texas was free but poor. Nor did Mexico recognize the independence of her erstwhile state. In 1842 a Mexican force captured and temporarily held San Antonio. In retaliation Texas undertook a raid into Mexico. *Opposite* we see the Texans crossing the Rio Grande.

MIER EXPEDITION DESCENDING THE RIO GRANDE.

Thomas J. Green, *Journal of the Texian Expedition Against Mier.* 1845

But at Mier, just across the river on the Mexican side, the Texans were captured. Every tenth man was shot, and the remainder were imprisoned.

Thomas J. Green, *Journal of the Texian Expedition Against Mier.* 1845

## The Oregon Trail

Through the expedition of Lewis and Clark (see page 97), the establishment of Astoria (see page 124) and other approaches, the United States exercised a claim over the Oregon Country —jointly with Great Britain. Missionary settlements in the 1830's aroused wide interest in the region, and by 1842 a steady stream of emigrants was rolling westward. The Oregon Trail started from Independence, Mo., the outfitting place for the Santa Fe traders, and for some distance followed the old Santa Fe Trail—splitting off from it and crossing the Kansas River near presentday Topeka, Kansas.

INDEPENDENCE - COURTHOUSE
MISSOURI

Charles A. Dana, *United States Illustrated.* 1853

From the crossing of the Kansas, the trail went northwesterly to the Blue River, and reached the Platte at Grand Island. Prairie fires were common dangers of the Trail.

*Right,* Prairie Fire

From a painting by George Winter
*Courtesy,* The William Henry Smith Memorial Library of The Indiana Historical Society, Indianapolis

Prairie chickens and wild turkeys were everywhere, as were, also, grasshoppers

PRAIRIE CHICKENS.
William E. Webb, *Buffalo Land.* 1874

Howard Stansbury, *Exploration and Survey of the Valley of the Great Salt Lake of Utah in 1849-50*

WILD TURKEY.
William E. Webb, *Buffalo Land.* 1874

## The Oregon Trail (*Continued*)

Having reached the Platte River, the emigrant trains followed that river's southern bank to slightly beyond the fork of the South Platte, where they crossed over and again followed the southern bank of the North Platte. Near present Bridgeport, Neb., they passed between the river and a famous landmark—Court House and Jail Rocks.

Jail Rock                        Court House Rock

CHIMNEY ROCK

A few miles farther up the river, Chimney Rock stood out against the sky.

John C. Fremont, *Report of the Exploring Expeditions of 1842 and 1843-44*

Scotts Bluff

*Courtesy, The Managing Editor*

Another day's march brought them to Scotts Bluff, where the badlands forced them away from the river and through a picturesque pass.

Rattlesnakes abounded

*U. S. Senate, Executive Document, 33rd Congress, 1st Session*

## The Oregon Trail (*Continued*)

Another forty miles brought the emigrant trains to Fort Laramie (see page 285) which, in the view *below*, we see as it appeared to John C. Fremont when he went up the trail in 1842.

FORT LARAMIE

Courtesy, The New York Zoological Society, New York

John C. Fremont, *Report of the Exploring Expeditions of 1842 and 1843-44*

The travelers were now in the foothills of the Rocky Mountains, and Rocky Mountain goats (or sheep) might be seen leaping from cliff to cliff above the Trail.

For another one hundred and forty miles the Trail followed the south side of the North Platte. Then it crossed over and shortly left the Platte, heading for the Sweetwater River at Independence Rock, a landmark on which were carved literally thousands of names. Buffalo had been met with earlier but here was their great range.

NORTH EAST VIEW OF INDEPENDENCE ROCK

*U. S. Senate, Executive Document No. 1, 31st Congress, 2nd Session*

## The Oregon Trail (Continued)

John C. Fremont, *Exploring Expeditions in the Years 1842 and 1843-44*

Devil's Gate

Along the Sweetwater was another interesting landmark, the Devil's Gate. The Trail crossed and recrossed the Sweetwater and from its headwaters was gently led to South Pass on the Continental Divide—west of which the streams ran toward the Pacific.

To avoid the mountainous country directly before them, west of South Pass, the wagon trains generally turned somewhat to the southward at that point, crossing the Green River and—after 1843 when it was established—passing by Bridger's Fort.

South Pass

*Courtesy,* National Park Service, Washington, D. C.

FORT BRIDGER BLACK'S FORK OF GREEN RIVER

Howard Stansbury, *Exploration and Survey of the Valley of the Great Salt Lake of Utah in 1849-50*

## The Oregon Trail (*Continued*)

When Fremont went out on the Trail in 1842, he turned off to the north just beyond South Pass and explored the Wind River Mountains.

VIEW OF THE WIND RIVER MOUNTAINS

John C. Fremont, *Report of the Exploring Expeditions of 1842 and 1843-44*

But the Oregonians were interested in nothing short of Oregon. From Bridger's Fort, they headed for the Snake River, striking it at Fort Hall, a trading post of the Hudson Bay Company.

OUTSIDE VIEW OF FORT HALL, ON SNAKE RIVER OR LEWIS FORK OF THE COLUMBIA RIVER

*U. S. Senate, Executive Document No. 1, 31st Congress, 2nd Session*

*U. S. Senate, Executive Document No. 1, 31st Congress, 2nd Session*

INSIDE VIEW OF FORT HALL

## The Oregon Trail (Continued)

From Fort Hall the Trail followed down the Snake River, crossed it, and came to Fort Boise, another Hudson Bay trading post.

VIEW OF FORT BOISSÉ ON SNAKE RIVER

A few miles beyond Fort Boise the road left the Snake River and went over the mountains to the Columbia River.

INSIDE VIEW OF FORT BOISSÉ ON SNAKE RIVER

Following the south side of the Columbia, the caravans came to the Methodist Mission at the Dalles, a series of falls in the river, beyond which navigation was sometimes possible.

Mission near Dalles

All illustrations on this page are from *U. S. Senate, Executive Document No. 1, 31st Congress, 2nd Session*

## Oregon

From the Dalles there was, by land, a hard pull of ninety miles over the Cascade Range to Fort Vancouver near the mouth of the Willamette River—up which most of the emigrants went, and on which the American Village (Oregon City) grew up.

THE AMERICAN VILLAGE

Sir Henry James Warre, *Sketches in North America.* 1849

At the mouth of the Columbia, where Astoria had stood, were a few houses, but Fort Vancouver (see page 286) was now the great trading post—still operated by the Hudson's Bay Company.

Charles Wilkes, *Narrative of the U. S. Exploring Expedition.* 1844

ST MARY'S AMONG THE FLAT-HEADS.   (See Letter N?2?

In the mountains of eastern Oregon (present Montana), among the Flathead Indians, was the Catholic Mission of St. Mary's, founded by Father DeSmet in 1841.

P. J. DeSmet, *Oregon Missions and Travels over the Rocky Mountains in 1845-46.* 1847

## California

John C. Fremont, several of whose pictures we have seen from the official report of his explorations of 1842, was sent on another expedition in 1843. On Nov. 25, 1843, he was at the Dalles —ready to return home with his party, but instead of going back over the Oregon Trail, he headed south along the eastern base of the Cascade or Sierra Range. On Jan. 13, 1844, his party was at Pyramid Lake with the high, snowbound Sierras to the west and an impassible desert to the east.

Fremont decided to go over the mountains to California, then a part of Mexico. It took the party a month to force its way through the snow-filled passes of the Sierra Range.

J. C. Fremont, *Report of the Exploring Expeditions of 1842 and 1843-44*

THE PYRAMID LAKE.

But on March 6, 1844, Fremont, on the American River in advance of his main party, approached the junction with the Sacramento River, where John Augustus Sutter, a Swiss who had lived in Missouri,

J. C. Fremont, *Report of the Exploring Expeditions of 1842 and 1843-44*

PASS IN THE SIERRA NEVADA OF CALIFORNIA

had the headquarters of a great ranch which he held under a grant from the Mexican government.

ENCAMPMENT ON THE SACRAMENTO,

Charles Wilkes, *Narrative of the U. S. Exploring Expedition.* 1844

*Above* is a view near Sutter's Fort as seen by a U. S. naval officer in 1841.

SUTTERS FORT.

J. M. Letts, *A Pictorial View of California.* 1853

# 9

# MANIFEST DESTINY

## 1845-1848

United States Magazine and Democratic Review, August, 1844

James Knox Polk

In the national election of 1844 the Democratic Party nominated James Knox Polk of Tennessee; the Whigs nominated Henry Clay of Kentucky. Polk won, and on March 4, 1845, became the eleventh President of the United States.

*Right.* Polk proceeding to the Capitol for the inaugural ceremonies.

The Weekly Herald, New York, March 8, 1845

*Left.* Polk proceeding to the White House after the inauguration.

The Weekly Herald, New York, March 8, 1845

## The Texas Question

*The Weekly Herald*, New York, Feb. 8, 1845
Discussing the Texas Question

Since Texas achieved its independence in 1836, there had been a strong sentiment both in the Republic of Texas and in the United States in favor of annexation to the Union. The question was a political issue in the campaign of 1844. Polk came into office committed not only to the annexation of Texas but to the acquisition of California. To Texas he promptly offered the privilege of entering the Union as a State.

## NEW-YORK DAILY TRIBUNE.

BY GREELEY & McELRATH.    OFFICE TRIBUNE BUILDINGS.    FIVE DOLLARS A YEAR.

VOL. V. NO. 75.    NEW-YORK, MONDAY MORNING, JULY 7, 1845.    WHOLE NO. 1319.

**Very Late and Important from Texas.**

By the United States Steamer *Princeton*, which arrived at Annapolis, Maryland, on Thursday afternoon at 2 o'clock, we have Texas dates to the 23d of June—from Washington to June 21, from Galveston to June 23. The news comes to us in a Postscript to The Union. The President of the United States received the official papers at half-past 8 o'clock on Thursday evening by a Special Messenger from Annapolis.

By this news it will be seen that the Annexation Resolution passed both Houses of the Texan Congress unanimously, and that the Senate had also unanimously rejected the proposed Treaty with Mexico. They judge correctly that they would be fools to turn their attention to Mexico, when they have so great a goose to pluck as Uncle Sam. It is stated that Capt. Waggaman had arrived at Washington, Texas, to select posts to be occupied by the U. S. troops. A Resolution had been introduced into both Houses of Congress, requiring the Executive to surrender all posts, navy-yards, barracks, &c. to the authorities of the United States.

Early in July, 1845, a duly constituted convention in Texas accepted the offer made by the United States, and, on December 29, Texas was formally admitted to the Union.

## NEW-YORK DAILY TRIBUNE.

BY GREELEY & McELRATH.    OFFICE TRIBUNE BUILDINGS.    FIVE DOLLARS A YEAR.

VOL. VI. NO. 25.    NEW-YORK, TUESDAY, MAY 12, 1846.    WHOLE NO. 1653.

### THE TRIBUNE.

From our Extra of Yesterday Morning.

## BY ELECTRIC TELEGRAPH!

CABINET AT WASHINGTON CONVENED ON SUNDAY MORNING.

## 50,000 VOLUNTEERS CALLED FOR!

## $10,000,000 TO BE RAISED!

## Additional and important particulars of War with Mexico!!!

REINFORCEMENT OF PT. ISABEL BY CREWS OF U. S. VESSELS FLIRT AND LAWRENCE!!

No Mexicans between Pt. Isabel & Gen. Taylor.

Gen. GAINES again in the Field.

## War with Mexico

Mexico, however, refused to recognize the boundary claims of her former state, and when in 1846 the President ordered the United States Army, under Gen. Zachary Taylor, to the Rio Grande, war between the two countries became a fact.

## Across the Rio Grande

Hostilities began on May 8, 1846, at Palo Alto, a few miles north of the Rio Grande, within the present state of Texas. American cannon won the field.

George Wilkins Kendall, *The War Between the United States and Mexico.* 1851
Battle of Palo Alto, May 8, 1846

The following day, near Resaca de la Palma, also north of the Rio Grande, a more serious battle occurred. The Mexicans were forced to cross the river. Then, for three months, General Taylor remained inactive while futile peace negotiations were carried on and an army assembled.

*The Weekly Herald,* New York, June 27, 1846
Battle of Resaca de la Palma

Negotiations having failed, Taylor, in August, struck into Mexico and, on Sept. 21-23, attacked and captured the city of Monterrey, 100 miles southwest of the Rio Grande.

George Wilkins Kendall, *The War Between the United States and Mexico.* 1851
Battle of Monterrey

## The Conquest of New Mexico

While Gen. Taylor was marking time on the Rio Grande, the Army of the West, under Gen. Stephen W. Kearny, was marching from Fort Leavenworth, on the Missouri River, charged with the conquest of New Mexico and California.

Courtesy, The State Historical Society of Wisconsin, Madison
Fort Leavenworth. About 1849

In addition to units of the regular army, there was a volunteer force and a Mormon battalion, the latter enlisted from the emigrants of that faith encamped on the Missouri River (see page 361). From Fort Leavenworth the route was down the Santa Fe Trail to Bent's Fort on the upper Arkansas River.

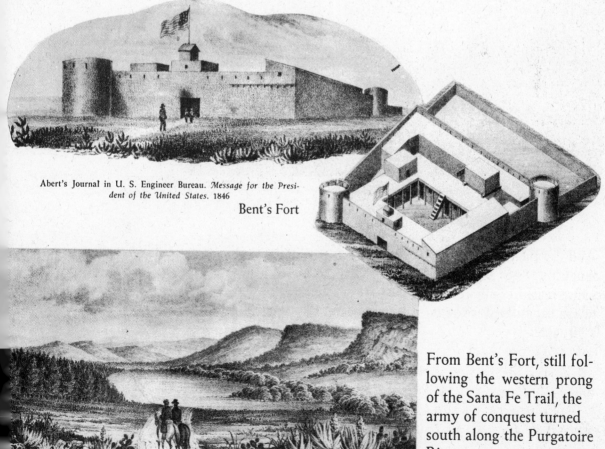

Abert's Journal in U. S. Engineer Bureau. *Message for the President of the United States.* 1846

Bent's Fort

From Bent's Fort, still following the western prong of the Santa Fe Trail, the army of conquest turned south along the Purgatoire River.

*U. S. Senate, Executive Document No. 438, 29th Congress, 1st Session*

Valley of the Purgatory

## To Santa Fe

On down the Trail, Kearny's army crossed the headwaters of the Canadian River.

View on the Canadian

U. S. Senate, Executive Document No. 438, 29th Congress, 1st Session.

It skirted the Sangre de Cristo Range.

View of the Santa Fe Road

U. S. Senate, Executive Document No. 438,
29th Congress, 1st Session.

And, by the middle of August (1846), the advance reached Santa Fe, which capitulated without a struggle.

SANTA FÉ.

U. S. Senate, Executive Document No. 41,
30th Congress, 1st Session.

## Kearny's March for California

At Santa Fe the army was divided. Kearny, with 300 dragoons, started (Sept. 25, 1846) for California.

THE LAST DAY WITH THE WAGONS

Crossing the Rio Grande at Albuquerque, he followed down the western side. Here he met Kit Carson, enroute from California to Washington with despatches from John C. Frémont reporting the successful conquest of California (see page 346).

Kearny decided upon a fast push for California. Sending back 200 of his men and his wagons, he turned toward the headwaters of the Gila River, equipped with pack mules only, and with Carson as his guide. The route took him through the Santa Rita Copper Mine, famous in southwestern history, but then deserted.

VIEW OF THE COPPER MINE

MOUTH OF NIGHT CREEK

Through the narrow valley of Night Creek, with mules already well broken down, the party reached the Gila River—a rough road for even the best conditioned animal.

All pictures on this page are from W. H. Emory, *Notes of a Military Reconnoissance, from Fort Leavenworth to San Diego*. Some of the sketches may have been made by Lt. W. H. Warner, later killed by the Indians in California; others were doubtless made by John Mix Stanley, celebrated painter of western subjects who accompanied the expedition as a draughtsman.

## Along the Gila

A TRIBUTARY OF THE GILA

Crossing and recrossing the Gila, between fantastic mountain ranges, the party pushed westward.

Gigantic cacti were a feature of the scenery.

"Chain of natural spires on the Gila"

PIMOS & COCO MARICOPAS INDIANS

On Nov. 11, the little army arrived at the village of the Pimas, the members of which tribe, together with their neighbors the Coco Maricopas, were peaceful, industrious Indians quite different from the wild Apache which infested the mountains to the eastward.

All pictures on this page are from W. H. Emory, *Notes of a Military Reconnoissance from Fort Leavenworth to San Diego*

## On to California

A dry march of twelve days from the Pima Village brought the party to the junction of the Gila with the Colorado River, which latter they were able to ford.

JUNCTION OF THE GILA & COLORADO RIVERS

W. H. Emory, *Notes of a Military Reconnoissance, from Fort Leavenworth to San Diego*

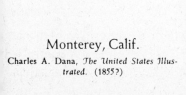

SAN DIEGO

W. H. Emory, *Notes of a Military Reconnoissance, from Fort Leavenworth to San Diego*

After another fearful march of some 150 miles, without adequate water, and a serious brush with a superior force of native Californians, Kearny's reduced and battered "army" was rescued by a relief expedition sent out by Commodore Stockton from San Diego, where the survivors arrived on Dec. 12, 1846.

It was found that after the first successes of Frémont and the naval forces in California, the native Californians had made counter attacks, and in part the conquest had to be made all over again.

Monterey, Calif.

Charles A. Dana, *The United States Illustrated.* (1855?)

## Frémont and the Bear Flag War

President Polk was intent on the acquisition of California. No officer in the U. S. Army knew the route to California better than Capt. John C. Frémont—Captain because of his successful exploring trip to California a year earlier (see page 337). The summer of 1845 saw Frémont, with sixty well-armed men, again on his way to California, where he arrived in December.

The Mexican officials, polite at first, soon ordered Frémont to get out. He refused, but, there still being no tidings of war, moved northward toward Oregon, making a camp on Klamath Lake.

John Charles Frémont, *Memoirs of My Life.* 1887
Frémont on Klamath Lake. 1846

Turning back toward California, Frémont found the American settlers ready to revolt against Mexico. The "California Republic" was declared, the Bear Flag created, and Mexican authority at an end in northern California.

*Right.* The Bear Flag
Courtesy, The Society of California Pioneers, San Francisco

John Charles Frémont, *Memoirs of My Life.* 1887
British and American Men-of-War in Monterey Harbor. 1846

Then, in July, came American naval units with news of the beginning of war. The American flag was raised over Monterey; the southern towns were taken—and Carson was sent east to announce the conquest (see page 343).

Later had come the counterblow of the native Californians—into which Kearny marched from the Gila (see page 345). However, a short time after Kearny's arrival, through the combined efforts of his forces, the naval units and Frémont's forces, the conquest was finally achieved.

## Cooke and the Mormon Battalion

Some three weeks after Kearny started from Santa Fe for California via the Gila, Col. Philip St. George Cooke, with the Mormon Battalion (see page 341) and the wagon train, also started for California—but by a longer sweep to the south where it was hoped the wagons could be got through.

GUADALUPE PASS SONORA

VALLEY LEADING TO SANTA CRUZ SONORA

This route led through the Guadalupe Pass, near the present southern boundary of New Mexico and Arizona. Except for the difficulty of getting through the pass, the road was reasonably passable, and Cooke established a new wagon road to the west.

The Battalion then turned up the dry valley of the Santa Cruz River through the village of Tucson and joined Kearny's route at the Pima Village—arriving in California the latter part of January.

From the Great Bend of the Arkansas to the Colorado River, both Kearny and Cooke had been crossing territory first explored by Coronado 300 years earlier.

Tucson

All illustrations on this page are from John Russell Bartlett, *Personal Narrative of Explorations and Incidents in Texas,* etc. 1854

## Doniphan's Expedition

In December, 1846, the volunteer army which had followed Kearny down the Santa Fe Trail was, after a brief visit to the Navaho, on the march south from Santa Fe—under Col. Alexander W. Doniphan. Following Kearny's route down the Rio Grande, Doniphan crossed to the eastern side at Valverde.

*U. S. Senate Executive Document No. 41, 30th Congress, 1st Session*

Valverde. 1846

From Valverde, the volunteers proceeded down the Jornada del Muerto (the journey of death), a ninety-mile detour away from the river and without water, to El Paso.

*Journal of William H. Richardson. 1848*

The Jornada del Muerto

BATTLE OF BRACITO.

Just north of El Paso, on Christmas Day, 1846, they were engaged by 600 Mexicans in what came to be known as the Batttle of Brazito— and won only after a brisk action.

John Frost, *An Illuminated History of North America.* 1854

## El Paso to Chihuahua

The volunteer army was made up mostly of Missourians, some 850 in all. The men were not accustomed to military discipline and the uniforms were far from uniform.

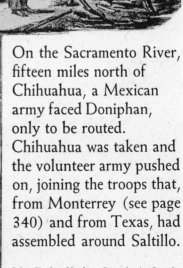

THE VOLUNTEER.

John Taylor Hughes, *Doniphan's Expedition.* 1848

Even Missourians learned something about mules.

John Taylor Hughes, *Doniphan's Expedition.* 1848

Wash day had its picturesque features.

*Journal of William H. Richardson.* 1848

CHARGE OF CAPTAIN REID, AT SACRAMENTO.

On the Sacramento River, fifteen miles north of Chihuahua, a Mexican army faced Doniphan, only to be routed. Chihuahua was taken and the volunteer army pushed on, joining the troops that, from Monterrey (see page 340) and from Texas, had assembled around Saltillo.

John Taylor Hughes, *Doniphan's Expedition.* 1848

## The War in Mexico

From Monterrey (see page 340) Gen. Taylor had advanced toward Saltillo. At a place called Buena Vista, on Feb. 22-23, 1847, the Mexicans, under Santa Anna, attacked in strength, only to suffer a severe defeat. Taylor became a popular hero in the United States, but the further conquest of Mexico was to be in the hands of Gen. Winfield Scott.

*Left*, Battle of Buena Vista

The strategy now shifted to that of a direct attack on Mexico City from the east. On March 9, 1847, Gen. Scott landed an army and a siege train near the port of Vera Cruz. Twenty days later the city capitulated.

*Right*, Bombardment of Vera Cruz

From Vera Cruz the army pushed westward along the National Road toward Mexico City. Santa Anna blocked the way at the mountain pass of Cerro Gordo. Again the Mexican Army was routed (April 18, 1847).

*Left*, Battle of Cerro Gordo

All illustrations on this page are from George Wilkins Kendall, *The War Between the United States and Mexico.* 1851. Kendall was part owner of the New Orleans *Picayune*, had been a prisoner of the Mexicans, and had no love for them. He was with Scott from Vera Cruz to Mexico City.

## To the Halls of the Montezumas

As the army approached the capital of Mexico, it swung around to the south and west of the City. At Contreras, Churubusco and Molino del Rey, battles were fought.

*Right*, Battle of Molino del Rey. Sept. 8, 1847

On Sept. 13, Chapultepec, a seemingly impregnable fortress guarding the western approach to the City, fell to the attacking American Army. The capital city, defenseless, surrendered.

*Left*, Storming of Chapultepec

On Sept. 14, 1847, Gen. Scott entered Mexico City. The war was over and by the Treaty of Guadalupe Hidalgo, ratified the following year, New Mexico and California were ceded to the United States.

*Right*, Gen. Scott's entrance into Mexico City

All illustrations shown on this page are from George Wilkins Kendall, *The War Between the United States and Mexico.* 1851

## Postage Stamps

In 1845 Congress authorized the use of adhesive postage stamps, and on July 1, 1847, the Post Office issued a five-cent stamp (bearing the head of Franklin) and a ten-cent stamp (bearing the head of Washington).

Prior to 1847 postage was, in general, paid in money and the fact of its having been paid indicated either in writing or by a rubber stamp (as *opposite*) on the envelope.

*A Description of United States Postage Stamps, 1847-1939*

There being sometimes a shortage of five-cent stamps, the user would cut a ten-cent stamp into two halves.

Letter postage was at the time five cents per ounce. The result was that many letters required a ten-cent stamp.

## The Sewing Machine

In 1845 Elias Howe, a twenty-six-year-old apprentice to a Boston watchmaker, invented a sewing machine, *below*, which could make 250 stitches a minute—five times the number of the swiftest hand sewer. But there was no demand for the machine, and Howe lacked the financial resources to promote its sale or manufacture.

However, the inventor persisted, and, borrowing money, made a second machine, *below*, which he took to Washington with an application for a patent. On Sept. 10, 1846, the patent (No. 4750) was granted.

Still the American public showed no interest in the invention, and in the autumn of 1846 Howe's brother took a third machine, *opposite*, to England, where the English rights were speedily bought, and the inventor sent for to adapt the machine to sewing leather. Falling out with his English employer, Howe worked his way home by cooking in the steerage. Ultimately his patent was recognized as basic for a universally used machine and Howe drew vast royalties from his competitors.

All illustrations on this page are shown through the *courtesy* of the U. S. National Museum, Washington, D. C.

## Plowing, Sowing, Planting and Cultivating

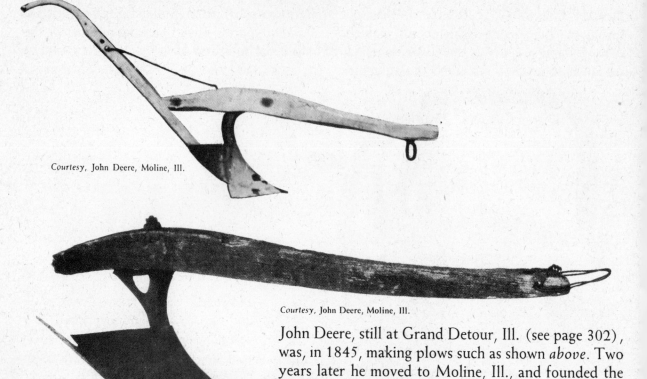

*Courtesy,* John Deere, Moline, Ill.

*Courtesy,* John Deere, Moline, Ill.

John Deere, still at Grand Detour, Ill. (see page 302), was, in 1845, making plows such as shown *above*. Two years later he moved to Moline, Ill., and founded the plant which made the name Deere synonymous with plows.

At Cincinnati on June 4, 1845, Hatch's sowing machine (shown *opposite*) was demonstrated. It sowed wheat, oats and grass, and "with such speed and perfect regularity, as surprised and delighted the numerous spectators".

*The Ohio Cultivator,* June 15, 1845

*Left,* Bachelder's Corn-Planter

*American Agriculturist,* February, 1846

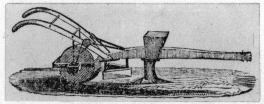

*The Ohio Cultivator,* Nov. 15, 1846

The *above* wheel cultivator, patented by Nathan Ide of Shelby, N. Y., was exhibited at the New York State Fair in 1846.

*American Agriculturist,* August, 1846

Pennock's Seed and Grain Planter planted wheat, rye, corn, oats, etc., and could be so regulated as to drop any required quantity to the acre.

## Reaping and Threshing

Andrew J. Cook, of Delhi, Ind., invented a reaping machine which was considered an improvement over McCormick's and Hussey's reapers because it had a revolving rake that swept the cut grain off the platform and deposited it in a heap suitable for binding.

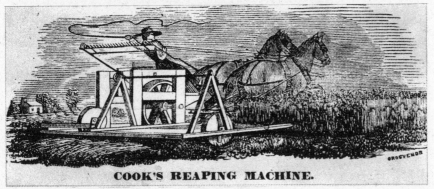

**COOK'S REAPING MACHINE.**

*The Ohio Cultivator, April 15, 1846*

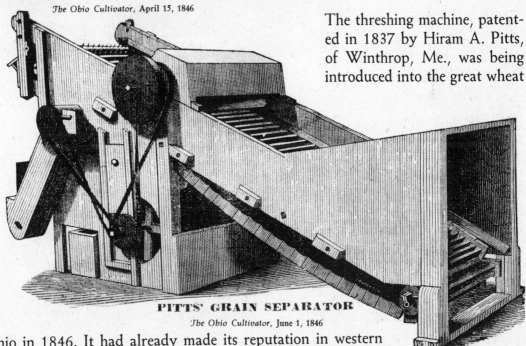

The threshing machine, patented in 1837 by Hiram A. Pitts, of Winthrop, Me., was being introduced into the great wheat

**PITTS' GRAIN SEPARATOR**

*The Ohio Cultivator, June 1, 1846*

region of Ohio in 1846. It had already made its reputation in western New York. In 1847 Pitts moved his factory to Alton, Ill., thus putting himself in the heart of the future grain belt.

Jerome I. Case, a young man from western New York, who had been selling threshing machines in eastern Wisconsin, rented a shop in Racine in 1844 and began building the machines which made the name J. I. Case standard on threshing equipment.

*Courtesy, J. I. Case Company, Racine, Wis.*

J. I. Case Threshing Machine and Horsepower. Manufactured by J. I. Case at Racine in 1848

## In the Barnyard

The farmer and stock raiser was keenly interested in keeping up and improving his livestock. *Opposite* is shown a draft stallion, "Sampson," imported from England in 1841 and in 1845 owned by a man in Columbus, Ohio.

*The Ohio Cultivator, Dec. 15, 1845*

*Right* is a New York prize Durham, with lettering to identify the various "points" considered in judging cattle.

**NAMES OF THE POINTS OF CATTLE.**

EXPLANATIONS.

A—Forehead.
B—Face.
C—Cheek.
D—Muzzle.
E—Neck.
F—Neck vein.
G—Shoulder point.
H—Arm.
I—Shank.
K—Elbow.
L—Brisket or breast.
M—Shoulder.
N—Crops.
O—Loins.
P—Hip or huckle.
Q—Crupper bone or sacrum.
R—Rump or pin bone.
S—Round bone, thurl or whirl.
T—Buttock.
U—Thigh or gasket.
V—Flank.
W—Plates.
X—Back or chine.
Y—Throat.
Z—Hind quarter.
a—Chest.
b—Gambril or hock.

The above outline is the portrait of a New York prize animal of the most approved style of Durham breed. The references illustrating the terms used in describing cattle will prove useful to farmers who are not familiar with the subject, and enable them to understand descriptions that would otherwise be incomprehensible to them. We have observed a great want of this knowledge among farmers, and especially judges at cattle shows. We shall at some other time give instructions respecting the standards or rules by which cattle are judged, with reference to the different breeds and the uses for which they are commended.

*The Ohio Cultivator, Jan. 15, 1846*

*Below* is a cross between the Woburn and Berkshire hog—considered "as perfect a specimen of the pork genus" as the editor of *The Ohio Cultivator* had seen.

*The Ohio Cultivator, Nov. 1, 1845*

*The Ohio Cultivator, Jan. 1, 1846*

Dorking Fowls, shown *above*, were being brought in from England and were said to be "decidedly the best breed for laying."

**New England in the 1840's**

VIEW OF NEWBURYPORT,

The building with the cupola, in the center of the picture *above* is the Putnam Free School, dedicated in 1848.

*Above*, The Water Celebration on Boston Common, Oct. 25, 1848, on the opening of the public water supply from Lake Cochituate (Long Pond). An ode written by James Russell Lowell for the occasion was sung by the school children.

New Haven, Conn., from Ferry Hill. 1848. East Rock is seen on the right.

**New York City**

*Courtesy, Stokes Collection, The New York Public Library*

Manhattan Island from Fort Columbus, Governor's Island. Castle Garden may be seen at the left between the two ships.

VAN AMBURGH & CO? TRIUMPHAL CAR.

PASSING THE ASTOR HOUSE, APRIL 20TH 1846.

*Courtesy, Eno Collection, The New York Public Library*

While P. T. Barnum was struggling to fame with the exhibition of Tom Thumb and othe[r] freaks, Van Amburgh, who had been in the show business since the 1820's, held the public gaze

**New York City**

From a drawing by J. W. Hill. 1848

New York from the steeple of St. Paul's Church. Barnum's Museum may be seen on the left. In the middle foreground just above the trees is the Daguerrian Miniature Gallery of Mathew B. Brady, later famous for his photographs of the Civil War.

Despite the *above* "proposal", it was twenty years before New York had an elevated railway.

Both illustrations on this page are shown through the *courtesy* of the Stokes Collection, The New York Public Library

**Baltimore in 1847**

VIEW OF THE CITY OF BALTIMORE

Courtesy, The New-York Historical Society, New York City

**Pittsburgh About 1848**

*Right*. Market and Court-house.

Courtesy, Historical Society of Western
Pennsylvania, Pittsburgh

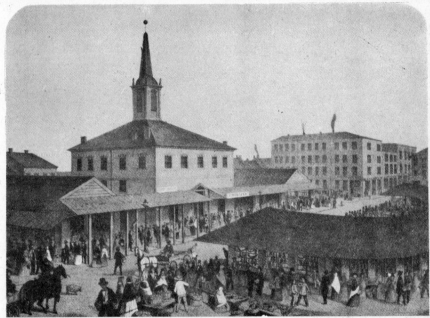

**Athens, Ga.
About 1845**

The view is from Carr's
Hill, showing buildings
of the University of
Georgia in background
and the terminus of the
Georgia Railway in
right foreground.

From a painting by George Cook
Courtesy, The University of Georgia,
Athens

## The Mormon Migration

As we have seen (page 327), the Mormons had built their capital city at Nauvoo, Ill. But even before the Temple was completed, Joseph Smith, the Prophet, was murdered by an unsympathetic mob, and the Mormons forced to leave Illinois. Leaving Nauvoo in the cold first weeks of 1846, they moved slowly across Iowa—seeking a new home somewhere in the West.

*Courtesy,* Church of Jesus Christ of Latter Day Saints, Salt Lake City

Mormons on Mosquito Creek, Iowa. 1846

At the site of future Council Bluffs, Iowa, they reached the Missouri River. *Below* is a view of the village and river as they appeared at the time.

On the western banks of the Missouri, where Omaha now stands, they established "Winter Quarters." Here they halted, living in wagons, tents and dugouts. From those assembled here, the Army recruited the Mormon Battalion which Col. Cooke marched from Santa Fe to California (see pages 341 and 347).

Frederick Piercy, *Route From Liverpool to Great Salt Lake Valley.* 1855

But the main body, with the coming of Spring 1847, again pushed westward, crossing the Loup River and following the northern bank of the Platte and North Platte—opposite the old Oregon Trail (see pages 330, 331, 332). At Fort Laramie their route joined the Oregon Trail, which they followed as far as the newly established Fort Bridger (see page 333), from which point they proceeded directly over the mountains to the Valley of Great Salt Lake, where they established a new Zion.

rederick Piercy, *Route From Liverpool to Great Salt Lake Valley.* 1855

Loup Fork Ferry

## The Upper Mississippi

There was no state of Minnesota in 1848, nor even a Territory of that name. The region, which successively had been a part of Michigan Territory, of Wisconsin Territory and of Iowa Territory, was then "unattached"—until the creation of Minnesota Territory in 1849. But there was a place called St. Paul's.

Henry Lewis, *Das Illustrirte Mississippithal*. 1854-57

### St. Paul (Minnesota). 1848

The view above was made in 1848 by Henry Lewis, an Englishman who had come to St. Louis about 1836. Between 1846 and 1848 Lewis planned and made a panorama of the Mississippi River, which he exhibited in the eastern United States and in Europe. Settling down in Germany he arranged for the publication of a great number of his illustrations in a book, *Das Illustrirte Mississippithal*, from which (the only source in most cases) the *above* and many other prints in the present volume are taken.

*Smithsonian Miscellaneous Collections*, Vol. 87, No. 3 (1932-1933)

The *above* picture shows an incident that occurred at Wabasha Prairie (Winona, Minn.) in June, 1848. The Winnebago Indians, being ordered to a new reservation, were invited by the Sioux to stay at Wabasha Prairie. Capt. Seth Eastman, then commanding at Fort Snelling, came down the river with a detachment of soldiers and forced the Winnebago to continue on their way. Eastman made the picture, and Lewis was present when the incident occurred—being then engaged in making his panorama as mentioned above. A number of other pictures by Eastman appear in the present volume, taken either from individual paintings or from Schoolcraft's *History, Condition, and Prospects of the Indian Tribes*, in the illustration of which Eastman spent five years.

## Down the Mississippi

Henry Lewis, *Das Illustrirte Mississippithal.* 1854-57

*Above.* Mouth of the Wisconsin River as seen by Lewis in 1848. Wisconsin was that year admitted as a state.

*Right.*
"Fishing on the Mississippi," by George Caleb Bingham, who as a boy was taken to Franklin, Mo., by his family and whose brush has given us inimitable views of the life along the Mississippi and Missouri from about 1830 to 1870.

Courtesy, William Rockhill Nelson Gallery of Art, Kansas City, Mo.

On the Iowa side of the river was the village of Dubuque, growing on the site of the lead mines worked by old Julien Dubuque fifty years earlier. Iowa was admitted to the Union in 1846.

Dubuque, Iowa, in 1848

Henry Lewis, *Das Illustrirte Mississippi-thal.* 1854-57

## Down the Mississippi with Henry Lewis

The night of July 26, 1848, the artist, descending the river in a canoe, camped near Muscatine, Iowa, *opposite*. In his Journal (published by the Minnesota Historical Society) Lewis stated that the soil was very favorable but there were few settlers, and they were largely along the river.

At Fort Madison, *right*, Lewis found a thriving town of near 2000 people. A few miles farther down the river, on the Illinois side, he visited the recently deserted Mormon capital of Nauvoo, his view of which is shown on page 327.

Some miles above the mouth of the Des Moines River was the village of Keokuk, named for the Sauk warrior who superseded Black Hawk after the uprising of 1832 (see pages 231 and 278). Keokuk, himself, however, had been removed to Kansas in 1845 and, at about the time Lewis painted the picture *opposite*, Keokuk, the Indian, died a hopeless drunkard.

All illustrations shown on this page are from Henry Lewis, *Das Illustrirte Mississippibal*. 1854-57

### *Huckleberry Finn's* Mississippi

When Henry Lewis made the sketch of Hannibal, Mo., shown *opposite*, Samuel Clemens (Mark Twain) was living there— a boy of thirteen. The vicinity of Hannibal is the setting for the escapades chronicled in *Huckleberry Finn* and *Tom Sawyer.*

Henry Lewis, *Das Illustrirte Mississippithal.* 1854-57

George Caleb Bingham was, at the same time, immortalizing the life that daily floated down the great river. *Opposite* is a print from his painting entitled "Raftsmen Playing Cards."

*Courtesy*, City Art Museum, St. Louis, Mo.

The engines of the river steamboats were fed from wood, cut and piled on the river banks. *Opposite* we see, from Lewis' sketch, a Mississippi steamer tied up at the shore and men carrying wood aboard.

Henry Lewis, *Das Illustrirte Mississippithal.* 1854-57

## Approaching the Mouth of the Missouri

On the eastern side of the Mississippi, a few miles above the entrance of the Missouri River, from the west, stood the promising town of Alton, Ill., free state competitor of the slave city of St. Louis. It will be recalled that Hiram Pitts established his threshing machine factory at this place in 1847 (see page 355).

Henry Lewis, *Das Illustrirte Mississippi-thal.* 1854-57

Alton, Ill. 1848

All too often the Mississippi steamboats were wrecked on snags or sand bars. *Opposite,* from Bingham's brush, we see a wrecked steamer in the river and crewmen guarding the cargo piled on shore.

Courtesy, The State Historical Society of Missouri, Columbia

The entrance of the Missouri from the west was a busy spot. Steamboats, flatboats, and other craft vied with each other for the channel.

Mouth of the Missouri

Henry Lewis, *Das Illustrirte Mississippi-thal.* 1854-57

## The Lower Mississippi

Passing by St. Louis, which we have viewed recently (see page 325) we have another view of Cairo, Ill., at the mouth of the Ohio River.

Cairo, Ill. 1848

Another 150 miles down the river, as the crow flies, but much farther by the winding Mississippi, the voyager of 1848 came to Memphis, backdoor of Tennessee. It is interesting to compare Lewis' view with that of Lesueur (page 275) made nineteen years earlier.

Memphis, Tenn. 1848

At the mouth of the Yazoo River was Vicksburg, thriving in the midst of one of the richest cotton-growing sections of the South.

Vicksburg, Miss. 1848

All illustrations shown on this page are from Henry Lewis, *Das Illustrirte Mississippthal.* 1854-57

## The Cotton Kingdom

From Vicksburg to Baton Rouge, cotton was king in the 1840's. *Opposite* we see a cotton plantation along the banks of the lower Mississippi.

*Right* is a view of Natchez from the river. Note the bales of cotton piled on the boat in the left foreground. Along the river's bank may be seen Natchez-Under-The-Hill, notorious in steamboat days for its gambling dens, brothels and other iniquities. On page 275 we had a view of Natchez-On-The-Hill, in 1835.

*Left* we see Baton Rouge as sketched by one of Lewis' assistants in 1848. Next, and last, of the great cities down the river was New Orleans, which we have seen in 1841 (page 320).

All illustrations shown on this page are from Henry Lewis, *Das Illustrirte Mississippithal*. 1854-57

## The Presidential Campaign of 1848

The Whigs, victors in 1840 but defeated in 1844, put forward as their candidate for the Presidency, Gen. Zachary Taylor, the hero of Buena Vista (see page 350). The Democrats nominated Lewis Cass.

From a painting by George Caleb Bingham. *Courtesy*, Boatmen's National Bank of St. Louis, Mo.

Stump Speaking

Stump speaking, which had become a recognized adjunct of political campaigning, played its part in the impending election.

County Election

From a painting by George Caleb Bingham. *Courtesy*, St. Louis Mercantile Library Association, and the City Art Museum of St. Louis

## The Verdict of the People

From a painting by George Caleb Bingham
*Courtesy*, The Boatmen's National Bank of St. Louis, Mo.

When the electoral votes were counted, Taylor had 163, and Cass 127. The Whigs had won.

Zachary Taylor

From a portrait by G. P. A. Healy
*Courtesy*, Corcoran Gallery of Art,
Washington, D. C.

*Opposite.* A view of Zachary Taylor's plantation on the Mississippi River, forty miles above Baton Rouge.

Henry Lewis, *Das Illustrirte Mississippi-thal.* 1854-57

# 10
# GOLD
## 1848-1853

Alex Forbes, *California: A History of Upper and Lower California.* 1839

The Mission of San Francisco

The Spring of 1848 opened in its usual languid manner in the newly occupied and very distant territory of California. Pastoral life went on around the old mission centers.

Ranch hands found their greatest excitement in contests with grizzly bears.

J. W. Revere, *A Tour of Duty in California.*
1849

A RANCHERO FEAT

SUTTER'S FORT - NEW HELVETIA.

There was no unusual activity even at Sutter's Fort on the American River—but Sutter and a few others knew what James Marshall had found, while up the river making a mill dam.

J. W. Revere, *A Tour of Duty in California.*
1849

## Gold! Gold!

Then about the middle of May the secret leaked out. Gold had been found on the American River! The first discovery—that by Marshall—had been made in January, 1848, near the present city of Coloma. With the secret out, there was a rush from the nearby California towns to the gold field. Ranch hands left their cattle; seamen deserted their ships; storekeepers left their shops, their clerks had already gone.

ON THE ROAD TO THE MINES—ENCAMPING FOR THE NIGHT.

LIFE AT THE "DIGGINS"—SUPPER TIME.

The towns were deserted; ships were stranded in the harbors; every able-bodied man was at the mines or on his way to them. Thousands of dollars in "dust" were being washed out of the gravel daily.

W. R. Ryan, del.

GOLD ROCKER—WASHING PAN—GOLD BORER.

Soon it was discovered that the whole region between the Sacramento and San Joaquin rivers on the west and the Sierras on the east was one great gold mine. Fortunes were to be had for the taking.

All illustrations shown on this page are from William Redmond Ryan, *Personal Adventures in Upper and Lower California in 1848-49.* 1850

## The News Travels

By letters, by word of mouth and by official reports the news of the discovery of gold in California travelled east. In a message to Congress on Dec. 5, 1848, Polk, the retiring President, included a report on the discovery. Newspapers throughout the country repeated the sensational news.

**WEDNESDAY MORNING, DECEMBER 6.**

### The Gold Fever.

The California gold fever is approaching its crisis. We are told that the new region that has just become a part of our possessions, is El Dorado after all.— Thither is now setting a tide that will not cease its flow until either untold wealth is amassed, or extended beggary is secured. By a sudden and accidental discovery, the ground is represented to be one vast gold mine.— Gold is picked up in pure lumps, twenty-four carats fine. Soldiers are deserting their ranks, sailors their ships, and every body their employment, to speed to the region of the gold mines. In a moment, as it were, a desert country, that never deserved much notice from the world, has become the centre of universal attraction. Every body, by the accounts, is getting money at a rate that puts all past experience in that line far in the shade. The stories are evidently thickening in interest, as do the arithmetical calculations connected with them in importance. Fifteen millions have already come into the possession of *somebody*, and all creation is going out there to fill their pockets with the great condiment of their diseased minds.

... no doubt in a fair way

### Daily National Intelligencer.

WASHINGTON; WEDNESDAY, DECEMBER 6, 1848.

#### · PRESIDENT's ANNUAL MESSAGE.

... union for ship building, owned by the United States, it must become our great western naval depot.

It was known that mines of the precious metals existed to a considerable extent in California at the time of its acquisition. Recent discoveries render it probable that these mines are more extensive and valuable than, was anticipated. The accounts of the abundance of gold in that Territory are of such an extraordinary character as would scarcely command belief, were they not corroborated by the authentic reports of officers in the public service, who have visited the mineral district, and derived the facts which they detail from personal observation. Reluctant to credit the reports in general circulation as to the quantity of gold, the officer commanding our forces in California visited the mineral district in July last, for the purpose of obtaining accurate information on the subject. · His report to the War Department of the result of his examination, and the facts obtained on the spot, is herewith laid before Congress. When he visited the country, there were about four thousand persons engaged in collecting gold. There is every reason to believe that the number of persons so employed has since been augmented. The explorations already made warrant the belief that the supply is very large, and that gold is found at various places in an extensive district of country.

Information received from officers of the navy and other sources, though not so full and minute, confirm the accounts

### Daily Evening Transcript.

PUBLISHED BY DUTTON & WENTWORTH, PRINTED TO THE STATE, NO. 37 CONGRESS STREET, BOSTON, MASSACHUSETTS, AT FOUR DOLLARS PER ANNUM.

VOL. XIX.      BOSTON, THURSDAY EVENING, DECEMBER 14, 1848.      5641.

FOR CALIFORNIA. The company of men who are to start from Boston for California, have regularly organized themselves and adopted rules for their government, &c. Each member is to furnish $300 capital, and to devote his energies to the interests of the company. They bind themselves not to gamble or use intoxicating liquors, on peril of expulsion. The government consists of a president, vice president, and eight directors, chosen for one year, and to have charge of the funds and property of the association. Eighty individuals have already enrolled themselves as members.

### Late and Interesting from California.

#### More of the Gold Region.

Among the passengers by the Titi from Vera Cruz was an American gentleman, Mr. James Cutting, who is direct from California. He left San Francisco on the 11th of October and proceeded to ... rated. The largest piece of native gold Mr. Cutting has known to be found weighed thirteen pounds. He was not so fortunate as to pick it up. He has known men well who have picked up $1800, $1500 and $1200 in a single day, but those were extreme cases of good fortune. The average ... is very much smaller than ...

battles, form codes of laws, wealth, and entirely regenerate country—the *man* has nothing ter at all. The harum-scarum peditions to Strasburg ... handle a score of ... ...

### THE COURIER.

#### CHARLESTON:

WEDNESDAY MORNING, DEC'R. 20, 1848.

#### CALIFORNIA MEETING.

☞ All those determined to go to California, and wish to go via Chagres from this port, are requested to meet at Baker's Exchange Coffee House, (up stairs) *This Evening*, at half past 7 o'clock. The object of the meeting is to ascertain if a sufficient number can be raised to secure a vessel for the voyage, to sail between the 1st and 5th of next month.      TEN WHO ARE GOING.

D 20

Gentlemen.—I have received from Col. A. H. Gladden, lately commanding the Palmetto Regiment, the books,

The "gold rush" was on: By sea with a short land trip through Central America; overland by wagons, pack horse or on foot; by organized companies; by families; or singly.

## Forty-Nine

The overlanders went by many routes, but by far the greater number converged on the already known Oregon Trail (see pages 330-335).

KANSAS

*Courtesy*, Stokes Collection, The New York Public Library

Independence, Mo., had given way to the nearer village of Kansas (present Kansas City) as an outfitting and starting point up the route that now came to be called The California Trail.

Weston, on the Missouri side of the Missouri River, about opposite Fort Leavenworth, was another outfitting and starting point for companies that came thus far by river boats.

*Courtesy*, State Historical Society, Madison, Wis.

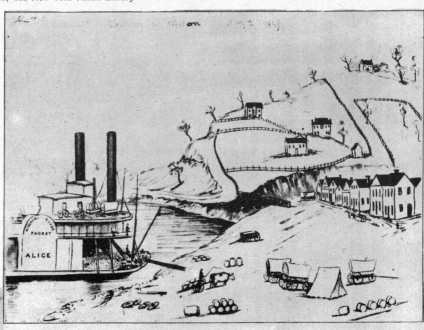

LANDING AT WESTON

Camp at St. Joseph (Black Snake Hill) Mo.

The Washington City Company, of which J. G. Bruff was captain, went on up the Missouri River to St. Joseph and even there found so many wagons ahead of them at the ferry that they travelled still farther up the river, looking for a place to cross.

From a sketch by J. G. Bruff
*Courtesy*, The Henry E. Huntington Library and Art Gallery, San Marino, Calif.

## Heading for the Platte

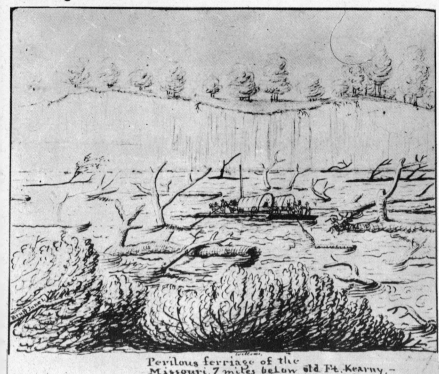

Perilous ferriage of the
Missouri, 7 miles below old Ft. Kearny.-
June 1.2.3.84th-1849, (during a great freshet)

From a sketch by J. G. Bruff
*Courtesy*, The Henry E. Huntington
Library and Art Gallery, San Marino,
Calif.

Near presentday Nebraska City Bruff's company found a ferry that took their 64 men, 16 wagons, 84 mules and 14 horses across the snag-filled Missouri.

Bruff's journals and sketches were published in 1944 with an introduction and voluminous notes by Georgia Willis Read and Ruth Gaines under the title of *Gold Rush* (two volumes, Columbia University Press).

The road from even this high point on the Missouri to the Oregon Trail on the Platte River was crowded with wagons. The high banks of some of the streams gave the outfits plenty of trouble.

*Courtesy*, State Historical Society, Madison, Wis.
"Letting the Wagons down a Declivity"

But at night the camping grounds frequently resounded with a new popular song by Stephen Collins Foster—

It rain'd all night de day I left,
De wedder it was dry;
The sun so hot I froze to def,
Susanna, don't you cry.

Original music of "Oh! Susanna" as published in 1848
*Courtesy*, The Foster Hall Collection, The University of Pittsburgh, Pa.

## Up The Platte

From the various starting places on the Missouri the gold seekers converged on the south side of the Platte River, somewhere between the present cities of Grand Island and Kearny, across from which latter place the Army was erecting Fort Kearny to protect the emigrants. Thence the route led up the south side of the Platte to a point somewhat beyond the forks of the river, where the wagons forded the South Platte and crossed over to the south side of the North Platte.

FORDING THE PLATTE

Courtesy, State Historical Society, Madison, Wis.

By this time buffalo had generally come into view, adding sport and food for the weary travellers.

H. R. Schoolcraft, *Information respecting Indian Tribes of the United States.* 1851-57

Cholera was taking its toll on the Trail. Just beyond the ford of the Platte, Bruff copied the death notice *opposite*

In memory of
Daniel Maloy
of Gallitin Co. Ill.
Died June 18th
1849, of Cholera
Aged 48

Platforms upon which the Indians placed their dead (beyond the reach of wolves) were seen along the way.

H. R. Schoolcraft, *Information respecting Indian Tribes of the United States.* 1851-57

## The California Trail

On up the Platte crept the heavy wagons—past Fort Laramie, no longer a trading house of the American Fur Company (see pages 285 and 332), but now a United States military post.

U. S. Senate, *Executive Document No. 1, 31st Congress, 2nd Session*

Fort Laramie

T. Green,
of Cholera,
Jackson Co., Mo.
20, June

Cholera still raged. Bruff copied many notices of deaths, among them that of T. Green.

MIDNIGHT SERENADE ON THE PLAINS.

Wolves serenaded the campers at night.

William E. Webb, *Buffalo Land.* 1874

SCENE IN THE BLACK HILLS  BITTER CREEK VALLEY

West of Fort Laramie the route lay through what were then called the Black Hills, but later named the Laramie Mountains.

Howard Stansbury, *Exploration and Survey of the Valley of the Great Salt Lake of Utah*

## The Crossing of the Platte

CROSSING OF THE PLATTE MOUTH OF DEER CREEK.

Howard Stansbury, *Exploration and Survey of the Valley of the Great Salt Lake of Utah*

Some one-hundred miles, according to the winding of the road, beyond Fort Laramie the Trail crossed to the north side of the Platte—at the mouth of Deer Creek and generally by ferry, the approach to which was littered with discarded wagons, stoves, trunks, food, everything imaginable.

Then on to the Sweetwater, through South Pass, and either by way of Bridger's Fort or by a shorter road called Sublette's Cutoff, the California road followed the Oregon Trail (see pages 332-334) to a point southeast of Fort Hall, where the California Trail turned westward toward the Humboldt River.

From a sketch by J. G. Bruff. *Courtesy,* The Henry E. Huntington Library and Art Gallery, San Marino, Calif.

CANTONMENT LORING

From a sketch by J. G. Bruff. *Courtesy,* The Henry E. Huntington Library and Art Gallery, San Marino, Calif.

Bruff, however, rode up to Camp Loring, a new military post near Fort Hall, to get information concerning the best route to California.

## Lassen's Road

Bruff's decision, as captain of the Washington City Company, was, after reaching the Humboldt, to follow Lassen's Road, a long detour to the north, rather than to continue down the Humboldt and cross the mountains opposite Sacramento.

THE RABBIT-HOLE SPRINGS,
(Wells in a desert)

Courtesy, The Henry E. Huntington Library and Art Gallery, San Marino, Calif

But even Lassen's Road brought its disasters, as the *above* sketch by Bruff all too vividly shows.

Winter overtook the long line of wagons in the mountains. Oxen and mules fell by the road side; wagons were abandoned; men, women and children struggled on afoot.

Grizzly Bear

*Courtesy*, New York
Zoological Society

Courtesy, The Henry E. Huntington Library and Art Gallery, San Marino, Calif.

Bruff stayed with the wagons; existed on long-dead oxen; avoided grizzly bears; considered eating an Indian; and finally stumbled into Lassen's Ranch more dead than alive.

LASSEN'S RANCHO

From a sketch by J. G. Bruff. *Courtesy*, The Henry E. Huntington Library and Art Gallery, San Marino, Calif.

The ranch house of Peter Lassen, who had come to California in about 1840, stood on the Sacramento River some 125 miles north of Sutter's Fort.

## From Bridger's Fort to Great Salt Lake

Many of those bound for California left the Oregon Trail at Bridger's Fort (in present southwestern Wyoming) and proceeded through the new Mormon city of Salt Lake by southern routes.

FIRST VIEW OF GREAT SALT LAKE VALLEY  FROM A MOUNTAIN

*Opposite* we see the road as it wound through the Wasatch Mountains.

And here are two views of Salt Lake City as it appeared in the summer of 1849.

STREET IN GREAT SALT LAKE CITY – LOOKING EAST

BOWERY, MINT & PRESIDENT'S HOUSE GREAT SALT LAKE CITY

Few of the Mormons went to the gold fields, but they did a lucrative business re-outfitting the wagon trains that passed through.

All illustrations shown on this page are from Howard Stansbury, *Exploration and Survey of the Valley of the Great Salt Lake of Utah*

## Through Death Valley

LEAVING DEATH VALLEY. — THE MANLY PARTY ON THE MARCH AFTER LEAVING THEIR WAGONS.

Some of the Forty-Niners who passed through Salt Lake City proceeded southward to the Old Spanish Trail (running between Santa Fe and Los Angeles) and reached California in that way. Others cut across the desert, and, after fearful suffering, won through Death Valley—or left their bones and those of their oxen on the desert.

Both illustrations on this page are from William Lewis Manly, *Death Valley in 49.* 1894

PULLING THE OXEN DOWN THE PRECIPICE.

## The Southern Route of '49

The Missouri River was not the only gathering place for the gold seekers. The Spring of 1849 found many companies organizing in the vicinity of Fort Smith on the Arkansas River. From this point a military escort under Capt. R. B. Marcy guided them across presentday Oklahoma to Santa Fe—following in general the Canadian River and the route taken by Gregg in 1839 (see page 328).

From a sketch by H. B. Mollhausen. *U. S. Senate, Executive Document No. 78, 33rd Congress, 2nd Session*

Fort Smith

VIEW OF SANTA FE AND VICINITY FROM THE EAST

*House, Executive Document No. 45, 31st Congress, 1st Session*

## The Southern Route to California

From Santa Fe the Forty-Niners who came across from Fort Smith followed the routes that Kearny and Cooke took in 1846 (see pages 343-345 and 347) and for the same reasons, namely, whether they travelled by pack mule or by wagon.

JUNCTION OF THE GILA AND COLORADO RIVERS. LOOKING UP THE GILA.

John Russell Bartlett, *Personal Narrative of Explorations and Incidents in Texas, etc.* 1854

LOS ANGELES

Courtesy, Stokes Collection, The New York Public Library.

Arriving in California at Los Angeles, they hurried northward to the mines.

## The California Gold Mines

*Left.* The Stanislaus Mine

William Redmond Ryan, *Personal Adventures in Upper and Lower California in 1848-49.* 1850

*Right.* Golddiggings on the Mokelumne River in California.

Charles A. Dana, *The United States Illustrated.* (1855?)

Mormon Bar, on the North Fork, American River.

J. M. Letts, *A Pictorial View of California.* 1853

**Hunting For Gold**

Placer Ville
(Hang Town).

J. M. Letts, *A Pictorial View of
California*. 1853

The Yankees House at
Hang Town.

"So much lower than their
heads they had to crawl in
and double up like jack
knives."

J. M. Letts, *A Pictorial View of
California*. 1853

*Opposite* we see "Old
Pete" Lassen's party resting during a hunt for gold
in the northern fields. The
man stretched out with his
arm over his head is Las-
sen. Bruff, who made the
picture, sits by the tree on
the right. For our identifi-
cations we are indebted to
*Gold Rush*, edited by
Georgia Willis Read and
Ruth Gaines.

*Courtesy*, The Henry E. Huntington
Library and Art Gallery, San Marino,
Calif.

**Traders, Gamblers, Prospectors**

### Trading Post in the Mines.

William Redmond Ryan, *Personal Adventures in Upper and Lower California in 1848-49.* 1850

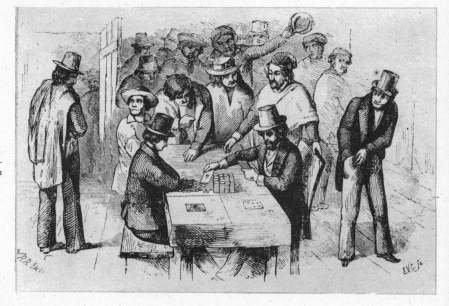

### Gambling Scene in San Francisco.

William Redmond Ryan, *Personal Adventures in Upper and Lower California in 1848-49.* 1850

### Between Sacramento, and the Mines.

J. M. Letts, *A Pictorial View of California.* 1853

## Sacramento and San Francisco In '49

**POST OFFICE, SAN FRANCISCO, CALIFORNIA.**

A FAITHFUL REPRESENTATION OF THE CROWDS DAILY APPLYING AT THAT OFFICE FOR LETTERS AND NEWSPAPERS.

**SACRAMENTO CITY Cᴬ**

FROM THE FOOT OF J. STREET.

SHOWING I. J. & K. STˢ WITH THE SIERRA NEVADA IN THE DISTANCE.

**SAN-FRANCISCO**

1849.

DRAWN ON THE SPOT BY HENRY FIRKS, FOR

W. H. JONES, ESQ.

OF SAN-FRANCISCO U.S.

In 1850 California was admitted to the Union as a State.

All illustrations shown on this page are through the *courtesy* of the Stokes Collection, The New York Public Library

## Greater Distance, Greater Speed

The settlement of California and the demand for speed in getting there brought a marked development in the construction of stage coaches and the building of clipper ships. In 1826 the firm of Abbot, Downing & Co. began making stage coaches which were widely used where other transportation was lacking. In 1847 the firm was dissolved, the Abbots and the Downings setting up separate businesses. Nonetheless, the stage coach shown *opposite*, made in 1848 and now housed in the Smithsonian Institution, is an Abbot-Downing, the body having been made by the Abbots and the gear by the Downings.

*Courtesy*, Smithsonian Institution, Washington, D. C.

Clipper ships were making records that steamboats of the day could not equal. *Opposite* is the *Surprise*, 1850.

*Courtesy*, The Mariners' Museum, Newport News, Va.

The *Staghound*, built by Donald McKay at East Boston in 1850, was 226 feet over all and of 1354 tons burden.

*Courtesy*, Peabody Museum of Salem, Mass.

## Riot, Train Wreck, Fire

William C. Macready, an English tragedian, was playing at the Astor Place Opera House on May 10, 1849. Admirers of Edwin Forrest, an American actor, gathered outside to protest. A riot followed in which many casualties occurred. Americans just did not like the English in 1849.

GREAT RIOT AT THE ASTOR PLACE OPERA HOUSE, NEW YORK.

Courtesy, Eno Collection, The New York Public Library

ACCIDENT ON THE BALTIMORE & OHIO RAILWAY

Alfred Bunn, *Old England and New England.* 1853

On the Baltimore & Ohio Railroad, along the Cheat River, west of Cumberland, Md., two passenger cars fell over a cliff with "a frightful list of killed and wounded."

On May 17, 1849, a fire destroyed the St. Louis water front and much shipping in the river. The *Minnehaha,* in which Henry Lewis floated down the Mississippi in 1848 (see pages 362-366), was one of the casualties.

Henry Lewis, *Das Illustrirte Mississippithal.* 1854-57

## State Fairs and Farm Implements

VIEW OF SHOW GROUNDS AT SYRACUSE, 1849.

*New York State Agricultural Society Transactions.* 1849

*The Genesee Farmer,* September, 1851

*Above.* Seymour's Grain Drill, which took first prize in three state fairs and was widely used in western New York.

*Below.* Stewart's Patent Stump Machine would pull a hundred stumps in a day. In a country where "clearings" were still recent, stump pullers were a part of the farm equipment.

*The Genesee Farmer,* April, 1851

*Left.* Wheeler's Horse Power operating a threshing machine in 1851.

*The Genesee Farmer,* April, 1851

## Milk and Its Condensation

In each succeeding Westward Movement, from the settlement of Connecticut in 1635 to that of California in 1849, "Old Bossy" had gone along—an indispensable adjunct to the commissary department. It took a man from the frontier to make milk available where liquid milk could not be preserved.

From a painting by George C. Bingham.  *Courtesy*, City Art Museum, St. Louis, Mo.

*Courtesy*, The Borden Company. New York City

Gail Borden, a surveyor and newspaper publisher in Stephen Austin's colony in Texas, and later agent for a land company at Galveston, returned in 1851 to his native state of New York. He soon began experimenting with the condensation of milk and in 1853 applied for a patent "on a process of evaporating milk in vacuum." *Above* is one of the earliest pieces of equipment used by Borden.

*Right.* The condensing pan with which Borden made his first condensing experiments at the Shaker Village, Mt. Lebanon, New York, in 1853. Alononzo Holister, who stands beside the pan, was present when Borden made the experiments.

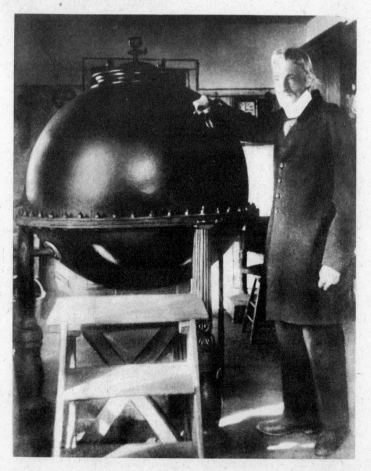

*Courtesy*, The Borden Company. New York City

## A President Dies—and the Telegraph Carries the News

From a portrait by J. B. Carpenter
Millard Fillmore

On July 9, 1850, President Taylor died and was succeeded by Millard Fillmore, the Vice-President.

The news of the President's death was carried over the country in a theretofore incredibly short time, due to the recently strung-up wires of what was known as the "magnetic telegraph." (See page 312.)

Taliaferro P. Shaffner, *The Telegraph Manual.* 1859

The telegraph was still in an experimental stage. The lines were flimsy—sometimes on poles, sometimes on trees, often down. *Below* we see a line inspector of the 1850's.

Taliaferro P. Shaffner, *The Telegraph Manual.* 1859

By 1851, however, there was a telegraph line across the Missouri River. *Right* we see the cable being carried over.

Taliaferro P. Shaffner, *The Telegraph Manual.* 1859

## Coal and Iron

As a fuel for the growing industries of the country, wood was giving place to coal. During the 1850's the use of anthracite (hard coal) far exceeded that of bituminous (soft coal).

A Coal Breaker

*Right.* Coal Miner

LEBANON IRON WORKS.

The increased demand for machinery gave an impetus to iron works.

Ever lengthening railroads called for iron for rails and rolling stock.

All illustrations shown on this page are from Eli Bowen, *The Pictorial Sketch Book of Pennsylvania.* 1854

SAFE HARBOR IRON WORKS.

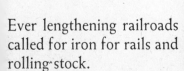

## The Slave Trade

Despite congressional prohibitions, slaves were bought in Africa and smuggled into the southern states.

AUDIENCE TO THE PERRY'S OFFICERS, BY THE QUEEN OF AMBRIZETTE.

Andrew H. Foote, *Africa and the American Flag*. 1854

*Opposite* we see the Queen of Ambrizette receiving the officers of the U.S.S. *Perry*, which from 1849 to 1851 was off the coast of Africa engaged in the suppression of the slave trade. Commanding the *Perry*, and doubtless under the umbrella in the picture, was Andrew H. Foote, later famous in the Civil War.

*Right.* From a book published in 1852 we have a contemporary conception of the domestic slave trade.

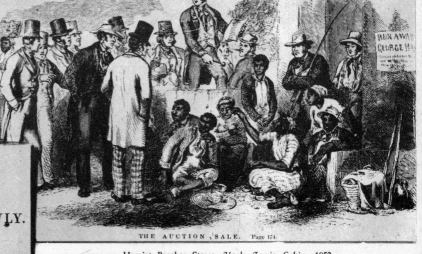

THE AUCTION SALE.    Page 174.

Harriet Beecher Stowe, *Uncle Tom's Cabin*. 1852

UNCLE TOM'S CABIN;

OR,

LIFE AMONG THE LOWLY.

BY

HARRIET BEECHER STOWE.

VOL. I.

BOSTON:
JOHN P. JEWETT & COMPANY.
CLEVELAND, OHIO:
JEWETT, PROCTOR & WORTHINGTON.
1852.

Three hundred thousand copies of *Uncle Tom's Cabin* were sold within a year of its publication.
*Opposite* is a reproduction of the title page of Volume I, in the first edition. The book had a tremendous effect on public opinion and unquestionably contributed to the state of mind which brought about the Civil War.

# How the Ladies Dressed

Godey's Paris Fashions Americanized

*Godey's Lady's Book, 1849*
Courtesy, The New-York Historical Society, New York City

*Godey's Lady's Book, 1849*
Courtesy, The New-York Historical Society, New York City

Bloomerism or the New Female Costume of 1851

*Bloomerism, 1851*

In 1851 Elizabeth Smith Miller, at Seneca Falls, N. Y. introduced a new style of feminine dress, which in addition to other features was intended as a symbol of the woman suffrage movement. The attempt of Amelia Bloomer, feminist editor, to popularize the style, attached the name of "Bloomer" to the costume —which was, all in all, a little ahead of its time.

## Great Salt Lake

The Mormon settlement on Great Salt Lake in 1847 (see page 361), the acquisition of the Utah country from Mexico in 1848 (see page 351), and the gold rush of 1849 (see pages 374 to 383) made a survey of Great Salt Lake desirable.

ENTRANCE TO THE VALLEY OF THE WEBER RIVER

In 1849 Captain Howard Stansbury of the Topographical Engineers was sent out with a party to make the survey.

We have already seen some of his pictures as he wound up the Trail from Fort Leavenworth to Fort Bridger—passing and repassing the trains of emigrants on the way.

*Above* we see the valley of the Weber River, which enters Great Salt Lake from the east.

GREAT SALT LAKE CITY FROM THE NORTH

*Above* is a distant view of Salt Lake City as Stansbury saw it in 1849.

*Left* is a Mormon fort south of Salt Lake City and which in 1849 served as a protection against the Utah Indians.

All illustrations shown on this page are from Howard Stansbury's *Exploration and Survey of the Valley of the Great Salt Lake of Utah.* 1852

## The Survey of Great Salt Lake

In the two views next *below* we have, from Stansbury's report, scenes of the activities of his party in making the survey.

Landing to Encamp.
Shore of Great Salt Lake
Bear River Bay

Howard Stansbury, *Exploration and Survey of the Valley of the Great Salt Lake of Utah.* 1852

Camp No. 4. Near
Promontory Point
Great Salt Lake

Howard Stansbury, *Exploration and Survey of the Valley of the Great Salt Lake of Utah.* 1852

Courtesy, Stokes Collection, The New York Public Library

*Above* is a view of Salt Lake City in 1853. The large building at the extreme right is the first Mormon Tabernacle.

## Exploring Red River

From the time of the Louisiana Purchase (see page 93), the course of Red River—a somewhat natural boundary between Mexico and ourselves—had been of concern to the Government. As we have seen (page 99), Pike was sent out in 1806 to find the head of the Red River and did not find it. In 1820 Major Long led an expedition in search of the headwaters of the river and he did not find them (see pages 199-200). Both had assumed that the river headed in the Rocky Mountains. In 1852 Capt. R. B. Marcy was made leader of a new expedition. Starting

ENCAMPMENT ON 6th JUNE

from a point well up on what he knew was the Red River, he proceeded towards its source. He soon found that there were two main forks and pursued the more northerly.

*Opposite* we see an encampment of Marcy's party on the north branch. With him as his assistant was a junior captain named George B. McClellan, who later became Marcy's son-in-law and in 1861 was the General-in-Chief of the Union Armies with his father-in-law acting as his aide.

Marcy and McClellan found that the headwaters of both branches of the Red were in the borders of a high and desolate tableland lying in western Texas and eastern New Mexico, known as the Llano Estacado or Staked Plains.

BORDER OF EL-LLANO ESTACADO

WITCHITAW VILLAGE ON RUSH CREEK

Returning from their survey, Marcy and McClellan visited the village of the Wichita Indians a few miles east of presentday Lawton, Oklahoma. A comparison of the picture *opposite* with Catlin's picture of what he called the Pawnee Picts (see page 276) would indicate that the two were identical.

All illustrations shown on this page are from Randolph B. Marcy, *Exploration of the Red River of Louisiana, in the Year 1852*

## The Pueblo Country

The acquisition of New Mexico brought within the United States a region first made known to white men by Coronado's expedition of 1540-42.

In 1849 a small army was sent into the region west of Santa Fe. The main purpose was to bring the Navaho into submission. With the party went Lt. Simpson of the Topographical Engineers, from whose journal our pictures are taken.

PUEBLO OF JÉMEZ
from the East Aug 20.

YOU-PEL-LAY, OR THE GREEN CORN DANCE OF THE JÉMEZ INDIANS.
Aug 19

Some twenty-six miles west of the Rio Grande the expedition reached Jemez (*above*). There they found the pueblo much as Espejo, a Spanish explorer, had found it two hundred and sixty-seven years earlier.

While at Jemez, some of the party witnessed the Green Corn Dance of the Indians. Lt. Simpson rode northward a few miles and examined the ruins of a church at Ojo Caliente (Warm Spring).

All illustrations shown on this page are from *U. S. Senate, Executive Document No. 64, 31st Congress, 1st Session*

THE OJO CALIENTE
twelve miles above Jémez

## The Ruins of the Montezuma?

SOUTH EAST VIEW OF THE RUINS OF THE PUEBLO WEJE-GI IN THE CAÑON OF CHACO.
Aug. 27 - Nº 2.

Some seventy-five miles northwest of Jemez in the Chaco Canyon, Lt. Simpson found many ruins of great buildings constructed of stone in a manner wholly different from anything known by the natives. Simpson's Pueblo guide told him that they had been built by the Montezuma.

In one of the ruins was found a room in an almost perfect state of preservation. It was 14 feet long by 7½ feet wide and 10 feet high. The entrance door was 3½ feet high by 2¼ wide. There had been 124 such rooms on the first floor of the pueblo and it had been four stories high.

INTERIOR OF A ROOM IN THE NORTH RANGE OF THE PUEBLO CHETHO-KETTE (THE RAIN).
Aug. 28ᵗʰ - Nº 5.

RESTORATION OF THE PUEBLO HUNGO PAVIE, (CROOKED NOSE)
Cañon of Chaco No. 4.

However, as the restoration shows, the upper stories doubtless were terraced, thus making each succeeding story somewhat smaller than that below.

All illustrations shown on this page are from U. S. Senate, Executive Document No. 64, 31st Congress, 1st Session

## The Stronghold of the Navaho

CAÑON OF CHELLY,
eight miles above the mouth–Sept 8th

U. S. Senate, Executive Document No. 64,
31st Congress, 1st Session

The Canyon de Chelly, in present-day northeastern Arizona, was famed as the place where the Navaho gathered to resist any invader of their country. After a show of force and a few cannon shots, Lt. Simpson's party rode several miles up the Canyon in 1849.

He found it averaging two hundred yards wide with perpendicular walls five hundred feet in height.

At one place he saw the ruins of a pueblo on a shelf fifty feet from the bed of the Canyon, overhung by the walls of the Canyon and accessible only by ladders.

RUINS OF AN OLD PUEBLO
in the Cañon of Chelly–Sept 8th

Two years later the Government established Fort Defiance a few miles south of the Canyon as a check on the activities of the Navaho.

U. S. Senate, Executive Document No. 64,
31st Congress, 1st Session

FORT DEFIANCE at CANONCITO BONITO, NEW MEXICO

H. R. Schoolcraft, Information respecting Indian Tribes of the United States. 1851-57

## Zuñi

PUEBLO OF ZUÑI.
Sept. 15

From the Canyon de Chelly, Lt. Simpson's party turned south to the pueblo of Zuñi—a distance of about one hundred miles. Here they were among Coronado's "Seven Cities of Cíbola." *Opposite* we have a view of Zuñi in 1849. Note the ladders used for entering the pueblo. There were no doors on the ground floors.

## Inscription Rock

From Zuñi the expedition turned back toward Santa Fe. Lt. Simpson made a slight detour to visit Inscription Rock, so named because of the many inscriptions carved on its sides. One of these was dated as early as 1606.

NORTH FACE OF INSCRIPTION ROCK.
Sept. 17th

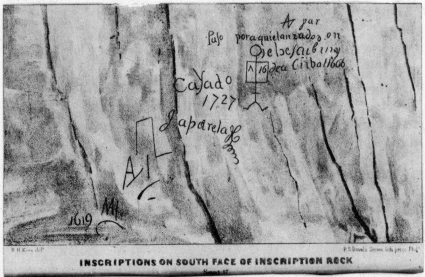

INSCRIPTIONS ON SOUTH FACE OF INSCRIPTION ROCK

Together with R. H. Kern, one of two brothers, both of whom were artists and both of whom accompanied the expedition, Lt. Simpson copied the inscriptions and included them in his journal.

All illustrations shown on this page are from *U. S. Senate, Executive Document No. 64, 31st Congress, 1st Session*

## An Unseen Wonder

In 1851 Capt. Sitgreaves of the Topographical Engineers was ordered to make a survey from Zuñi to the Colorado River of the West. R. H. Kern went along and made the pictures. *Opposite* is another view of Zuñi, showing the Buffalo Dance as well as the pueblo.

BUFFALO DANCE.
Pueblo de Zuñi - N.

CASCADE OF THE LITTLE COLORADO RIVER, near Camp 13.

Sitgreaves' party followed the Little Colorado River westward to the beginning of the canyon of that river, when, hearing reports of what was ahead, he turned off across the mountains south and west.

Striking the main Colorado River in the Mohave country, Sitgreaves found the Mohave men to be as tall as Diaz (one of Coronado's captains) had reported three hundred years earlier. But Sitgreaves did not see the Grand Canyon and verification of Cardenas' description of that wonder awaited a later exploration.

All illustrations shown on this page are from *U. S. Senate, Executive Document No. 59, 32nd Congress, 2nd Session*

MOHAVE INDIANS     N M

## Frank Pierce, President

In 1852 the Whig Party nominated General Winfield Scott for the Presidency. But the day of the Whigs was done. Franklin Pierce of New Hampshire, nominated by the Democrats, won the election and became President in 1853.

*Democratic Review*, June, 1852

Note the name "Frank", which was commonly used at the time.

*Opposite*. Chamber of Representatives, Washington, D. C., about 1853.

Charles A. Dana, *The United States Illustrated*. (1855?)

THE NEW CAPITOL

The north and south wings of the Capitol were begun in 1851 from designs by Thomas U. Walter, whom we recall as the architect of Girard College (see page 256).

Charles A. Dana, *The United States Illustrated*. (1855?)

## The Smithsonian Institution

James Smithson, an English scientist, died in Genoa, Italy, in 1829. By his will an estate of over half a million dollars was left to the United States "to found at Washington an establishment, under the name of the Smithsonian Institution, for the increase and diffusion of knowledge among men." The legacy was duly collected, brought to America in gold coin and deposited in the Mint.

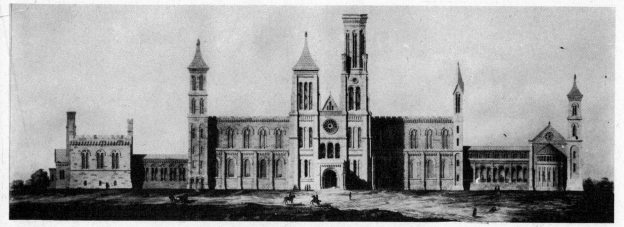

*Courtesy, Smithsonian Institution, Washington, D. C.*

By an Act of Congress in 1846 the Smithsonian was organized, and in 1847 the cornerstone of the building was laid. *Above* is a view painted from the architect's plans.

## The Washington Monument

Planned as early as 1833, the cornerstone of the Washington Monument was not laid until 1848. The picture *opposite*, from the *Illustrated News* of Jan. 8, 1853, shows the state of the Monument at that date.

## Perry to Japan

TO-RI-GA-SA-XI, YEDO BAY

Wishing to establish commercial relations with Japan, which had long excluded foreign traders, the United States Government sent Commodore Perry with a naval squadron to visit that country.

Arriving at Yedo Bay (Tokio) in July, 1853, Perry, after a threat of force, delivered a letter from the President to the representatives of the Japanese Emperor.

DELIVERY OF THE PRESIDENT'S LETTER

COMMO PERRY MEETING THE IMPERIAL COMMISSIONERS AT YOKUHAMA

Returning the following year, Perry concluded a treaty which ended the Japanese policy of seclusion.

All illustrations shown on this page are from *Narrative of the Expedition of an American Squadron to the China Seas and Japan. Performed in the Years 1852, 1853 and 1854*

## In the Mississippi Valley

the last considerable piece of Indian Country was organized as the Territory of Minnesota in 1849.

By the Treaty of Traverse des Sioux (1851) the Upper Sioux Indians restricted themselves to a reservation along the Minnesota River.

From a painting by Frank B. Mayer who was present at the Treaty
*Courtesy,* The Minnesota Historical Society, St. Paul, Minn.

Treaty of Traverse des Sioux

*Below* is a view of St. Paul (Minnesota) as it appeared in 1853.

*Courtesy,* Stokes Collection, The New York Public Library

*Right* is a view of Moline, Ill., in the early 1850's. As we have seen (page 354), John Deere had been making his plows at this place since 1847.

Charles A. Dana, *The United States Illustrated.* (1855?)

## Chicago

the future metropolis of the Middle West, was still but a small city of about 30,000 inhabitants. But the Illinois and Michigan Canal had been completed in 1848, and the Galena & Chicago Union Railroad started building west in the same year. In 1851 railroads from the east entered the city—and its eminence as a railroad center became evident.

*Opposite* we have a view of the City in 1853, looking southwest from the City Hall Tower.

*Above.* The Tremont Hotel, southeast corner of Lake and Dearborn Streets. 1850.

Both illustrations on this page are shown through the *courtesy* of the Chicago Historical Society, Chicago, Ill.

## Showboats

had cruised the western rivers since the 1830's.

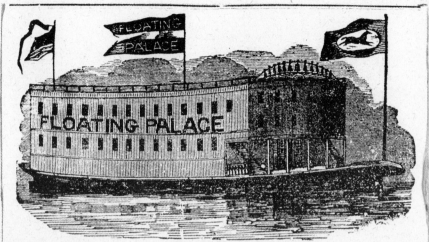

SPALDING & RODGERS CIRCUS CO
ON BOARD FLOATING PALACE,
WILL Exhibit in Terre Haute on **Saturday, April 23d,** at 2 and 7 o'clock, P. M.
PRICE OF ADMISSION.
Dress Circle, all armed Chairs............................50 cen
Family Boxes, Cushioned Seats.........................25 "

*Courtesy,* Emeline-Fairbanks Memorial
Library, Terre Haute, Ind.

*Opposite* we see the well-known circus of Spalding & Rodgers advertising a show on April 23, 1853, in their Floating Palace at Terre Haute, Ind., on the Wabash River.

## Wheeling

where the Cumberland, or National, Road (see pages 189-90 and 267) crossed the Ohio, dedicated a suspension bridge in 1849. In the lower left part of the view the National Road is seen winding up the hill— eastward bound.

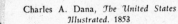
WHEELING in VIRGINIA

Charles A. Dana, *The United States
Illustrated.* 1853

## Pittsburgh

at the Forks of the Ohio, was by 1849 showing unmistakable signs of its future industrial eminence.

*Courtesy,* Stokes Collection, The New York
Public Library

## Richmond, Va., in 1852

Here, too, we see a growing city in which the state capitol is but one of many buildings. It is interesting to compare this view with that made by St. Mémin in 1804 (see page 100).

*Courtesy, Stokes Collection, The New York Public Library*

## Salem, Mass., in 1853

after two hundred and twenty-seven years of existence, still retained the look of a New England village.

S A L E M ,  Mass.

*Courtesy, Stokes Collection, The New York Public Library*

*Opposite.*

## Desert Rock Light-House

off the coast of Maine.

Charles A. Dana, *The United States Illustrated.* (1855?)

## The Starucca Viaduct

on the Erie Railroad, was 1,200 feet long and 110 feet high. The view from the viaduct was accounted one of great natural beauty.

Begun in 1835, the Erie Railroad reached its objective on Lake Erie (at Dunkirk, N. Y.) only in 1851. The following year a connection was made with Buffalo.

*53*

Charles A. Dana, *The United States Illustrated.* (1855?)

## Baltimore, in 1853

The view *opposite* is of Baltimore and Calvert Streets.

*Courtesy,* Stokes Collection, The New York Public Library

## Trenton, N. J., about 1853

VIEW OF TRENTON, N. J. FROM MORRISVILLE PA.

*Courtesy,* Stokes Collection, The New York Public Library

## Fruits of the Erie Canal

The traffic which flowed back and forth on the Canal since its opening in 1825 (see pages 208-213) created many great cities. *Below* is a view of Utica in 1850.

Rochester in 1853, shown *below*, may well be compared with Rochester of 1825 shown on page 210.

ROCHESTER.

## New York City

*Below* is a bird's eye view of the City in 1850. North of 42nd Street was still open country. Castle Garden is shown on the extreme left.

*Courtesy, Stokes Collection, The New York Public Library*

Somewhat to the left of the incoming train, shown within the circle in the upper-right-hand corner of the picture *above*, may be seen, where the New York Public Library now stands, the Croton Water Reservoir, pictured in more detail *below*.

In its Egyptian lines the Reservoir reflected the many Old World cross-currents which influenced American life in architecture, place names and other ways. Another example of Egyptian architecture of the period will be found in the picture of the Tombs on page 414.

*Courtesy, Eno Collection, The New York Public Library*

## New York, in the 1850's

ASTOR HOUSE

Charles A. Dana, *The Scenery of the
United States.* 1855

BROADWAY

Charles A. Dana, *The United States
Illustrated.* (1855?)

THE TOMBS

HALLS OF JUSTICE
NEW YORK

Charles A. Dana, *The United States
Illustrated.* (1855?)

## The Hippodrome

*Courtesy, Eno Collection, The New York Public Library*

INTERIOR VIEW OF THE NEW YORK HIPPODROME—OPENING NIGHT.

*Illustrated News,* May 14, 1853

**New York,** in the 1850's

*Left.* Union Square in 1850.

*Courtesy, Eno Collection, The New York Public Library*

Firemen's Parade on Broadway in 1853. Note the fire engine; also the gigantic advertising photographing instrument on the front of Brady's Gallery (see page 359).

*Illustrated News,* November 12, 1853

Barnum's American Museum, at Broadway and Ann Street, was the outstanding place of amusement for New Yorkers and country visitors— ". . . the ladder by which I rose to fame", said Barnum.

*Illustrated News,* October 29, 1853

## Jenny Lind

In 1850 Jenny Lind, the famous singer, known as "the Swedish nightingale", opened an American tour at Castle Garden, N. Y., under the management of P. T. Barnum.

*Courtesy, Stokes Collection, The New York Public Library*

*Above* Castle Garden. In 1850 it was a place of entertainment. Later it became an immigration office, and more recently it was known to New Yorkers as the Aquarium.

FIRST APPEARANCE OF JENNY LIND IN AMERICA.
At Castle Garden Sept'ʳ 11ᵗʰ 1850

*Courtesy, Eno Collection, The New York Public Library*

## The Crystal Palace Exhibition

held at New York in 1853, was the first international exhibition in the United States. Its official title was The Exhibition of the Industry of All Nations.

NEW YORK CRYSTAL PALACE.
FOR THE EXHIBITION OF THE INDUSTRY OF ALL NATIONS.

*Courtesy*, Eno Collection, The New York Public Library

The Crystal Palace, of glass and iron construction, was located west of the Croton Reservoir (see page 413)—presentday Bryant Park.

By the emphasis which it placed on industrial progress, this Exhibition not only recorded the already well-advanced movement away from an age of handicraft but it did much to speed the coming of an industrial era which in many ways revolutionized the life and thought of America.

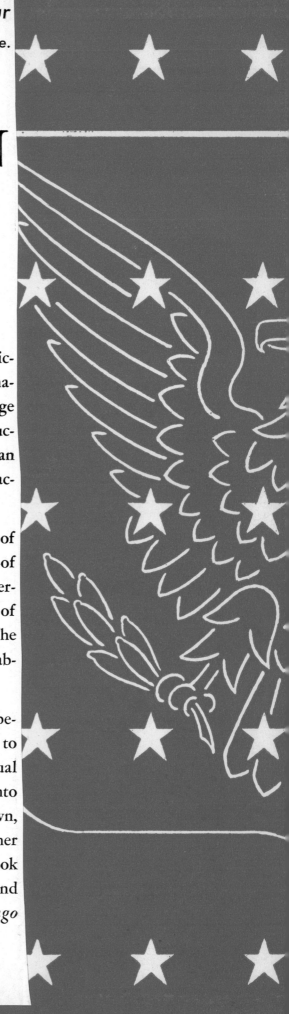

"A magnificent picture book of our social past."— New York Herald Tribune.

# ALBUM OF AMERICAN HISTORY
## (Colonial Period)

### James Truslow Adams
#### Editor in Chief

"History in pictures, authentic pictures; pictures that tell more and quicken the imagination more than many pages of text. The average reader will find this one of the best introductions to a real understanding of American social history; certainly it is the most attractive."—*Los Angeles Times*

"It is impossible to overestimate the value of this collection of authentic pictorial records of our early days . . . It is just as impossible to overestimate its fascination. The scholar will of course recognize it at once as indispensable. The ordinary reader will find himself utterly absorbed."—*Philadelphia Inquirer*

"A picture-museum of America's colonial period . . . a visit through its pages will bring to you as nothing else can, a sense of the actual lives of the colonists . . . It is a visual look into America of another day. This is a book to own, to keep on your bedside or library table rather than on your bookshelves. It's the sort of book in which you discover new wonders and delights each time you pick it up."—*Chicago Sun*

*With more than 1400 illustrations*